Hallmark

A CENTURY OF CARING

At the heart of Hallmark is the strong belief that its products and services must enrich people's lives. This book is dedicated to the thousands of Hallmark employees and retailers, past and present, whose collective spirit brings that mission to life and inspires future chapters in Hallmark's ongoing story.

A CENTURY OF CARING

by Patrick Regan

ANDREWS McMEEL PUBLISHING, LLC

Kansas City • Sydney • London

09 10 11 12 13 POA 10 9 8 7 6 5 4 3 2 1

ISBN-13: 978-0-7407-9240-3
ISBN-10: 0-7407-9240-7

Library of Congress Control Number: 2009931087
www.andrewsmcmeel.com

ATTENTION: SCHOOLS AND BUSINESSES

Andrews McMeel books are available at quantity discounts with bulk
purchase for educational, business, or sales promotional use. For
information, please write to: Special Sales Department, Andrews McMeel
Publishing, LLC, 1130 Walnut Street, Kansas City, Missouri 64106.

Produced by Lionheart Books Ltd.
5200 Peachtree Road
Suite #2103
Atlanta, Georgia 30341

Book design by Michael Reagan

Cover design by Jim Langford

Chapter openers design by Rick Cusick

Text by Patrick Regan

Printed in China
through Asia Pacific Offset

First edition, January 2010

Table of Contents

Acknowledgments

Telling the story of Hallmark Cards' first one hundred years was a fascinating but daunting experience. The product with which the company is so closely associated, the greeting card, seems so simple at first blush—picture, words and paper—but anyone who delves into the process of creating and selling greeting cards finds one of the most complex businesses imaginable. The story of this iconic American company proved to be similarly multi-layered. As the scope and scale of this book grew, so too did the list of people who helped bring it to completion.

The Hallmark story begins with the Hall family, and its members must be the first to be acknowledged. Their candor, spirit, humor, and heartfelt affection for the family business and for each other made the countless hours spent among them a genuine pleasure. As a native Kansas Citian, I have long been grateful for Don and Adele Hall's commitment to making this city a great place to live. After nearly two years of working on this book, I am even more grateful for their friendship and their faith in me to get this story right. It has been an honor and a joy getting to know them.

Additional thanks go to Margi Pence, Barbara Hall Marshall and Elizabeth Ann Reid for providing tremendous family history and insight.

Don Hall, Jr. and David Hall helped me to further understand the intricacies of the greeting card business and found time for me even in the midst of very busy days.

Dozens of interviewees spent countless hours recounting their career experiences. Each provided a unique glimpse into the company. Their names are featured throughout the book so will not be repeated here—with one exception. Jeannette Lee served as an incredible source of first-hand Hallmark history dating back to the 1930s. She is a jewel and an inspiration.

Along the way, a host of Hallmarkers has been instrumental to making this book happen. They lent their talents to this book even as they attended to their fulltime jobs at Hallmark. Heartfelt thanks to Jim Langford, Shelley Shrock, Johne Richardson, Kelda Jackson, Dale Forton, Dan Foster, Guy Giunta, Barbara Bennett, Kristi Ernsting, Terry Lee, Brent Harris, Eileen Drummond, Sally Groves, Linda Odell, Carly Jossund, Lynley Farris, Wanda Taylor, Brad Moore, Jan Parkinson, Toni Houghton, and Mary Carrington-Harris.

Thanks to Hallmark archivist Sharman Robertson and designer Rick Cusick who contributed skill and sweat to this project from day one. Thanks also to Judy Vroom for many hours of interview transcription.

Special thanks to John Peterson, my "inside guy" at Hallmark, for tireless and timely research and writing and for guiding me—literally and figuratively—through Hallmark's sometimes perplexing corridors. John deftly authored many of the sidebar features included herein.

Thanks also to Steve Doyal whose encyclopedic knowledge of Hallmark past and present was an invaluable resource.

Thanks are also due to a few key contributors outside of Hallmark. Lisa Reagan somehow managed to keep this complex book organized and on track. She was ably assisted by Elana Maxwell.

My wife, Sarah Regan, propped me up when this project threatened to beat me down, and my mother, Patty Regan, served the vital role of first reader.

Finally, two people above all were instrumental in getting this book off the ground and keeping it on course. Thanks to Bill Hall, master diplomat, dam-breaker, and whip-cracker. I wish I had you in my court on every project. And thanks to Michael Reagan of Lionheart Books for persuading me that together we could create a truly different kind of corporate history book—and then making it happen. Nobody does books better.

—*Patrick Regan, 2009*

Introduction

WHEN THE HISTORY OF AMERICAN INDUSTRY IS WRITTEN AND REVEALED, AT THE CORE OF THOSE FOUNDATIONS WILL BE FOUND A GENIUS OF DARING AND AMBITION. THIS BOOK COULD BE USED AS A PRIMARY RESOURCE FOR HOW TO BUILD A NATION AS WELL AS HOW TO CONSTRUCT A SUCCESSFUL INDUSTRY.

J.C. Hall, who was born into a poor but hard-working family, became a consummate salesman. He set a standard of work, which the whole family supported and emulated. While it was said that he was not the usual salesman. He was neither bombastic nor gregarious. He was hard-working and disciplined. He found that selling anything well, whether paper, candy, popcorn, or greeting cards, would reward him with loyal customers and continuous orders. Hall set a standard which is maintained one hundred years later in the halls and offices of the Hallmark Company. The ideas of loyalty to his family, product and his customers, have been respected and adhered to throughout the years.

There are accounts in this book of the entire Hallmark family that reveal the interdependence of the family members, their respect for each other and the workers in their plants. There are stories of family members who used their own money to help needy employees.

I have read few biographies which have moved me as much as the Hall family saga. They have, over a century, sought the high road insisting upon quality over quantity. The standard of their products has never been allowed to fall below the level of the best they can produce.

It would be easy to think a greeting card company could in no way be as important as a pharmacological business or an automobile industry, or a giant oil corporation, but years ago I learned how important the greeting card company was.

My mother left California to visit me in North Carolina. I invited her into my office, and there, my mail had been separated into piles of letters and piles of greeting cards.

As I sat with my secretary dictating responses to the letters I received, my mother looked at the large basket filled with greeting cards. She interrupted my dictation, asking in a very sweet voice, "Baby, are you saving these cards for later?"

I said, "Yes."

She asked, "Why?"

I said, "Because people who really wanted answers had sat down and written letters, so I respond to them immediately. These cards have simply been bought and the sender did not have to think of what their messages were. They bought them, signed them, and sent them to me, and I will get around to answering them."

My mother's voice became very quiet. She asked me, "Do you realize the pains it takes to send off a card? First the sender must want to communicate with you, but may find it impossible to say what needs to be said in an elegant and direct way. So, the sender goes to a card store in comfortable shoes, because the selection may take half-hour or longer. The sender reads through thirty or forty cards before finding the one which fits the occasion. The sender pays for the card, signs the card and addresses the envelope, goes to the Post Office, puts a stamp on it and sends it off. Don't you think that is enough effort to warrant your attention?"

I was embarrassed at my high-handedness. But I did learn a lesson quickly and irrevocably. I realized that I had to look at the greeting card business with the same respect that I showed for other American industries.

Today, after over one hundred years of superb family leadership, Don Hall, Jr., now President and CEO of Hallmark, shares the same values and shows the same steadfastness, honesty, and willingness to do the hard work which was required of his forefathers. Upon reading this book, I think that Don Hall, Jr. is a replica of his grandfather J.C. Hall. I have talked to him and worked with him over a period of nine years and I find him accessible, of gentle wit, resolute, but not inflexible. He carries on caring for his family, his business, his people, and his community.

My best wishes to Hallmark for its future and my complete thanks to Hallmark for its "Century of Caring."

—*Maya Angelou*

CHAPTER ONE

Starting from Scratch

(1891–1909)

> *"The history of every country begins in the heart of a man or woman."*
>
> — *Willa Cather,* O Pioneers!

THE STORY OF HALLMARK BEGINS WITH THE STORY OF A FAMILY, A FAMILY THAT MANAGED TO RISE ABOVE ORIGINS THAT WERE SO inauspicious that to call them humble would be overly generous. The family would eventually build an iconic American company in a bustling city, but this story begins far from there. It begins on the hardscrabble, slate-flat great plains of the American Midwest. And though the company began in 1910, the story picks up some 30 years earlier.

David City, Nebraska sits on windswept table-land about 10 miles south of the Platte River valley and 60 miles west of Omaha. It was, in the latter part of the 19th century, as it is today, corn and wheat farming country. European immigrants—predominantly German and Czech—had first settled the virgin prairies of the Nebraska Territory in the mid-1800s. Desiring a central location for their county seat, Butler County officials platted and incorporated David City in 1874.

Over the next 15 years, three different railroads would lay track through the town of just under 2,000 people, cementing its position as a regional hub of transportation and commerce. For

pioneers, farmers, ranchers, and merchants west of the Mississippi, a rail line was nothing less than a lifeline. And though they didn't yet realize it, for the Hall family of David City, the rail lines would bring their best opportunity to someday escape the dire circumstances that held them fast to this windy little town.

The paint was still fresh on the David City town hall when George Nelson Hall and wife Nancy Dudley Houston welcomed their second child, a son named Rollie, in 1882. An earlier child had died in infancy. Another son, William, would follow two years later. Seven years would pass before their third son, named Joyce, arrived. A final child, Marie, was born four years after that. The children were born into poverty. On the Nebraska plains, prosperity was usually tied to a family's holdings in acreage or livestock. The Hall family, crowded into a small clapboard house on the corner of C and 6th Streets, had neither. One of the few advantages they did have was a proximity to the children's

LEFT: *The historic joining of the east and west rail lines on May 10, 1869, at Promontory Point, Utah.*

ABOVE: *Grandpa Adam Hall (center with beard) in front of the David City Livery Stable.*

grandparents. Adam Hall was a retired farmer, a taciturn prohibitionist, but loving to his grandchildren and a steady presence in their lives. He and his wife, Nannie Bozarth Hall, lived in a tidy home kitty-corner from his son's family.

George and Nancy Hall began their family during a period of enormous, historic change in America. And even in isolated eastern Nebraska, evidence of that change was arriving in town every day, courtesy of the ever-increasing railroad traffic.

By the 1880s, America had fully embraced the Industrial Revolution. In 1882, the same year that Rollie Hall was born, Thomas Edison's Pearl Street Power Company first brought electricity to New York City. Alexander Graham Bell had successfully transmitted the first telephone message only six years earlier. In 1889, German engineers Gottlieb Daimler and Karl Benz each unveiled their own versions of a new gasoline-powered vehicle called the motor car. Three absolutely history-changing technological breakthroughs in a 13-year period—it was not for nothing that this was called a revolution.

People across America marveled at this endless parade of innovations and inventions. And by 1889, a public newly fascinated by wealth and consumerism could keep track of the blooming financial empires of families like the Rockefellers, Vanderbilts, and DuPonts in a new daily newspaper called the *Wall Street Journal*.

But railroad or no, it was a long way from Wall Street to C Street in David City.

George Nelson Hall had tried his hand at various occupations as his family grew, but nothing stuck. After a failed attempt at running a hardware store in nearby Brainard, Nebraska, he turned his attention toward preaching, which meant traveling. As an adult, what Joyce Hall remembered most about his father was his absence.

Joyce would later say that though his father found no success as a retailer, he may well have passed along the inclination toward

"HE WOULD TRAVEL TO VARIOUS METHODIST CHURCHES AND BE GONE FOR AS LONG AS SIX MONTHS. WE WEREN'T POOR BECAUSE MY FATHER COULDN'T MAKE A LIVING— WE WERE POOR BECAUSE HE LET US BE. ALTHOUGH HE ALWAYS SEEMED TO HAVE MONEY FOR HIMSELF, HE SENT VERY LITTLE TO US. HE TOLD MY MOTHER THAT SHE NEEDN'T WORRY— 'THE LORD WOULD PROVIDE.' I FOUND OUT THEN THAT IT WAS A GOOD IDEA TO GIVE THE LORD A LITTLE HELP."

— *Joyce Clyde (J.C.) Hall*

LEFT: *Nancy Dudley Houston Hall.*

MIDDLE: *William and Rollie in their Sunday best pose for a portrait typical of the era.*

RIGHT: *Joyce Hall at age ten in David City.*

"SHE WAS A WONDERFUL MOTHER WHO SAID VERY LITTLE, BUT WHAT SHE SAID SHE MEANT. WHEN FOOD WAS SCARCE IN OUR HOUSE, SOMEHOW MY MOTHER WOULDN'T HAVE AN APPETITE. AND IF THE NIGHT GOT COLD, I WOULD WAKE UP WITH ANOTHER BLANKET."

— *J.C. Hall*

ABOVE: *The railroad brought the circus to towns throughout America's hinterland. Everyone turned out for the parade, and youngsters like J.C. Hall flocked to the circus grounds as the big tents went up, offering to perform chores in exchange for a ticket to the show.*

business to his sons. Perhaps they were just more hungry than their father.

If their father was a haphazard presence around the Hall family home, their mother more than made up for his unreliability. Nancy Dudley Houston Hall was a quietly resolute woman—a direct descendent of Texas soldier and statesman, Sam Houston. But, while her resolve was consistently strong, her health wasn't. Not long after giving birth to her last child, her health failed to the point where a doctor informed her that she wouldn't live much longer. "Yes, I will," she said. "I'll see my my children raised." She was right. She lived to age 56. Marie, her youngest, was 21 when their mother died.

His daughter was just three years old and Joyce seven when George Hall left home for good. But by then, the resourceful children and their mother were well used to making it—if just barely—on their own. While not yet a schoolboy, Joyce had learned from his older brothers a hatful of ways to hustle enough spare change to keep the household intact. By age eight, he had followed his brothers' lead in running an unofficial popcorn concession on the passenger trains that came through town. With a few cents' investment in popping corn, he'd pop a big batch, bag it in small paper sacks, and walk out to the water tower a

RIGHT: *An illustration from* Harpers *magazine depicts a typical passenger rail car in the late 1800s. In that era it was often called the modern ship of the plains.*

10

mile outside of town. When the trains stopped to take on water, Joyce would board with his bags of popcorn and walk the aisles, selling bags for a nickel apiece. Other times he'd sell homemade sandwiches, fruit, magazines, and newspapers—anything that he could buy or make cheap and sell for a bit more. Profits were turned over to his mother.

As Joyce recalled, there seemed endless opportunities for a boy who wasn't afraid of a little hard work.

"I always had some kind of job. On Sundays at the ball park, I would sell lemonade. You could make a whole tub of lemonade with the juice of one lemon, a little bit of citric acid, and about twenty-five cents worth of sugar. When the circus came to town—if you got up and out before dawn—you could usually get a job, with payment being a free ticket. I set up stakes for the tents, carried water, and fed the animals."

Because of the steady railroad traffic, David City was a popular stopover for traveling salesmen. On evenings when the weather was fair, the "drummers," as they were called, would sit outside the Perkins Hotel on Courthouse Square and swap yarns about their adventures on the rails and on the road. Young Joyce often listened in on their conversations and found himself

dreaming of the bustling world that loomed farther down the railroad track.

At age nine, Joyce Hall took the first step toward joining that worldly fraternity of drummers. A woman representing the California Perfume Company came to town to recruit an agent to sell the company's products door-to-door. She called on Mrs. Hall as a prospect, but as Joyce remembered, his mother was practically an invalid by then. "And she wouldn't have had the five dollars to buy the sample case needed for selling anyway." But Joyce wasn't about to let the opportunity pass. The 40 percent sales commission was too enticing.

"When I heard about it, I raced over to see my grandfather. He listened carefully to my story without saying a word. Then he got out his wallet and gave me five dollars. I approached the woman about being the agent and had to sell pretty hard. She said, 'Well, I haven't got one here anyway, and I might as well let you try it.' So I got the job because no one else in town wanted it."

In the sample case were cosmetics, lilac cologne, lemon extract, soap, and tooth powder. On Saturdays and on evenings after school, Joyce would walk the streets of David City and sell.

A BOY NAMED JOYCE

Growing up poor with a largely absent father and sickly mother, Joyce Hall was dealt a rough hand as a child. But one of the toughest burdens he had to bear was a first name he despised. On the day he was born, a Methodist clergyman, Bishop Issac W. Joyce, was visiting David City. So impressed was his mother by the preacher, that she chose his surname for her newborn son.

The name would bring Joyce Hall no end of despair as a child—and a good share of taunting from schoolmates. Like the eponymous character in Johnny Cash's "A Boy Named Sue," young Joyce, though a temperate child by nature, learned to answer the taunts with his fists.

"I was fully grown before I wasn't ashamed of my name."

Using his middle name wasn't an option. Like his brother Rollie, he hadn't been given one. One day, Rollie decided that was an oversight they could fix. He had a teacher named Beatrice that he favored, so he took that as his own middle name. Inspired by one of the railroad lines that passed through town, Joyce selected Burlington, and set about stamping JOYCE BURLINGTON HALL onto his school books. But Rollie wasn't convinced. After some thought, he assigned his young brother a different middle name: Clyde. Joyce preferred his own choice but deferred to his admired older brother. J.C., he reasoned, was a vast improvement over his given name.

And while he muddled through the lower grades of primary school, Joyce continued his more formative and practical education one customer at a time.

"I didn't know anything about credit, but I learned. If a lady said, 'Leave the perfume and I'll pay you next Monday,' I thought she'd do just that. But I soon found out what 'poor credit risk' means."

For Joyce Hall, class was always in session. And he would later count his tenure selling for the California Perfume Company among his most influential early experiences. The company did pretty well too, incidentally. It would later change its name to Avon Products.

At the turn of the 20th century, Joyce Hall was eight years old. His hometown of David City, Nebraska, was barely a generation removed from the western edge of the settled United States. The tall grass prairies, home and hunting ground to Plains Indian tribes just 50 years earlier, had been put into production to feed a booming nation. Just 60 miles east, wholesale businesses in Omaha supplied a growing number of retail stores with everything from John Deere's newest shovel plow to engraved stationery. The huge wholesale warehouses that flanked the city's narrow 9th Street created a man-made, industry-born canyon of commerce. Because of the wholesale "jobbers" who worked in the massive brick structures, the area was widely known as Jobbers' Canyon.

A jobber, as defined by *Webster's Unabridged Dictionary*, published in 1913, was "one who buys goods from importers, whole-salers, or manufacturers, and sells to retailers."

Joyce Hall had never been to Omaha, but no one had to tell him or his brothers the meaning of the word *jobber*. They'd figured out

ABOVE: *A postcard from David City, c. 1907.*

BELOW: *The Hall family home in David City.*

OPPOSITE PAGE: *The Snow store in Columbus, Nebraska, c. 1905.*

the middleman game early on. And in just a few years, their mastery of "jobbing" would put them on a path to creating a company that would become synonymous with an entire industry.

But for Joyce, there was first the matter of getting through the third grade. And that first meant helping his family meet the basic needs of shelter and food. Winters in rural Nebraska could be brutal, but summers he recalled a bit more fondly.

"The heat was easier to cope with and we had more food. We managed to have some hens and a few fryers. We had a small vegetable garden and raised raspberries and rhubarb, and we had cherry and plum trees—and once in a while we'd get a catch of catfish. Butter was cheap, but we didn't always have it. After eating cornbread without butter for a number of days, we'd scare up a dime for a pound of butter that was scooped out of a community tub."

The close of the 19th century also saw an addition to the retail landscape in David City. In 1898, a traveling candy salesman named L.W. Snow and his wife set up a millinery and notions shop in town. Although the store was fairly humble in its offerings, it—and its owners—would have an outsize effect on the Hall family.

Rollie and William Hall, then 17 and 15 years old, were soon working at the Snow store on Saturdays and after school. Not long after that, Snow bought out a bookstore in Columbus about 20 miles from David City. He persuaded Rollie to leave high school and move to Columbus to run the store for him.

Nine-year-old Joyce worked as a seasonal employee for Snow, selling fireworks in the week leading up to the Fourth of July and leaving school a week early to help with the Christmas rush. His first "shopkeeping" job further stoked his fire for business, and the small details that spelled commercial success were not lost on the tall, quiet boy.

"Of course what we have a right to expect of the American boy is that he shall turn out to be a good American man. Now, the chances are strong that he won't be much of a man unless he is a good deal of a boy. He must work hard and play hard. He must be clean-minded and clean-lived, and able to hold his own under all circumstances and against all comers. It is only on these conditions that he will grow into the kind of American man of whom America can be really proud."

—*Theodore Roosevelt,* The Strenuous Life, *1900*

The boyhood of Joyce Clyde Hall was not one that any parent would likely wish for his or her child. But with the hard work of his brothers and the boy's own willingness to bear his share of the load, the Hall family steadily, incrementally rose their family's station. As an adult, J.C. Hall would look back on his childhood with pride and no small amount of gratitude. "Poverty for me was a tremendous spur," he would say. "It actually gave me an advantage over a lot of folks when I was starting out."

By 1900, William Hall had joined his brother at Snow's store in Columbus. Snow himself was a traveling candy salesman and in town only a few days each month.

Two days before Christmas in 1900, Rollie wrote to his mother from Columbus:

> *Dear Mama,*
>
> *Enclosed you will find a Christmas present—$10 from Willie and I.*
>
> *Mr. Snow has offered Willie $15 per Mo. & board to work in the store and me $40. He said that he would try us in Jan. and if us two could make things go would rather have us than anybody else, but if we can't make things go, keep up trade, etc., Willie loses his job, but Mr. Snow says there is no reason why we can't.*

Later in the letter he writes of his 16-year-old brother, "I hate to see Willie go out of school but at the same time it may do him more good in here than in school."

The brothers did make a go of it in Columbus, and William, like his brother before him, left school early to join the workforce full time.

As store manager and de facto buyer, Rollie spent significant time with the many drummers who called on the store while passing through town. He saw, in their restless energy and enthusiasm for the sale, a lot of himself. After all, he had been selling one thing or another since he started working trains and baseball games at age eight. When he heard drummers talking about bringing in $400 or even $500 a month, he was certain that his future did not lie behind a shop counter.

"COLUMBUS WAS BIGGER THAN DAVID CITY AND SORT OF MAGICAL TO ME. I HADN'T SEEN MUCH TO COMPARE WITH THE STORE BEFORE. IT WAS THE ONLY BOOKSTORE IN TOWN, AND IT ALSO CARRIED MAGAZINES, CANDY, CIGARS, AND A FEW OTHER THINGS. MR. SNOW WAS A GOOD MERCHANT. HE'D REPLACE POOR SELLING PRODUCTS PROMPTLY WITH SOMETHING BETTER. HE KEPT THE CANDY CASE FULL, THE GLASS SPARKLING, AND THE FLOOR SWEPT."

— *J.C. Hall*

TOP: *13 year-old Joyce Hall. He got his first dog, Teddy (above), when the homeless pup scratched forlornly at the door of the bookstore on a bitter winter night. They quickly became constant companions. The dog, like so many of the day, was named for the sitting president, Theodore Roosevelt.*

THEODORE ROOSEVELT

Forty-two-year-old Theodore Roosevelt, historian, naturalist, explorer, hunter, author, and soldier, became the youngest president ever in 1901 when President McKinley was assassinated. He went on to become an extremely popular figure. He dissolved 40 monopolistic corporations as a "trust buster," and his "Square Deal" promised a fair shake for both the average citizen (through regulation of railroad rates and pure food and drugs) and the businessman. He was the first U.S. president to call for universal health care and national health insurance. He considered the construction of the Panama Canal his greatest achievement. In 1906 he was the first American to be awarded the Nobel Peace Prize for negotiating the peace in the Russo-Japanese War.

One of his most lasting contributions was the permanent preservation of unique natural resources in the United States. The area of the United States placed under public protection by Roosevelt was approximately 230,000,000 acres.

LEFT: *President Roosevelt on horseback during a visit to Yellowstone Park in 1904.*
BELOW: *Thomas Moran's painting of* The Canyon of Yellowstone, *c. 1911.*

In 1901, a year or so after moving to Columbus, Rollie took the train to Omaha, signed on with the Marshall Paper Company, picked up a 40-pound sample case, and hit the rails. His territory included Nebraska, Kansas, and South Dakota. The drummers' life suited him from the start. And the money was just as good as the glib salesmen had boasted. After a short stint selling paper, he traded it out for a candy line, working for the same company that employed his old boss, Mr. Snow.

While Rollie was out selling—and making valuable contacts in every town in his vast territory—William Hall tended to business at home. He was appointed store manager after his brother's departure, and the vocation suited him more than it had Rollie. Will Hall showed good instincts about inventory and merchandising, and he was popular with the local customers as well as the steady stream of drummers and sales agents that called on the store.

One frequent visitor was William S. Jay, a distributing agent for the *Nebraska State Journal*, who called on the store every six to eight weeks. On one of his stops, he asked Will Hall if he'd like to own a store of his own. Hall was interested but at the time had only about $300 to his name. Jay offered Will a business loan at 2 percent interest. The two began scouting nearby towns for likely properties, eventually finding a bookstore for sale in Norfolk, about 60 miles north of David City. Willie Hall put up his $300, and W.S. Jay loaned him $2,700 for the balance of the purchase. It was the spring of 1905 and 21-year-old William Hall was in business for himself.

LEFT: *Rollie, Marie, and J.C. Hall in front of the family store in Norfolk.*

On May 20, 1905, the *Norfolk Daily News* introduced the new proprietor to its readers:

> *"Mr. Hall, the manager, has been in a business similar to that of the book store for many years and is acquainted with it from the ground up. He comes highly recommended by a large number of Columbus friends, and will be heartily welcomed in Norfolk."*

When school was out, 13-year-old J.C. Hall went to work at the store, and soon after the entire family moved to Norfolk, leaving David City for good.

Norfolk was about twice the size of David City, and while the latter was a rather sleepy farm town, the former had a reputation as a rowdy outpost. For J.C., this reputation was borne out before he set foot in the town.

> *"The day I left David City by train, a man boarded a few stations before Norfolk. It was clear he hadn't neglected his thirst. He made a few loud remarks that he thought were funny, but there was something about him that was frightening. I couldn't take my eyes off him. It wasn't uncommon in those days to carry a gun, but shooting it was another matter. Suddenly he pulled a revolver from his hip pocket and took three shots right down the aisle. As we all ducked behind the seats, I could almost feel the bullets whizzing over my head."*

No one was hurt in that incident, and a brakeman on board administered swift justice by pistol-whipping the man from behind. J.C. took it all in, wide-eyed, like watching a dime novel about the Wild West come to life in front of him. In the next few years, he would witness an impressive array of lawless behavior in Norfolk—bare-knuckle brawls in the streets and even an honest-to-goodness shootout sparked by a disagreement over the poker table. That incident happened just a few doors down from the family store and resulted in a draw—both men died from gunshot wounds. Norfolk would not lack for excitement.

Even if there was ample opportunity for trouble in Norfolk, for J.C. Hall there was no time for it. During the school year, he worked at the store before the class day began, sweeping and dusting, and returned at noon so his brother could take a lunch break. After school, he worked until the store closed at 10:00 ᴾᴹ, taking only a short break at 6:00 ᴾᴹ to have dinner at home with his mother. His salary was $18 per month—a small fortune to him—and he started saving.

ROLLIE HALL

Slight of build and standing only around five-and-a-half feet tall, Rollie B. Hall was an unimposing man. But in the annals of Hallmark, few loom larger than Mr. R.B. Hall.

Much of the now-legendary path trod by J.C. Hall—the schoolboy businesses of selling popcorn and magazines to train passengers and lemonade at baseball games—was, in fact, first tramped by his nine-year-older brother.

Rollie Hall was not a stereotypical salesman. While he had an easy manner with people, he was not gregarious, boisterous, or possessed of a born closer's killer instinct. Learning of his hardscrabble youth and his workmanlike response to those conditions, you get the feeling that he was drawn to the drummer's life not out of a yearning for an adventurous life but for the simple fact that it was a trade he'd mastered early and that rewarded hard work. Selling—whether paper, candy, postcards, or greeting cards—was a good job for a disciplined, well-organized, self-reliant man who was comfortable with his own company. The vocation suited R.B. perfectly.

A consummate gentleman in the "old-fashioned" mode, R.B. Hall endeared himself to his accounts with his honesty, his dry wit, and his gentle rapport. His integrity was legendary. Perhaps, though, what truly set Rollie apart was his capacity for work.

For R.B. Hall, work meant travel. For many decades, he virtually lived on the road. In the years before Hall Brothers, selling for the Marshall Paper Company, and later for Vogel and Dinning Candy Company, Rollie had a three-week territory—meaning it took that long to call on each account once. He lived in hotels and worked seven days a week—a schedule he maintained throughout his career.

> *"Rollie was a terrific worker. He would never stop, day or night."*
> —Willam F. Hall

Rollie moved to Kansas City and into the family company full time in 1911. At age 29, he was already a veteran salesman. His account contacts, relentless drive, and just as importantly, his seed capital, helped get the fledgling company on its feet and on a course to make history.

R.B. Hall would stay with the company, as vice president of sales and trusted counselor to his brother J.C., for 43 years, retiring in 1954. At the time of his retirement, approximately 250 salesmen worked for the company. Mr. R.B. knew them all on a first-name basis. To this day, the top salesmen and women in the company are annually awarded the R.B. Hall Award.

Of all his accomplishments, perhaps none was more important than his role in raising his younger brother. As the oldest son in a fatherless household, Rollie taught J.C. by example—not only about sales and profits, but about people, impressing upon his charge the absolute necessity of maintaining integrity in business and personal affairs.

THE QUIET PHILANTHROPIST

Rollie Hall tended to avoid the spotlight, so much so that many of his contemporaries were never aware just how much impact he had in the lives of others—especially the young and disadvantaged. When Hall Brothers employees came up against unexpected financial hardships, his R.B. Fund, drawn from his personal accounts, would often make up the difference on a mortgage owed or a debt outstanding. His philanthropy was always done quietly, with no fanfare, and with the utmost respect for dignity.

R.B. Hall received many awards and honors in his lifetime, but perhaps the closest to his heart was the Boy Scouts of America's Silver Beaver Award for distinguished service to young men. Donald Hall remembers his eldest uncle as a champion of the sales force and one of the most honest and gentle men he ever knew. "To this day, I always think of Uncle Rollie when I see a silver dollar. Whenever he was around kids, he would slip one in our pockets without us ever feeling a thing. He was very quiet, very small, and a very fine man."

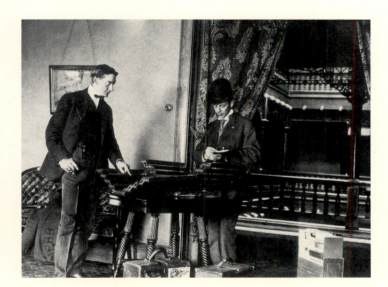

Of course, there was downtime in the store, and Joyce took full advantage. He devoured the constantly refreshed assortment of books and magazines. His favorite was the monthly *American* magazine, which began publication in 1906 and often featured profiles of prominent men in business, the arts, and sports. He paid as much attention to the advertisements as to the stories and credited his lifelong interest in advertising to those boyhood days in the bookstore.

Winter meant less activity in the store and afforded him time to delve into the best-selling books of the day. Favorite authors included Harold MacGrath, Mark Twain, Zane Grey, Booth Tarkington, and Harold Bell Wright.

Books and magazines sold well in the store but the real business was at the cigar counter. Joyce and William played dice poker with customers who could either win a free cigar or end up paying double. Results tended to come out even, but the sales technique helped sell more cigars.

Norfolk was good for the Halls. The family lived with William when they first arrived in town, but before long they had moved into a comfortable, two-story house with central heating and an indoor bathroom. Both Rollie, who was on the road selling candy, and William had respectable incomes. In addition to school and his work at the store, Joyce would take on extra jobs whenever he could. One memorable job was selling newspapers on Saturday night.

On Saturday nights in Norfolk, Joyce Hall found himself the most sought-after person in town. After all, he was the kid who delivered the funnies. By the beginning of the century, some of the country's largest newspapers had begun running comic sections in their Sunday editions. The nearest to Norfolk was the *Chicago American*. On Saturday nights, the Hall bookstore would sell as many as 400 copies of the Sunday edition. Joyce would ride his bicycle to the railroad junction about a mile outside of town, load a teetering stack of newspapers on his bike, and ferry them back into town—delivering them to the waiting crowd. It usually took him a couple of trips to get all 400 to the store.

"We didn't get the newspapers to the store until about eight o' clock, but the crowds started gathering by seven, marching up and down the street and generally having a good time. People made a big event of their Saturday night funny papers."

Rollie Hall spent only about one weekend a month at home; the rest of the time he lugged his candy cases across his sales territory of western Nebraska, Wyoming, and the Black Hills of South Dakota. During Joyce's second summer in Norfolk, Rollie decided to take him along on his route. For Joyce, it was the adventure of a lifetime.

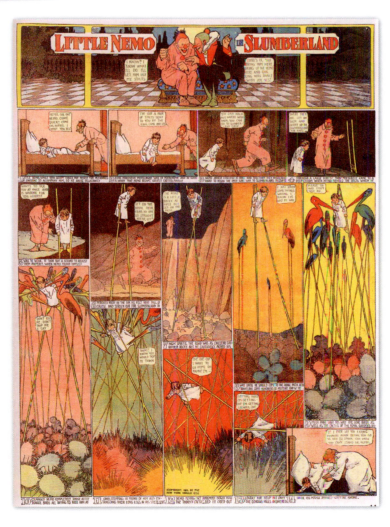

FAR LEFT: *Lyonel Feininger, an American artist based in Munich, Germany, drew a beautiful comic strip filled with oddly shaped characters modeled after the popular* Katzenjammer Kids. *Feininger's* Kin-der-Kids *debuted on May 6, 1906, in the* Chicago Sunday Tribune *with the cartoon characters sailing out of New York's harbor in a bathtub.*

NEAR LEFT: *The* Sunday Comic Weekly. *In 1894, Joseph Pulitzer installed a color printing press and introduced color comics into the Sunday papers. Each Sunday, the front page of the comic supplement featured a full, one-panel, color cartoon, which addressed current social topics, popular culture, or politics.*

By 1908, 75 percent of the Sunday papers in the United States featured comic strips.

LOWER LEFT: *Winsor McKay's* Little Nemo in Slumberland *was one of the most popular serial comics of its day. It ran in newspapers from 1905 to 1914. Translated into seven languages,* Little Nemo *spawned a Broadway musical, several animated films, dolls, and games. McKay's genius lay in his ability to break out of the conventional comic form of uniformly sized stills to capture the surreal dreams of the quiet, anxiety-ridden Little Nemo and his impish, cigar-smoking, dreamland companion, Flip.*

TOP LEFT: *The* American *magazine was one of young J.C. Hall's favorites, c. 1906.*

MIDDLE LEFT: Huckleberry Finn, *as depicted by E. W. Kemble in the original 1884 edition of the book by Mark Twain, considered by many to be one of the greatest American novels ever written.*

LEFT: Secret Service *was one of the most popular color-covered "nickel weeklies," c. 1903.*

19

Before the trip was through, he would learn the drummer's trade firsthand—and see that his brother was a first-rate practitioner.

Rollie had an ulterior motive. He wanted to introduce his younger brother to his customers so the boy could handle his territory the following summer while he took a month's vacation—the first one in his life. Joyce was thrilled. He'd devoured Zane Grey's stories of the wild west while passing time in the bookstore. Now he was going to see the real thing: the wide-open prairie, the Badlands, Deadwood, South Dakota, and, most thrilling of all, Indians! He even packed a .22 revolver (unbeknownst to his brother), just in case.

The trip did not disappoint, but his experience on the Pine Ridge Indian Reservation in the Badlands disavowed him of any romantic notions surrounding the Indians. While there, he saw the desperate conditions the reservation offered and the poor health it virtually guaranteed.

He vividly remembered one particular example:

"Rollie always got a good order here since no other candy man ever showed up. While it was illegal to sell liquor to Indians, there was no law against selling lemon extract, but it must have had a lot of alcohol, because it had the same effect. The drummer who handled it sold it by the wagonload. The sides of the road were so littered with empty bottles that you could hardly see the ground. The sad thing was that it took a good part of the Indians' government allowance to buy the extract."

The following summer, Joyce came back to work the territory alone. Rollie had taken him to Omaha first, to pick up the samples and another provision he deemed essential for a serious salesman—a pair of long pants. Up to that time, J.C. had always sported the knee britches of a schoolboy. But the kind of teaching that took place in the notoriously untamed western territory required a boy to grow up fast.

"Fortunately, most of Rollie's customers had become his good friends, and they would give me an order. A few even gave me extra orders, either to make me feel good or to have something to kid Rollie about."

On his first solo selling trip, Joyce spent some nervous nights in plenty of rough western towns. He remembered a particularly restless night in Lander, Wyoming, when some high-timing cowpunchers galloped their horse down the wooden walkway just on the other side of the wall, shooting holes through the walkway's tin awning.

But when morning came, Joyce got right to business. And he found business, for the most part, to be good. In nearly every town, and on every train in between, he met other drummers

No. 1638. "The Deadwood Coach."
Photo. and copyright by Grabill.

OPPOSITE PAGE: *On his first sales trip alone covering his brother's territory, 16 year-old Joyce rode the legendary Deadwood Stagecoach in the Black Hills of South Dakota. "This was the territory of Buffalo Bill, Calamity Jane, and Wild Bill Hickok, and there were still plenty of similar characters around," said Hall. "I rode with a couple of them the day I took the coach and couldn't take my eyes off of them. It was exciting to see this untamed territory, but it was also a relief to leave."*

selling everything from packaged seeds to patent medicines. Lots of the veterans took a shine to the slim, serious kid from Norfolk, and they were generous with their advice. But one sales technique Joyce picked up put him in hot water with his brother. After writing a small order from a conservative merchant, a fellow drummer suggested that Joyce double the order to boost his sale. The mis-order technique worked just as promised, and Joyce soon tried it out on another customer. This one complained to Rollie about his surrogate's upselling scam, and in Joyce's own words, "the practice ended abruptly." Rollie wasn't about to have the Hall name tarnished by any slippery sales tactics. For Joyce, it was another lesson learned. In his own words, "Play it honest, and work around the clock."

Despite that momentary lapse of judgment, Rollie was impressed with his brother's work ethic. When Joyce returned home to Norfolk, Rollie rewarded him with a Howard pocket watch worth $45, an extremely expensive timepiece for its day. J.C. Hall cherished the memento his entire life.

That fall, news came to town that the Rosebud Indian Reservation would be opening for settlement. A lottery to draw for home sites was to be held in Bonesteel, South Dakota, a town near the reservation. Passenger trains filled with settlers would come through Norfolk on their way to South Dakota every evening for a week—two trains a night. Joyce smelled another profit-making opportunity. He pulled a borrowed popcorn wagon to the junction

ABOVE: *Edward Curtis' photograph of Red Cloud and other Lakota chiefs on the Pine Ridge Reservation in the Black Hills of South Dakota, c. 1905. Beginning in 1866, Red Cloud orchestrated the most successful war against the United States ever fought by an Indian nation. The war ended in 1868 with a victory by the Lakota. The U.S. signed the Treaty of Fort Laramie and agreed to withdraw completely from Lakota territory. The treaty's remarkable provisions mandated that the United States abandon its forts along the Bozeman Trail and guarantee the Lakota their possession of what is now the western half of South Dakota, including the Black Hills, along with much of Montana and Wyoming. The peace, of course, did not last. Custer's 1874 Black Hills expedition's discovery of gold again brought war to the northern Plains, a war that brought an end to independent Indian nations.*

a mile outside of town and popped corn as fast as it could pop. He sold small bags for a nickel. At the end of the week, he had earned a remarkable $180—this in an era where average adult annual wages in the rural Midwest hovered around $600 per year. But for Joyce Hall, that $180 would come to mean even more. In just a few months, his popcorn money would become seed money.

The Man in the Derby Hat

One spring evening in 1905, Joyce Hall was working alone in the store when a sharply dressed young man in a derby hat walked in.

When told that the proprietor was presently unavailable, the man in the derby hat settled in to wait, passing time chatting with Joyce. The dapper man had come from Chicago. He represented a large New York-based importer of picture postcards and had been calling on an account in Fremont, Nebraska, 60 miles down the road. The Chicago man was looking to sign up a wholesaler for his product, but the Fremont meeting had been a bust. He impressed upon the young man how much money there was to be made in "jobbing" postcards. Postcard collecting and sending had become a full-blown national craze. Maybe, he suggested, this Norfolk outfit might be up to the job.

The man showed Joyce his samples. They were large, vividly colored lithographs imported from Germany. Joyce was sold. He asked the man how much money it would take to set up the wholesale business. He said the deal in Fremont would have taken about $1,000 in inventory to get up and running but suggested they might be able to make a go of it for less.

Joyce kept the store open late hoping his brother would show up, but the man grew tired of waiting and said he'd return in the morning. When Joyce saw his brother at home later that night, he breathlessly recounted the meeting with the postcard man, and offered to put up every penny he had to buy into the business.

Will did not share his excitable brother's enthusiasm. "Will just didn't take the postcard business—or me—very seriously," J.C. recalled.

But the Chicago man proved a better salesman than Joyce. After a few hours with the man the next morning, Will Hall was convinced. The initial capital investment would be $540. Will, Joyce, and Rollie would each contribute $180 (the precise amount of Joyce's recently acquired popcorn money). That morning, Joyce and William picked out $540 worth of cards for the initial order of the firm that Joyce had already named the Norfolk Post Card Company. A day after the man in the derby hat walked through the door, the Hall brothers were in the postcard business.

ABOVE: *In 1898, the U.S. government reluctantly gave up its monopoly on printing postcards, which sparked a postcard publishing boom as new publishers rushed into the market. While eager to transfer the burden of card production, but conflicted about the loss of revenue, the government issued new postal regulations with many added restrictions. Starting on July 1, 1898, postcards could be sent through the mail for only one cent regardless of whether they contained a message or not. The words "Private Mailing Card —Authorized by the Act of Congress on May 19th, 1898" were required to be printed on the back of all cards not issued by the government.*

ABOVE: *On December 24, 1901, new regulations were issued and the words "Post Card" replaced "Private Mailing Card" on the backs of privately made cards. Government-issued cards would retain the title "Postal" though the public would soon use both names interchangeably. As the images gracing the front of postcards grew larger, only a small blank border, usually along the bottom or side, remained to write a message as postal regulations allowed for only the address to be written on the back.*

TOP: *William F. (Will) Hall and family, c. 1910.*

THE PICTURE POSTCARD CRAZE

Picture postcards were first produced in Austria in 1869. Their popularity spread across Europe rapidly in the 1870s.

In the U.S., the post office had sold plain, prepaid postcards for decades. But it would be nearly 30 years after the rise of picture postcards in Europe before the practice of sending privately produced postcards—and the hobby of collecting them—caught on in the United States.

When the trend did arrive in America, it would become the most extraordinary collecting phenomena the nation had ever seen. People feverishly collected the color lithographed cards, which sold for anywhere from two cents to twenty-five cents each. Postcard albums were proudly displayed in the parlors of grand homes and on dining tables in modest shacks alike.

Consider this staggering statistic: official figures from the U.S. Post Office for the fiscal year ending June 30, 1908, cite 677,777,798 postcards mailed. At the time, the total population of the U.S. was 88,700,000. That's an average of nearly eight postcards for every person in the country!

At the time, postcards were more about the image than the message. In fact, writing personal messages on the address side of a postcard was forbidden by the U.S. Post Office until 1907. This is why you'll often see personal messages written over the images on postcard fronts. Postcards with a divided back, which permitted room to write, were finally permitted beginning March 1, 1907. The mailing rate at the time was two cents. The plain postal service cards, known as "penny postcards," sold for one cent each.

The product to feed America's postcard addiction came largely from abroad. At the height of the craze, European publishers accounted for more than 75 percent of all postcards sold in the U.S. Germany, a nation with a highly advanced lithographic process, was the undisputed world leader in postcard production. This dominance of the industry continued until World War I brought an end to German card production. English and U.S. publishers moved in to fill the void, but no one could match the Germans' quality.

By around 1915, that lack of quality product, combined with the rise of the telephone as a quick, easy, and novel form of communication, spelled an end to the craze that captivated the nation.

THE PANIC OF 1907

The explosion of postcard publishing in the early years of the 20th century reflected a broader national economic boom that began with the end of the Spanish American War. The optimism and greed of this time translated into the growth and formation of a vast number of new companies, often propped up by unwise extensions of credit.

The Panic of 1907, also known as the 1907 Bankers' Panic, was a financial crisis that occurred when the New York Stock Exchange fell close to 50 percent from its peak the previous year. There were numerous runs on banks and trust companies. The 1907 panic eventually spread throughout the nation when many state and local banks and businesses entered into bankruptcy. Primary causes of the run included a retraction of market liquidity by a number of New York City banks, loss of confidence among depositors, and the absence of a statutory lender of last resort.

The crisis occurred after the failure in October 1907 of an attempt to corner the market on stock of the United Copper Company. When this bid failed, banks that had lent money to the cornering scheme suffered runs that later spread to affiliated banks and trusts, leading a week later to the downfall of Knickerbocker Trust Company—New York City's third-largest trust. The collapse of the Knickerbocker spread fear throughout the city's trusts as regional banks withdrew reserves from New York City banks. Panic extended across the nation as vast numbers of people withdrew deposits from their regional banks.

The sight of a desperate mob besieging a bank became common in the following weeks. Meanwhile, a coterie of New York financiers, led by J. P. Morgan, raised enough cash to import $100 million in European gold to finance the stricken banks. In Washington, President Teddy Roosevelt assured the nation that its financial institutions were secure. Just to make sure, he authorized Secretary of the Treasury George Cortelyou to transfer massive sums directly to struggling New York banks and to issue $150 million in low-interest government bonds. The cash infusion reassured skittish depositors, and they stopped their withdrawals.

The following year, Senator Nelson W. Aldrich established and chaired a commission to investigate the crisis and propose future solutions, leading to the creation of the Federal Reserve System.

TOP: *Worried investors gather outside the New York Stock Exchange in October 1907.*

ABOVE: *Edward Steichen's famous portrait of J.P Morgan, c. 1905. What looks like a knife in his hand is actually the arm of the chair.*

ABOVE: *As the public's desire for postcards grew, the businesses supporting this demand grew. Decorative storage boxes and albums of all kinds flooded the market. Many clever devices were also made for the display of postcards. The most enduring was the revolving metal card rack, invented by E.I. Dail in 1908. (A similar rack sits on the counter behind an unknown shopkeeper.) It allowed self-service of merchandise while taking up less space than conventional wall racks. Dail sold 5,000 racks in the first nine months of production. With all of the newer innovations that have come to pass, the simple basic design of the postcard rack has endured.*

"ONE OF THE GREAT SELLERS IN THE STORE SOON WAS POSTCARDS— BIRTHDAY GREETINGS, SCENIC VIEWS OF STREAMS, MOUNTAINS, ROADS, LAKES, TREES; CONGRATULATIONS CARDS, CHRISTMAS, EASTER, VALENTINE... THE RACK HELD AN ESTIMATED 500 DESIGNS AND IT WOULD BE NOTHING UNUSUAL FOR SIX OR TWELVE PEOPLE TO BE AROUND IT AT ONE TIME."

—*William F. Hall*

Looking back on the meeting more than half a century later, Hall recognized the weight of destiny in the moment.

"Many times since, I've wondered where I'd be and what I'd be doing if he hadn't stopped in our store that night."

Rollie Hall learned of the new business, of which he was one-third partner, when he returned from working his territory. As the brothers had hoped, he added the postcards as a sideline business and added a fat binder to his sample load. He soon found that the cards sold well enough to make the extra effort worthwhile.

Back in Norfolk, William and Joyce encouraged every drummer who called on the store to carry the postcards as a sideline in a similar fashion. Soon the Norfolk Post Card Company was being well represented throughout the region.

William Hall also made certain that his Norfolk customers were well supplied with postcards. He offered a mix of custom-made cards with local views along with generic cards bought from wholesalers. Most cards sold two for a nickel.

In 1907, the *Norfolk Daily News* reported that, "The postal card craze retains its hold on Norfolk with undiminished vigor, boosting post office receipts and bringing joy and coin to the card dealers."

So intense was the passion of postcard buyers that William Hall decided to remodel the entire back half of the store to accommodate inventory. The news was significant enough to warrant coverage in the *Daily News*:

"A balcony, 20' x 25', is to be built in the rear of the store over the present packing and storage room. The wholesale postal card business will occupy this balcony."

Meanwhile, Joyce carved out a territory for himself closer to home. He'd call on a merchant in a nearby town on Friday evenings and hit two or three others on Saturdays. When school let out for the summer, he'd take one- and two-week trips through Nebraska and South Dakota. On one of these trips, he met an amiable man from Cedar Rapids, Iowa, who was selling a product he'd not heard of before: sweeping compound. A simple mixture of saw dust, sand, and paraffin oil, sweeping compound was made to sprinkle onto wood floors before sweeping. The coarse sand cleaned the floor, and the oil and sawdust kept the dust down.

In a time when most streets were unpaved and most floors were bare wood, keeping floors clean was a constant struggle. The compound worked, and according to Joyce's new acquaintance, it sold. Customers paid $3.50 for a 100 pound keg. The man agreed to sell Joyce a carload of the compound at a discount and give him an exclusive on his territory.

Joyce repeated the man's sales pitch to his brothers, but he couldn't talk them into the venture. Undeterred, he visited the local bank. He walked out with a loan of "a few hundred dollars." That, combined with some savings of his own, was enough to buy a carload of the compound. The banker provided the 17-year-old with a rubber stamper to endorse checks. It read: Norfolk Brokerage Company—J.C. Hall, Manager.

In the summer of 1909, Joyce headed out with Rollie again—this time selling postcards and sweeping compound while his brother sold candy. He did eventually sell out his stock of the cleaning compound, but it became increasingly clear to Joyce that the market for postcards had considerably more potential.

"I thought that I might combine my sweeping-compound business with my 'popcorn empire.' Now, of course, I realize what a serious mistake these ventures would have been. Popcorn machines were only successful while they were a novelty. And sweeping compound only took an empty shed and a few dollars' worth of sand, sawdust, and paraffin oil—and anyone could get in the business."

In August, the two brothers made a stop in Omaha, and Rollie managed to track down their father. They hadn't seen him since Joyce was seven—over 10 years earlier—and this would be the last time they ever would. They told their father about their various business ventures, and Joyce eagerly explained their growing postcard business. The elder Hall was impressed by his sons' successes but had a suggestion for them: relocate to Omaha.

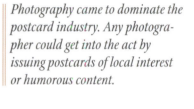

Photography came to dominate the postcard industry. Any photographer could get into the act by issuing postcards of local interest or humorous content.

The beginning of the 20th century was also the start of an age of mass consumerism. Vacations and trips were now a marketed commodity. Railroads, in particular, made efforts to associate travel to the proper locations with becoming a better citizen.

164. Watching the progress of fire from Lafayette Square, Apr. 18, 1906. San Francisco, Cal.

Applying paint by hand was commonly done on postcards begining in 1902. Each colorist was responsible for one hue, which would be applied by hand to a printing block in production-line fashion. The blocks were then used to make the finished postcard.

With the growth of the middle class, more women began to receive an education, and their desire to step out into the world increased. But it was also a time of expectations outpacing social realities. Depictions of women were changing, but they were still confined to a number of prescribed roles.

Greetings from Ocean Grove. The yacht was in Howard

Norfolk, he pointed out, was too small to support a wholesale business. Joyce, in particular, took that advice to heart. He had already been thinking the same thing.

And a move to Omaha might well have been the next step for the fledgling business were it not for one more chance encounter. This one would happen a few months later, in Norfolk. In December of 1909, a cigar salesman from Kansas City called on the store. His name was John H. Conway, and he held particular fascination for Joyce because of his previous job. He had been a professional baseball umpire in the National League.

The drummer and the young man fell into easy conversation. Joyce told him of his plans to move the company to Omaha in the new year. Conway liked the plan but told Joyce he had picked the wrong town. He then launched into a description of Kansas City so effusive that it might have made the head of the chamber of commerce blush.

He talked about the indomitable enthusiasm of the city's residents and leaders, something he and others referred to as "the Kansas City spirit." He pointed out that the city had gotten the railroad built across the Missouri River at Kansas City instead of Leavenworth or St. Joseph, where it had been planned. Even more impressive was the mind-bogglingly fast rebuilding of the convention hall that the city had pulled off nine years earlier. When the newly built hall had been destroyed by fire just three months before the scheduled 1900 Democratic National Convention, business leaders vowed to have a new facility ready in time, then made it happen. Yes, sir, Kansas City was the place for an ambitious young man with a head full of dreams.

J.C. Hall was impressed with the lofty talk. But, in truth, he had another, slightly less lofty, reason for preferring Kansas City to Omaha. Marie Tracy, whom Hall called "the prettiest girl in my class," had moved there with her family six months earlier.

Whatever the motivation, Kansas City was undeniably an ideal spot for a wholesale business. Its location in the center of the country and its extensive rail network made it a natural hub for conducting a growing business.

Though nearly an adult, Joyce sought his family's approval for a move. It took some of his best selling skills to close the deal. His ace-in-the-hole, in fact, was a promise to attend business school in Kansas City. By the end of the year, Joyce had made his case. On January 9, 1910, he boarded a train headed south from Norfolk. Onboard, the conductor collected a one-way ticket to Kansas City.

19 07

Christmas Greetings
and all Good Wishes
for the New Year

Merry Christmas
and
A Happy New Year

Hearty
Congratulations
on the DATE

Hearty Congratulations,
and wishes most sincere,
For health and luck
continued through
The year TODAY
is bringing you,
And many a future year!

JOY AHEAD!

THE YEARS HAVE WINGS, BUT KINDLY ONES,
THAT SPEED US ON TO HAPPY SCENES,
AND EACH NEW YEAR BRINGS BRIGHTER SUNS,
AND SO THIS BIRTHDAY ONLY MEANS
THAT YOU HAVE COME TO BLUER SKIES,
WITH EACH NEW DAY A GLAD SURPRISE!

CHAPTER TWO

That Kansas City Spirit

(1910 – 1915)

> *"It's a funny thing about life; if you refuse to accept anything but the best, you very often get it."*
>
> — *W. Somerset Maugham*

O n Monday morning, January 10, 1910, Joyce Hall stepped off the train in Kansas City, Missouri, and into a new world. He was met by no one but disembarked into a crowded, noisy terminal that had nothing in common with the sleepy Norfolk, Nebraska, station save the steel rails running into its roundhouse.

As most train passengers did, he had arrived at the city's Union Depot, an imposing, Victorian behemoth of a building nearly 400 feet long—as long as an entire town block in Norfolk and half again. A four-sided clock tower, 125 feet high, loomed over the entrance. When it opened in 1878, the local *Kansas City Star* had declared it the "handsomest and largest railroad depot west of New York."

But by 1910, the grand station was frankly a grimy dump. Plans were already being drawn up for a station to replace it, and the old Victorian lady was showing unmistakable signs of neglect. Union Depot stood not in the city's downtown but in the sandy soil of the city's sprawling, flat lowlands west of town near the

confluence of the Missouri and Kansas Rivers, an area known as the West Bottoms. And the Bottoms were known for the industry that had put Kansas City on the map: meat packing.

In 1910, Kansas City was second only to Chicago among the nation's meat-packing centers. A constant stream of railcars brought cattle, hogs, and sheep from Kansas, Colorado, and Texas, and they all ended up in the West Bottoms, first in the vast stockyards for fattening up, and then into the slaughterhouses for processing. The sheer numbers were staggering. In 1907 alone, an estimated 7.5 million animals—more than 20,000 each day— rolled into the stockyards. Some animals were moved farther east, but the great majority met their end in the Kansas City stockyards.

Union Depot stood just east of the endless stockyards, but for out-of-town passengers arriving there, the first impression of the city wasn't the site of endless, fenced feedlots and rendering houses. The first impression was the smell. The stench rising from the yards and rendering plants was thick, acrid, and relentless. But

to plant owners and railroad magnates that shipped the meat to big eastern cities, it was the smell of money.

Stepping out of the station onto Union Avenue on that cold January day, J.C. Hall and his fellow passengers were greeted by a seedy row of beer halls and cheap hotels. The street, with its 23 saloons, was known as "Kansas City's wettest block."

The scene was loud, lurid, grimy, smoky, and smelly. It assaulted the senses in every way.

"I asked the price of a horse-drawn cab, but it was too much. I trudged up the long wooden chute to the streetcar line. That got me to elevated tracks over the railroad, then through another wooden chute and up a huge bluff to the downtown business district. Things began to look better. My confidence in the Kansas City spirit was renewed."

ABOVE: *A train arriving at Kansas City's Union Depot, c. 1900.*

TOP: *The West Bottoms looking down the elevated streetcar line from the bluffs. Union Depot is on the top left.*

LEFT: *Union Depot, c. 1900.*

With the bustling city laid out before him, J.C. gripped his two heavy bags tightly and headed straight for The Baltimore Hotel, a Louis Curtiss-designed jewel with a reputation so lofty that it had even reached rural Nebraska. He was awed by the Carrara marble columns and great fountain.

Then he walked out of the grand hotel and set out to find the local YMCA. It stood a few blocks away at 10th and Oak Street. He secured a corner room on the top floor. Then, stashing his bags, he set out to explore his new hometown.

He bought a much-needed overcoat at one store and a pair of shoes at another and continued to walk the busy streets. He passed theaters, restaurants, and opulent hotels. As he walked, he was careful to dodge the clacking cable cars as they careened down hills and around corners. He stopped in a cafeteria—the first he had ever seen—to get some lunch and marveled at its efficient operation, a choreographed system of moving dishes, food, and diners.

KANSAS CITY IN 1910

When he wasn't working, 19 year-old J.C. Hall found plenty of diversions and a city on the move.

On summer nights, residents flocked to Heim's Electric Park at 45th and Paseo Boulevard. Billing itself as the Coney Island of Kansas City, the amusement park was famous for its fountains and dramatic light displays—it was said to be illuminated by over 100,000 bulbs. Even more impressive, it featured draught beer piped in directly from the nearby Heim Brewery.

Kansas City was a top-notch theater town. The Willis Wood, the Shubert, and the Grand hosted musical and vaudeville greats and touring productions of Broadway shows. Guided by a young landscape engineer, George Kessler, Kansas City was at the forefront of a national "city beautiful" movement. The movement's legacy would be Kansas City's remarkable network of boulevards, parks, and greenspaces.

In Swope Park, at the city's southeastern edge, Kansas City's first municipal zoo opened in 1909. Its 60 acres and single stone building were home to Asian elephants, lions, monkeys, and a bear purchased from a traveling circus.

The minor league Kansas City Blues baseball team played at 20th and Olive Street on the city's east side.

The 1910 U.S. Census reported 248,381 Kansas City residents, ranking it as the country's 20th most populated residential area.

Kansas City ranked as the nation's second-largest railroad terminal.

In 1909, a new train station was approved by the city council and voters. The new Union Station—just a few blocks away from Hallmark's future headquarters—was completed in 1914.

After lunch, J.C. walked down a two-block stretch of 11th Street that was home to the city's most fashionable shops. The postholiday sales were on. At the Woolf Brothers clothing store, window posters announced $25 suits marked down to $18.25. At Paul Kessel furriers, a mink muff and neck piece set was marked down from $50 to $20. And around the corner at the J.W. Jenkins & Sons Music Company, a new Steinway piano could be had for $550.

On the ground floor of the Altman Building, Hall found a multichair barbershop and stopped in for a haircut.

"The man who cut my hair was one of the proprietors, Earl T. Hedrick. When I told him I'd just arrived in Kansas City, he backed way, pointed his scissors at me and said, 'Young man, I'm going to give you such a good haircut that when you need another, you'll come back to me.' And I did—for almost fifty years."

His first few hours in the city provide a revealing insight into a young man who absolutely couldn't wait to make a go of it in the business world. He was curious, energetic, intrigued by technology and progress, and, as his new barber would learn over the years, loyal to a fault.

The next day, J.C. Hall walked to the New York Life Building and registered at Spalding Commercial College.

Hall signed up to study courses in the commercial department. His coursework ran the spectrum from spelling to commercial law.

The founder of the school, George E. Spalding, was a lively, charismatic man whose long, curly white hair and cowboy hat made him a ringer for Buffalo Bill. His personal slogan was printed on a tin sign that hung above an old grandfather's clock:

"Time is money—Save time." J.C. Hall would take the message to heart.

"That simple slogan made a great impression on me. As my own business grew, I adopted it and changed it to read: 'Time is everything—save time.' I had already seen that the difference between failure and success was making the best use of time. I never could sit around waiting for things to happen; it's more fun making them happen."

Truth be told, it was pretty difficult for J.C. Hall to sit around Spalding Commercial College, too. The school offered coursework in three-month terms. By the time spring rolled around at the end of his first term, he couldn't wait to get back to selling full time and building his business. After all, he hadn't come to the city chasing the dream of becoming a flawless speller.

As soon as the term ended, J.C. began spending three or four days out of every week on sales trips. He'd ride the Hannibal and St. Joseph Railroad through central and northern Missouri on one trip and take the MKT (Missouri, Kansas, and Texas Railroad) as

OPPOSITE PAGE : *Kansas City's Petticoat Lane as J.C. would have first seen it in 1910.*

BELOW: *Map of West Bottoms, published in 1895, shows the stockyards, processing plants, and the vast train infrastructure that supported it and the rest of Kansas City. The circled area on lower left is the Union Depot.*

"EVERYTHING'S UP TO DATE IN KANSAS CITY. THEY GONE ABOUT AS FER AS THEY CAN GO. THEY WENT AN' BUILT A SKYSCRAPER SEVEN STORIES HIGH, ABOUT AS HIGH AS A BUILDIN' ORTA GROW. EVERYTHING'S LIKE A DREAM IN KANSAS CITY—IT'S BETTER THAN A MAGIC LANTERN SHOW."

—Rodgers and Hammerstein, "Kansas City" from Oklahoma!

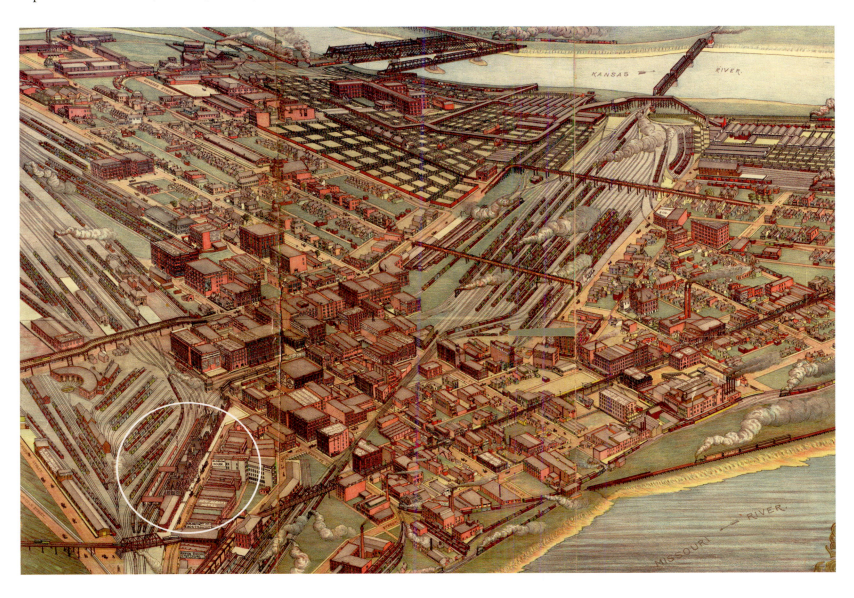

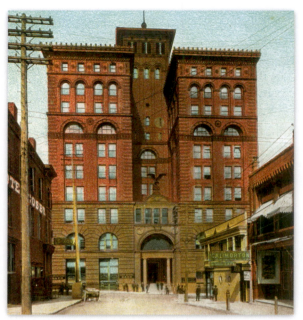

far west as Wichita, Kansas, on the next. He'd stop in every town with a station, selling to every shop he could find. Then he'd roll back into Kansas City to fill the orders and keep the books.

It was an impossible schedule to maintain. And as hard as he pushed, he knew he could never hit the majority of the small, rural towns he needed to reach to keep business growing. He wished Rollie were there and told his brother so in occasional letters home. He tried to convince his brother that together they could make something big in Kansas City. But Rollie, while still selling postcards as a sideline, had a good thing going in the candy business. For now, at least, J.C. was on his own.

J.C. did have one idea that he thought might solve his distribution problem. It involved the U.S. mail. His plan was simple but somewhat risky. And definitely brash. Here's what he did:

He received cards from his suppliers in decks of 100—all of the same design. Thousands of different designs were available. He took 100 of these decks and made up his own assortments: one hundred sets of 100 different cards. All of this inventory was stored in boxes stacked floor-to-ceiling in his room at the YMCA.

The risky part was the distribution. J.C. purchased maps of Missouri, Kansas, and four surrounding states. He made lists of every town with a population over 1,000 and under 10,000.

He identified what he thought would be worthwhile but overlooked markets. The obvious problem was that he didn't know the names of any of the retail establishments in these towns. He decided to take a gamble with his inventory. He addressed each package of one hundred cards to "The Leading Post Card Dealer" along with the town name and state. An enclosed invoice listed "100 assorted Post Cards, amount due $1.08"—a penny a piece for the cards and eight cents for shipping. His room at the YMCA became considerably more roomy. Now there was nothing to do but sit back and wait.

Some of the packages came back just a few days later, undeliverable due to incomplete addresses. Other parcels were returned by angry merchants who couldn't believe the cheek of sending unordered merchandise, payment due. Still other packages were received as if they were gifts—the recipients never bothered paying at all.

A few tense weeks passed before the first check arrived: payment in full for delivery of merchandise. Then a few more trickled in. Then a steady stream. Eventually, about a third of the cold-called accounts paid for the cards.

It wasn't a windfall, but enough. Enough to restock inventory, enough to keep business afloat. The accounts that paid got a new shipment the next month and each subsequent month, and gradually a client list of mail-order customers was built. J.C. Hall's gamble had paid off.

It wasn't long before the YMCA began to object to Hall running a mail-order business from his room. He learned of a small second-story room available in the Braley Building just a few blocks down 10th Street. This was the same building that housed The Crafters print shop that had printed invoices and stationery for the Halls' postcard company. J.C. signed a lease and now the Norfolk Post Card Company had a legitimate Kansas City address. Soon it had an employee, too. A young man named Kim Barnes who had worked at the Hall bookstore in Norfolk moved to Kansas City in the spring of the same year to help sort and fill orders. By summer's end, the company had outgrown its tight quarters and rented an adjoining room to accommodate its expanded operation.

J.C. was impressed by the work that came out of The Crafters print shop. The company had only one small press and a hand cutter, but they were good typesetters. Though the Norfolk Post Card Company had always been jobbers—selling postcards purchased from large publishers in Europe and back east—J.C. had long toyed with the idea of publishing his own cards. He had noticed a drop off in the quality of the product available and knew that publishing cards himself would put him in control. He selected some of his favorite quotes from famous men and hired The Crafters shop to print them.

The softening postcard market lead to other innovations as well. One notable attempt to recapture the public's interest was a line of leather postcards with burned-in designs. The cards retailed for 10 cents and featured what was, for the day, fairly bold humor—a new area for the company. While they were produced with high quality, they were not exactly high-minded. A popular

ABOVE: *The Braley Building, the first real address for the Norfolk Post Card Company and ultimately the Hall Brothers.*

BELOW: *A leather postcard from 1907.*

one read: "The Cowboy's Creed—Live every day so you can look any man in the eye and tell him to go straight to hell."

J.C. Hall would later credit the novelty postcards with "keeping us alive for a time." One of their bestsellers bore a simple message in bold type: "SMILE, damn you, smile." It's advice that Hall admits he had difficulty taking himself.

"There were not many light moments during those early years—and I suffered all my life from just barely smiling when I should have grinned and grinning when I should have laughed."

But if the addition of these novelty cards helped, they didn't address an even larger concern. J.C. was becoming increasingly convinced that postcards in general were a passing fancy. Because of their limited writing surface, they were a poor form of communication. As collectibles, their appeal was fading as their novelty wore off. It would be a few more years before the trend became obvious to most, but to someone so intimately familiar with the business, it was clear that the decade-long craze was becoming played out.

Still, for the time being, Hall's strategy was to work harder, travel more, and make up volume by adding accounts. Any notion he had of returning to school in the fall of 1910 was out of the question. "It may seem a strange statement," he admitted, "but I couldn't afford to go back to school. If I hadn't spent all my time running the business, I probably would have lost it altogether."

Despite the tough market, he still believed—in himself and his company. And he attributed much of his willingness to hang on to the city he had grown to love. He'd found the Kansas City spirit to be very real. And contagious, too.

J.C. knew he needed help, especially on the sales end. Not surprisingly, he turned to the best salesman he knew—his brother, Rollie. In occasional letters home, he had kept his family apprised of his successes in Kansas City. He had been hoping all along that they would join him. But as autumn turned to winter, he pressed the case harder.

In a letter to Rollie, he stressed the easy money to be made and pushed for a move sooner rather than later.

> *Dear Rollie,*
>
> *I think you will find it an easy matter to sell $200 a week and after you get the business worked up there will be no limit to what you can sell. I will have our line in fine shape by the first of the year and it won't be such a hard graft as you have now.*
>
> *I think that you had better plan to leave Norfolk with Mama and Marie on Christmas morning or even sooner. You could help Mama pack the mornings of the week before Christmas and then you could be all ready Christmas morning and get in here the day after Christmas. I expect you had better ship the household goods the day before Christmas so that they will be here by the time you get here.*
>
> *You want to be sure and be here in plenty of time so as to be ready to go on the road Monday the 2nd as the first weeks in the year ought to be good when the people are getting new cards to take the place of the Christmas and New Year cards.*
>
> *Love to all,*
>
> *Joyce*

His efforts paid off. When 1911 arrived, Rollie, sister Marie, and their mother joined J.C. in Kansas City. They bought a comfortable house on Troost Avenue. For Rollie, it hadn't been an easy decision. He had been making $5,000 a year from his well-established candy-selling business—a lot to give up. J.C. knew that throwing in with him full time was a risky proposition.

Rollie's impact on the business was felt immediately. As J.C. had suggested in his letter, the eldest Hall brother set out directly after the new year. Rollie organized a three-week territory covering the most productive towns in the surrounding states. J.C. ran the office and took shorter selling trips close to home. He bought himself his first car, a four-door Hupmobile. Despite frequent breakdowns, the car proved to be an efficient alternative to trains on these shorter trips. At least, that's what J.C. told himself. The real truth was J.C. simply loved "automobiling," despite the hassles that came with it. On one memorable trip across the state to St. Louis, he racked up 11 flat tires—all of which had to be laboriously hand patched and reinflated by the roadside.

J.C. Hall, c. 1911

The first three employees of Hall Brothers: (l. to r.) Marion Pond, Kim Barnes and (probably) Julian Raines.

Postcard publishers were forever seeking a competitive advantage, a product that others didn't have. So the novelty postcard came into being. They took many forms. Some were made from an unusual material such as metal, celluloid, leather, or wood. Others had attachments of feathers or fabric, and still others utilized songs, pop-outs, cut-out shapes, or an exotic technical process.

OPPOSITE PAGE TOP: *Among the more popular novelty postcards were the mechanical ones. These were cards with moving parts. At the base of this card is a tab that can be pulled and the image changed.*

MIDDLE LEFT: *A Tuck patented press-out postcard featuring birds with press-out wings.*

MIDDLE RIGHT: *A song card.*

BOTTOM (FROM LEFT): *Leather postcards were a very popular novelty. The rose is draped with an embossed and foiled gold locket. A Message from Butte features a cut-out to insert a photo and an envelope for a letter.*

Rollie's presence also lent some gravitas to the company. J.C. was still a lanky 19 year-old and by his own account looked even younger. They made a decision in 1911 to hire some in-house salesmen, but as J.C. remembered, "a veteran salesman—who might be twice my age—would take one look at me and shake his head. How could a boy run a business?" With Rollie on board, the company gained a legitimacy and a world of experience in sales.

He could never have guessed the impact his particular selling style would have on generations of Hallmark sales personnel that would follow, but, according to his brother, Rollie set a permanent standard for the company's sales philosophy.

"He never used pressure. He sold his product because he believed in it, and he never sold anything that he didn't think a dealer could sell himself. His customers were his friends, and I can't recall Rollie ever losing a customer— or a friend. As a salesman, he was not particularly imaginative or aggressive, but he was industrious and every ounce a gentleman."

Despite their sales push, by 1912 postcard sales were down. The craze was crashing, and no amount of effort by the Hall brothers was going to renew the public's interest. Part of the problem came from the supply side. Manufacturers had started cheapening the quality, and discount stores flooded the market with cards that retailed for 10 cents a dozen. Basic cards had typically sold two for five cents up to that point. Customers no longer felt compelled to wallpaper rooms with postcards or even display them in albums.

Though they hadn't acquired the name yet, greeting cards had been around for years. The vast majority were sold for Christmas and Valentine's Day and, as with postcards, most came from Germany and England. The Halls' Norfolk store had introduced what it called "Christmas letters" as something new for the holidays in 1911.

For the two brothers in Kansas City, adding greeting cards with envelopes to their line was an obvious next step.

Of course, the tiny Kansas City company wasn't alone in picking up the new trend. In fact, not far from its modest downtown office, another Kansas City family operation, headed by a bookseller named Fred Rust, had begun selling cards in 1906. The Rust Craft Company would grow to become the second-largest card company in the country by the mid-1950s. Through a series of mergers and acquisitions, it has since been absorbed into other companies and no longer exists.

Having seen encouraging sales with their first forays into the Christmas card business in 1912 and 1913, the Hall brothers were convinced that this new business was the way to go, and they were ready to bet their future on it.

J.C. Hall took a trip to Chicago to make a deal with the Murray Engraving Company—a prestigious publisher of high-end cards—to become their exclusive wholesaler to the industry. He thought the deal was done, and the company prepared for a big influx of new offerings and customers leading into Christmas. But when a salesman from Murray came to town, it was obvious that the deal had not come off as expected. "He wanted our order, but only as retailers, not wholesalers."

J.C. rushed back to Chicago to try to set things right, but to no avail. "Once again," said Hall, "it looked as if we were in trouble. We had to have engraved cards—and soon."

Hall knew of a small engraving company in Kansas City that he thought could handle the job. He quickly pulled together a handful of designs—a poinsettia, a holly wreath, and a few others—and added a variety of sentiments. In all, it gave them a line of 20 cards. On the back of each was the inscription:

Published by Hall Bros., Kansas City, Mo., Made in U.S.A.

It was the first time the Hall name had appeared on a card they had sold. With that humble and quickly assembled offering, the Hall brothers became more than jobbers. They were in the publishing business. And they'd never look back.

"SEVENTEEN THOUSAND DOLLARS BEHIND SCRATCH"

By 1915, the five-year-old company founded by the Hall brothers had become a pretty fair reflection of the city it called home. Hustling, successful, confident, and, above all, hard-working. It was the Kansas City spirit made flesh. The company had faced, and overcome, its share of obstacles, and midway through the century's second decade, the future looked bright.

After a successful 1914 Christmas selling season, the firm was gearing up for the next holiday. By early January, they had received all their shipments of valentine cards and were ready to start filling orders. But in the predawn hours of January 11, 1915—nearly five years to the day after J.C. Hall had arrived in the city—everything changed.

"About five o'clock in the morning I had a call from Reed Gentry, an officer in the small bank that occupied half of our building. He was an easygoing fellow and said, 'Hall, your place is on fire.' I'll be right down, I said. 'Don't hurry,' he said. 'It's all burned down.'"

Hall pulled a pair of pants over his pajamas and rushed down to the store. By the time he arrived, everything that could burn had. Several feet of water stood in the basement, partially covering a small iron safe that held all of their accounts, orders, and a little cash.

Before long, the rest of the company's small staff had assembled in front of the building. The thermometer stood frozen near zero degrees. The entire stock of valentines, for which the company was heavily in debt, had been destroyed. As the sun came up on their burned-out building, they wondered if it had set on their business.

Hall would later write that he was almost in a state of shock but noted "there's a big difference between being shocked and being whipped."

The first concern was whether the account files and orders had survived the fire. He hired a team of dray horses to haul the safe out of the flooded basement. The safe's dial was still hot enough to burn Hall's fingers. But their luck ticked up a bit. The safe proved both fireproof and waterproof—its contents were spared. So they still knew who had ordered their valentines, even if they had no stock to send them. The next stroke of luck bordered on the unbelievable. J.C. Hall remembered it nearly 60 years after the fact with a sense of wonder still intact.

"At this point, a well-dressed young man introduced himself as Willard Rupe, the manager of the Starr Piano Company, which was located a few doors from us on the second floor of the old Kansas City Star *building. He said he had leased part of his space for future use; then added some of the nicest words I've ever heard: 'You're welcome to use the space without any charge.' He even furnished a typewriter, some tables, and chairs. This was probably the most generous thing anybody had ever done for me. We stayed there several years and paid rent every month in spite of Rupe's reluctance to take it."*

Chalk up another one to the Kansas City spirit—this time manifested as the spirit of giving.

By 10 o'clock the same morning, they were operating again. Hall called their two principal valentine suppliers, explained the situation, and asked if they could duplicate their shipments. He said he didn't know when they could pay for the replacement inventory but assured them they would. Both took him at his word, and orders were shipped by express the same day.

After the smoke had cleared, Hall had a chance to assess their position. They were bloodied, to be sure, but not beaten. Even with a $9,000 insurance settlement, he estimated that they were $17,000 in debt.

"Someone said, 'Hall, you're starting all over again from scratch.' 'That isn't so,' I told him. 'We're starting from seventeen thousand dollars behind scratch.'"

ABOVE: *In 1914, the Hall brothers opened their first retail store in Kansas City on the ground floor of the Corn Belt building, 1019 Grand Avenue. The company's wholesale operations occupied the building's rear balcony and basement. After the building burned, they moved next door to the Starr Piano Company.*

"IF WE WERE GOING TO QUIT, THIS WOULD HAVE BEEN A GOOD TIME TO DO IT."

—*J.C. Hall*

"I THINK HE THOUGHT THAT THAT WAS THE END OF HIS BUSINESS. HE DIDN'T KNOW HOW HE WAS GOING TO GET BACK."

—*Evert Wampler, on J.C. Hall immediately after the fire of 1915.*

"YOU KNOW, I'VE KNOWN MR. J.C. HALL FOR A LONG WHILE. I NEVER KNEW A MAN IN MY LIFE THAT COULD GET IN AS MANY RAT HOLES AND GET OUT OF THEM AS WELL AS HE COULD."

—*Robert Dominick, of Trader's Bank, the banker who loaned J.C. Hall the money to pay off his debts after the fire.*

A Short History of Greeting Cards

The custom of exchanging written greetings goes back nearly to the invention of writing itself. In the palace of Egyptian pharaohs sentiments were conveyed on papyrus scrolls, and good will wishes for the New Year were exchanged at the court of ancient Chinese emperors.

John Calcott Horsley

Today it's estimated that Americans give about 6.5 billion greeting cards each year. Modern printed cards have roots in handmade greetings that go back to the European Middle Ages. These masterfully crafted artworks usually celebrated romantic love, but others were given as souvenirs for birthdays, Saints' Days, or proposals of marriage. By the early 1400s, handmade paper greeting cards were being exchanged in Europe, while German artisans were printing New Year's greetings from woodcuts.

Esther Howland

Although the first handmade paper valentine card can be traced back to 1415, it wasn't until the early 1800s and the advent of affordable postal service that valentines became popular. By the middle of the 19th century, fancy stationers had cornered the market for ready-made valentine cards complete with novel attachments and embossed paper lace.

The custom quickly crossed the Atlantic Ocean. Young Esther Howland of Massachusetts became the first regular publisher of valentines in the United States. She sold her first handmade valentine in 1843 and soon built a successful publishing firm specializing in elaborately decorated cards that sold for as much as $50 each.

With the valentine business in full swing, the production and popularity of Christmas cards soon followed. The first known published Christmas card appeared in London in 1849, when Sir Henry Cole hired artist John Calcott Horsley to design a holiday card that he could send to his friends.

The greeting card, as we now know it, is a product of the 19th century during the reign of Queen Victoria in England (1837—1901). Several factors coincided to produce this boom in greeting card popularity: increasing literacy, a new consumerism fueled by economic prosperity, advances in printing technology, and postal reform. By the 1850s, the greeting card was transformed from an expensive, handmade, and hand-delivered gift to an affordable means of personal communication.

Kate Greenaway

By 1870, hundreds of European card manufacturers were producing cards to sell at home and to the American public. German immigrant Louis Prang is given credit for popularizing greeting cards in America through his Boston lithography business. By 1875, Prang's reproductions were equal to the best work in the U.S. and Great Britain, and in that year he introduced the first complete line of Christmas cards to the American public.

Prang's cards reached their height of popularity in the early 1890s. That's when cheap imitative imports began flooding the market, forcing Prang to abandon his greeting card business. Between 1890 and 1906, there was a marked decline in U.S. greeting card production.

The American business climate for greeting cards rebounded after 1906, an auspicious time to start a card company. Besides Hallmark, other important firms such as The Paul F. Volland Company, The Buzza Company, Rust Craft, American Greetings, and Norcross all arose in the first decade of the 20th century.

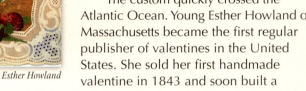

Louis Prang

Just a few months after the January fire, Hall learned that the Smith-Pierce Engraving Company in Kansas City was in financial trouble. After meeting with the principals, he agreed to take over payments on their presses and hire both men to work for Hall Brothers. He then hired several women to hand color the engravings.

With the addition of the Smith-Pierce equipment and expertise, and without really planning it, Hall Brothers had become a manufacturer. By the time the heavy selling season came around in mid-1915, they were creating and producing a portion of their own cards on their own presses. The five-year-old company was begining to adopt a more profitable business model. For a year that began with disaster, 1915 ended with healthy business and high spirits.

ABOVE: *Two of the first Hall Brothers greeting cards. They were all engraved with five steel dies, each printed separately on card stock that was beveled and paneled. The cards were printed on a 4' by 8' modern embossing press in 1915.*

EVERT WAMPLER

Evert Wampler was one of Hall Brothers' earliest employees and became the first (other than Hall himself) to complete a half-century of company service.

J.C. Hall had a favorite story about Wampler.

"On one occasion, I heard a lot of commotion in the next room and opened the door. Evert was armed with an oil-soaked rag and about to throw it at someone. He saw me, hesitated just a second, then threw it anyway. I had warned Evert I'd fire him the next time I caught him horsing around. But I didn't. I think I might have if he hadn't thrown it. It seemed to me that anyone with that kind of gumption in front of the boss must be a pretty good man."

Over the course of a 52-year career, Evert Wampler proved to be that and more. Wampler talked his way into a job with J.C. Hall in 1915, about six months after the fire that burned the young company back to its foundation. He had claimed to be 14 years-old but was, in fact, only 12. When J.C. told him he was too young to work, his only reply was, "Try me." Hall immediately saw a kindred soul in this high-spirited, hustling kid from a fatherless home.

"I never had anybody really care that much about me. In those days, I'd see him every day. He was a young man, but he was the best man I ever knew."
—Evert Wampler, on J.C. Hall

Wampler started, of course, at the bottom. He was hired on as a pressman's helper at $4.00 per week—a six-day, 54 hour week. Over the years, he would come to know every aspect of printing and production. He eventually ascended into supervisory positions but was always comfortable getting his hands dirty.

"I BEGAN TO SEE THAT GREETING CARDS WERE MORE THAN A FORM OF COMMUNICATION— THEY WERE A SOCIAL CUSTOM. WHILE THE CARRIAGE TRADE HAD NEVER TAKEN POST- CARDS VERY SERIOUSLY, THEY WOULD BUY GREETING CARDS OF THE FINEST QUALITY."

— J.C. Hall

CHAPTER THREE

Building Business and Breaking Ground

(1915–1932)

H AVING SURVIVED THE FIRE OF 1915, THE HALL BROTHERS SAW SURE AND STEADY GROWTH OVER THE NEXT DECADE—ENOUGH GROWTH TO KEEP THE COMPANY ON THE MOVE TO ever-larger quarters.

In 1919, the firm moved out of the space it had leased from the Starr Piano Company and into a larger office just a block south—a notable move for J.C. Hall as the new space was spacious enough to accommodate his first private office. Only four years after that move, the company would relocate again, this time to a brand-new, purpose-built building that would dwarf every workspace the firm had previously occupied.

Hall Brothers was growing creatively, too. By the early 1920s, the majority of their business was in greeting cards instead of postcards. As its market presence strengthened and its confidence grew, it took chances, experimenting with new formats. A line of nonfolding, heavy stock, laminated greetings, called "flat cards," introduced in 1924 was a retail success. But another effort from that same year—cards called "Greetaphones" with plastic phonograph records attached—was less successful. "One of the great flops of all time," J.C. Hall would unceremoniously call them.

Hall Brothers got into the greeting card business the same way it had entered the postcard trade—as jobbers who bought inventory from wholesalers and resold it to retailers. But after the purchase of equipment from Smith-Pierce Engraving, there was nothing keeping the company from turning out its own

ABOVE: *The Greetaphone Card from 1924.*

BELOW: *The 1915 floor plan of Hall Brothers in the Starr Piano Building after the fire.*

OPPOSITE PAGE: *Hall Brothers gift wrapping.*

OPPOSITE PAGE BOTTOM: *Greeting card written by J.C. Hall's first secretary, Lillian Sinai. It was a bestseller in 1916.*

A New Way to Wrap

Through the early 20th century, gift wrap—or "gift dressing" as it was then called—was fairly uninspired. Like other suppliers at Christmas, Hall Brothers offered customers a choice of tissue in white, green, and red. But as Christmas 1917 approached, the company found itself sold out of its entire stock of tissue and unable to obtain more before the holidays.

Scouring the production plant for anything that could be used as an alternative, Rollie Hall spotted a stack of brightly-colored paper sheets recently imported from France for use as envelope linings. He left the plant with an armload of the decorative papers and hustled them down to the Halls' one and only retail store, stacking them on top of a showcase near the cash register.

Priced at 10 cents a sheet, the papers flew off the shelf faster than they could be restocked. The following Christmas, though the company had stocked up heavily, they again sold out before the holiday arrived.

It has been observed that there is nothing so powerful as an idea whose time has come. And though it might be a stretch to say that Hall Brothers invented gift wrap, it is no exaggeration to say that in 1917 it started helping people see gift wrapping in an entirely new way. As J.C. Hall stated:

Rollie Hall, c.1922

"The decorative gift-wrapping business was born the day Rollie placed those French envelope linings on top of that showcase."

Decorative gift wrap became the first non-greeting card product that the company produced—just the beginning of a long line of innovations that continues to this day.

To Greet You Christmas Day

There are friends we meet as we journey along
Who like ships that pass in the night
We meet one day and they drift away
Silently out of sight

There are other friends whom we chance to meet
Who prove loyal and staunch and true
Who tug at our hearts when the Yuletide starts
Just such a friend are you

products. From 1915 on it started to take tentative steps in that direction, learning what worked along the way.

J.C. Hall was a quick study, and he realized that while a postcard's popularity depended primarily on the image it carried, a greeting card needed just the right message or sentiment to succeed. And when it came to sentiments, he was open to all sources. Hall's first secretary, Ms. Lillian Sinai, penned a bestseller in 1916—an eight-line Christmas verse referred to internally as "Ships that Pass in the Night."

Though not a writer himself, J.C. Hall developed a good ear for quality, saleable verse and prose. According to his son, Donald Hall, "It wasn't a natural instinct, but one he developed." The elder Hall was a stickler for just the right words. To this day, a maxim coined by J.C. Hall is deeply ingrained in the company's creative department: "A customer picks up a card for the design, but buys it for the sentiment."

There were no staff writers in those early days, and if an employee showed a flair for composing sentiment, he or she was expected to contribute.

Hall remembers how he inspired one of his salesmen to wax poetic.

"When we were in the Starr Piano Company, Jack Burroughs would climb down the fire escape to get into the back alley and across to the Cupper Hotel Bar. He would get to feeling poetic and start writing. I saw him writing once, so I said, 'Write some sentiments.' So he did, and they were pretty terrible."

But Burroughs' verse improved with a little practice, and soon he was turning out sentiments at a pretty steady clip. An early favorite read:

> I sit by heck, and scratch my neck
> And wonder what I'll send you
> Thots wander thru my muddled brain
> From buzz wagon to candy cane
> But none of these quite suit this year
> So I'll just send a word of cheer.
> *A Merry Christmas*

While the postcard business waned, the greeting card industry was expanding in just about every direction. Everyday cards—cards not sent on holidays but for birthdays, weddings, anniversaries, and expressions of sympathy—were becoming more popular. New reasons to send cards seemed to keep popping up. Hall Brothers did its share of moving the industry forward and adding new categories of cards.

In the three years of European conflict leading up to the U.S.'s entrance into World War I, the Hall Brothers retail store on 11th Street carried a small line of patriotic stationery. But there was never much demand for it. On April 6, 1917, all that changed.

Upon hearing of the U.S. declaration of war on that day, Blanche Taylor, a clerk at the store, was moved to display the patriotic product in the front window. In the few hours before she closed the store that evening, she had sold it all. For the Hall Brothers store—and especially for the jobbing business—it was clear that The Great War was going to have a great impact on business as well as on the lives of every American.

BELOW: Examples of an early birthday card with a general message and early specific sentiment cards.

"WE INTRODUCED THE CUSTOM OF SENDING CARDS SIMPLY EXPRESSING FRIENDSHIP IN 1919. THERE WAS NO PARTICULAR OCCASION ASSOCIATED WITH THEM, AND IT WASN'T LONG BEFORE THESE BECAME AN IMPORTANT PART OF OUR LINE. BIRTHDAY CARDS CARRIED GENERAL MESSAGES UNTIL WE INTRODUCED LINES EXPRESSLY FOR A MOTHER. THESE WERE FOLLOWED BY OTHER SPECIFIC SENTIMENTS FOR FAMILY MEMBERS AND FRIENDS."

—*J.C. Hall*

THE GREAT WAR: 1914–1918

British recruiting poster (1915) by E.V. Kealey

Historians still actively disagree over the fundamental causes of the Great War, as it was called at the time. The period leading up to the war was a complex tangle of diplomatic and political maneuvering—many countries debated over strategies and alliances until nearly the last minute—and the first few weeks of the conflict were similarly chaotic and confusing. However, historians agree nearly unanimously about the war's consequences: World War I led almost directly to World War II and set the stage for many other important events in the 20th century.

The war began on July 28, 1914, when Austria-Hungary declared war on Serbia. This seemingly small conflict between two countries spread rapidly. Soon, Germany, allied with Austria-Hungary, and Russia, Great Britain, and France were drawn in on the Serbian side largely because of treaties that obligated them to defend each other. Western and eastern fronts quickly opened along the borders of Germany and Austria-Hungary.

By 1915 the war was dominated by trench warfare in both the east and the west. Soldiers fought from dug-in positions, striking at each other with machine guns, heavy artillery, and chemical weapons. Though soldiers died by the millions in brutal conditions, neither side had any substantive success or gained any advantage.

In some respects, World War I was the last 19th-century war. Officers still carried swords, cavalrymen rode horseback, and kings and nobles played a major role in military affairs. But technologically it was a 20th-century conflict. Walled forts no longer provided security against massive howitzers. Infantry charges were suicidal against machine guns. Combat largely consisted of sitting in narrow, muddy holes while explosives rained from the sky. The War to End All Wars brought carnage on a scale unknown in human history and the first large-scale use of air power, submarines, posion gas, and machine guns.

American recruiting poster (1917) by James M. Flagg

By conservative estimates, around nine million soldiers died in battle and another 21 million were wounded—many of them defending entrenched front lines that were so stalemated that they rarely moved even a few yards in either direction. Civilian loss of life totaled an additional 13 million. Epidemics of influenza (which continued after the war) and other diseases, either induced or exacerbated by the war, raised the death toll by at least an additional 20 million. In total, counting battle casualties, civilian deaths, and victims of disease, the loss of life worldwide surpassed 40 million.

The shell-shattered area of Chateau Wood, Flanders (1917). Photograph by Frank Hurley

From the begining of the war, President Woodrow Wilson maintained a stated policy of neutrality, although trade with Germany was cut sharply and trade with Britian was massively increased. In February of 1917, Germany began waging submarine warfare against all merchant shipping in the Atlantic and sank three U.S. merchant ships. Then, British agents intercepted the so-called Zimmerman Telegram detailing a German plot to start a war between the United States and Mexico. By April, President Wilson asked Congress to declare war on Europe's Central Powers in order to "make the world safe for democracy," which they did on April 6, 1917. At the time, the American Army was fairly small, but within six weeks of the declaration Congress passed the first draft legislation since the Civil War. It took almost a year for American troops to reach the frontline in any significant numbers. By early 1918 more than one million U.S. troops and a massive reservoir of supplies reached the trenches in Belgium and France. By late fall, Germany signed the Armistice at Versailles, and the war was over.

Having financed and helped feed the allies, as well as breaking the battlefield stalemate, the United States emerged from the war as a major world power for the first time. Unlike its European allies, it had not been driven to economic ruin by four years of war and was now a creditor nation.

The United States had turned a corner with its participation in World War I. It now turned inward and welcomed an era of confidence and prosperity the likes of which the world had never seen.

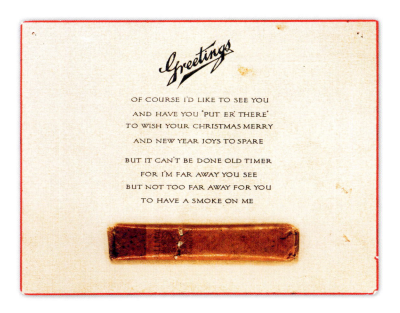

ABOVE: *Among the many cards designed for servicemen overseas during WWI, one of the most popular carried a cigarette wrapped in cellophane and glued to the front. Hall Brothers had thousands warehoused when a federal revenue inspector paid them a visit. Selling the cards, he explained, required individual cigarette tax stamps—a staggeringly expensive proposition. The entire stock had to be destroyed, and another costly lesson was learned.*

BELOW: *J.C. Hall, c. 1920.*

Immediately following the declaration of war, requests came from dealers for birthday cards appropriate to send to servicemen. Within a few months, cards bearing patriotic designs and text like "Greetings Soldier Boy On Your Birthday" were finding their way to sales counters across the country. Cards featuring eagles, ships, anchors, and other military emblems were gobbled up by a hungry market.

At first, J.C. Hall was content to include this growing assortment of patriotic product—stationery, paper hats, place cards, balloons, and cloth and metal flags—in his jobbing line. The company had its hands full as it was. But demand was so great that it soon became clear that if he was to be a greeting card manufacturer, he'd better get in on the production end of this patriotic boom. Once convinced, he moved fast. He had a variety of patriotic dies cut and the plant started printing a range of designs on flat, white—and later khaki-colored—cards.

Business soared during the roughly year-and-a-half until Armistice Day. And by the time the war was "over over there," the Hall Brothers company looked much different than it had at the beginning of the conflict.

By the end of the war, the firm had moved to a larger space on the third floor of the Meyer building at 1114 Grand. But it had also moved from adolescence into something like adulthood. The war, and its related upswing in business, had brought new processes, new employees, new customers, and new ideas—and in the postwar world, new horizons awaited the fast-growing company.

Grand Ambitions

The move to Grand Avenue meant something to J.C. Hall. In Kansas City, this was an important address. At 1114 Grand, the company's neighbors included high-end haberdashers and even national firms like Spalding, the athletic equipment maker, and the Columbia Graphaphone Company.

It looked impressive enough on the letterhead, but a peek inside the third-floor office would have revealed cast-off chairs, severely distressed tables, upended wooden crates serving as stools, and only three desks, all mismatched. Despite the build-up of business during the war, this was still a fairly ragtag operation—but no one outworked the crew at 1114 Grand.

As the 1920s rolled around, J.C. Hall had an even more pressing ambition than an aristocratic address. He wanted badly to extend his company's reach to the East Coast and, in fact, to markets nationwide. The company had established an eastern outpost by opening a retail store in Chicago in 1919 on the city's most storied street, Michigan Avenue, no less. But Hall wanted more—and knew that broad distribution, not retail, was the real key to expansion.

"No one in the greeting card business set out to benefit from the war, but in many ways it was an important turning point for the industry. People sought closer contact with one another and especially with their relatives and friends in the service. And servicemen themselves not only enjoyed receiving greeting cards but sending them as well. As a result many more men became permanent buyers of cards than ever before. And I saw something else in the custom—a way of giving less articulate people, and those who tend to disguise their feelings, a voice to express their love and affection."

—J.C. Hall

In the early 1920s, the Hall Brothers product line included 300 everyday card designs and 300 Christmas designs. Salesmen carrying the entire line lugged sample cases weighing about 90 pounds.

Crucial to this strategy was finding the right man to represent them in the biggest market of them all, New York City. J.C. Hall had heard about a salesman, a Brooklynite named Harry Lange, who he thought was just the man for the job. Hall traveled to New York to meet Lange, and though neither was entirely impressed with the other upon their initial meeting, the two men did—after getting to know one another a little better—come to terms. Lange was hired to cover New York City and state—a huge territory—but he didn't disappoint.

ABOVE: *Hall Brothers salesman Harry Lange with his two children.*

"New York buyers were tough, but Harry had the determination to hang on like a bulldog. He proved that New York could be sold by a Western manufacturer, which was not easy in those days."

Through Lange's connections, Hall Brothers was able to build a network that, by 1922, had grown to include 16 salesmen, doing business in all 48 states. Three years after the end of the war, the company had gone national. It was roaring into the twenties.

Another prominent addition to the Kansas City workforce in the early 1920s bore a familiar name. In 1921, William F. Hall sold his book and stationery business in Norfolk, Nebraska, and moved to Kansas City to join the family firm. He took on responsibilities as office manager and treasurer for the growing company. Eleven years after they began the company in Norfolk, the three Hall brothers were together again—and the rapidly growing company needed every one of them.

But what the company most needed was more space. It had outgrown six offices in its first decade, and by 1922, the firm was

"MY LIFE FROM THAT DAY ON TO THIS HAS BEEN IN J.C.'S HANDS. IT HAS BEEN TURBULENT AND UPSETTING AT TIMES, BUT WE GOT TOGETHER, STAYED TOGETHER AND ARE STILL TOGETHER."

— Harry Lange, 1955

operating out of a sprawling collection of work areas that included three stories in the building at 1114 Grand, a basement room in a building across the street, and another rented basement up the block. J.C. felt strongly that it was time to put the operation under one roof. Where that roof would be located, he decided to leave up to his employees.

> *"We took options on four pieces of property. The most desirable was at Twenty-sixth and Grand, about a mile from downtown Kansas City. We were concerned that our employees would consider this inconvenient, so we put the four locations to a vote. The result was strongly in the favor of Twenty-sixth and Grand. We didn't think about it at the time, but many years later we were told that this was a revolutionary thing to do."*

The building was completed in the summer of 1923. At five stories—each with 10,000 square feet of floor space—and designed to support six more stories if necessary, Hall was certain that this building would hold them forever. In less than two years, the company was using every available foot and leasing space in an adjoining building.

By the mid-1920s, the physical growth of the Hall Brothers operation mirrored the steadily expanding reach of its business. The company now bore little resemblance to the scrappy jobbing operation that young J.C. Hall had run out of a rented room a decade and a half earlier. It shipped cards to every state in the union and was beginning to seek business beyond the nation's borders. By 1928, Hall Brothers cards were being exported to Hawaii, the Philippines, Alaska, Mexico, and Asia. Product was sold into Canada despite a 40 percent import duty.

ABOVE: *The Hall Brothers building at 26th and Grand, under construction in 1923. The location was chosen by a vote of the employees.*

BELOW RIGHT: *J.C. Hall with his newborn Elizabeth Ann Hall in 1922.*

A Friend's Meeting

In 1917, an elderly man approached J.C. Hall with a poem and asked how much it would cost to have it printed on 100 greeting cards. Hall liked the verse and asked who had written it. When the man replied that he himself had, Hall made a deal to buy it for use on greeting cards. The sentiment was an immediate hit and became a perennial bestseller.

It wasn't until 1921 that Hall found out—courtesy of a very insistent and angry publishing executive—that the poem had in fact been written by popular author Edgar A. Guest. The piece, called "A Friend's Greeting," had originally been included in a collection of Guest's work titled *A Heap o' Livin'*. Reparations were demanded. A lawsuit was threatened. In desperation, Hall offered to buy the rights to use the sentiment for a then-unheard-of sum of $500.

"The going rate was about one dollar a line. It was probably the most money ever paid at that time for one sentiment." —J.C. Hall

The offer, Hall recalled, had "quite a stabilizing effect" on the man. So much so that he promptly pulled out the book in which the poem appeared and asked if Hall might be interested in any of Mr. Guest's other work.

The purchase of "A Friend's Greeting" turned out to be well worth the money. The sentiment remained in the Hallmark line in some form or another for an astonishing 69 years, finally being retired in 1986. It should surprise no one to learn that Mr. Hall and Mr. Guest became mutual admirers and lifelong friends.

Edgar A. Guest, c. 1930

ABOVE: *With 13 years experience as a manager at Kansas City's leading department store, Emery, Bird, Thayer, Charles B. Sefranka was a natural choice to manage the Halls' retail store. Joining the company in 1922, Sefranka also served as a road salesman and as the first head of the art department. A trusted advisor to J.C. Hall, he stayed with the company for 32 years—his last 15 as the firm's secretary.*

LEFT: *Early Hall Brothers sales-man Jim Short went to work for J.C. Hall in 1913 after the competitor he worked for, the Elite Card Company, went bankrupt.*

ABOVE: *When Charles Stevenson wanted to communicate with J.C. Hall—or make a note to him-self—he would do so by writing his message on a 3x5 index card. He reasoned that if he couldn't express the idea in that small a space, it wasn't clear or simple enough. Hall came to adopt Stevenson's use of 3x5s, as did other managers and associates. Today, the practice of writing ideas on 3x5s is deeply ingrained in Hallmark culture.*

BELOW: *All of the Hall brothers were reunited in 1921 when William Hall moved to Kansas City to work for the growing company as office manager and treasurer. From the left: J.C. Hall, brother-in-law Louis Pence, who married Marie Hall in 1920, William Hall, and Rollie Hall.*

THE SARGEANT STEPS IN

Charles Stevenson was fresh out of the army in 1919 when a mutual friend convinced J.C. Hall that the two should meet. Hall didn't have a job opening, but he agreed to interview the young man anyway—chiefly because he remembered Stevenson as a star player in the city basketball league in which both had played.

Hall quickly learned that Stevenson's skills went far beyond the two-handed set shot. After a few interviews, Stevenson was hired. But Hall still didn't know what to do with him. He assigned Stevenson an assortment of clerical tasks but knew that the bright, ambitious ex-sergeant was overqualified and underchallenged.

"Charlie would quit almost every Saturday afternoon. He'd tell me this was no place for him. I'd talk him into staying another week, but he'd be right back quitting the next Saturday."
—J.C. Hall

In desperation, Hall finally asked Stevenson what he wanted to do. In an earlier visit to the company's storage room, Stevenson had been appalled by its disorderliness. He set about making it right with military rigor.

Efficiency and order proved to be Stevenson's forte. In a company that had admittedly flown by the seat of its pants for nearly two decades—a company that had outgrown its start-up status but not its start-up operational structure—Stevenson brought order to the chaos.

"You get a job out on the table, and it's half done."
—Charles Stevenson

Stevenson's stature grew with the company, and he continued to define jobs for himself, by turns working in shipping, stock handling, and manufacturing. By the mid-1920s, Stevenson had been named general manager. He was J.C. Hall's right-hand man on the operations side of the business. And though the two weren't friends outside of work, by his own account, they were always together. "Mr. Hall and I did everything there was to be done," he said. "We worked seven days a week. I never left Saturdays until four o'clock—then he and I would walk up to the YMCA and play basketball."

Hall knew he had something special in Stevenson. Eventually, the young man who was hired for $25 a week as an order-lister became vice president of manufacturing and sat on the board of directors.

"Charles Stevenson taught us all better working habits," Hall would later write. "To this day, when people comment on the efficiency of Hallmark, I immediately think of him."

ELIZABETH DILDAY HALL

During the early years of building his business, J.C. Hall was a singularly focused young man. But in 1916, he met a girl who opened his eyes to more than just business. He had his younger sister, Marie, to thank. "Marie introduced me to her schoolmate, Elizabeth Ann Dilday. Marie was going to visit Elizabeth's two-year-old niece, Lucy Jean, who was a real charmer. It was love at first sight for me—with the niece that is. We all went for a ride in my Stutz."

After that first meeting, Hall started finding more time—an occasional evening or Sunday afternoon—to call on Lucy Jean and Elizabeth and take them for rides in his treasured Stutz Bearcat touring car. Barbara Hall Marshall understands her father's fondness for the toddler. "She was a beautiful child," Marshall explains. "Mother and Dad both adored her."

On those first few visits, if J.C. Hall was more interested in the darling Lucy Jean than in her pretty aunt, he figured it was all the same to Elizabeth. "I suspect the thing she really liked about me was my car," he once joked.

Before long, Lucy Jean's family returned to their home in Arkansas, leaving the Sunday drives to the young man and woman who were finding more and more in common. Then one day, not long after the child had left town, word arrived that she had become seriously ill. Elizabeth went to Arkansas to be with her. A short while later, she notified J.C. that the beloved child had passed away. "Sharing the loss of

that little girl brought us closer together," remembers J.C. The two were married in March of 1921.

Elizabeth Dilday's family had moved to Missouri from Kentucky (after a brief stint in Indiana) when she was a schoolgirl. True to her bluegrass state pedigree, Elizabeth was an avid horsewoman. "Mother loved to ride," her daughter Barbara remembers. "That was the main impetus for them moving to the country, so that they could have horses."

Elizabeth Hall loved the outdoors and maintained large flower and vegetable gardens at the family farm. The property's out-in-the-country setting attracted a steady stream of weekend visitors, and Mrs. Hall was always ready with food and drinks ("soft drinks, not hard" her daughter is quick to point out.) And though she wasn't overtly involved in the company, she was nonetheless a trusted advisor to her husband who consulted her on everything from greeting card designs to television scripts to personnel. "Dad always felt that Mother could size up people more quickly than anyone," says Barbara Hall Marshall.

Elizabeth was the quiet rock behind J.C. Hall and the anchor of her family. She died at age 79 on March 15, 1976. Her children remember her as playful, relaxed, and slow to anger. "But when she did get angry, watch out," said Barbara Hall Marshall with a laugh. "She was the real disciplinarian in our household," Don Hall recalls. "Dad would bluster, but Mother just had to say something once. She was tough but absolutely fair. She was a neat woman."

Elizabeth Hall maintained a quiet interest in the greeting card business, while concentrating most of her effort on raising her three children on the Halls' rural property south of Kansas City. Son Donald remembers her as a bit of a tomboy with a playful streak. Elizebeth Hall was a lifelong equestrian but she also had a fondness for the horseless carriage. Though pictured here with a different model, she loved to ride in J.C. Hall's Stutz Beareat.

RIGHT: *Elizabeth with their second child, Barbara Louise Hall, in 1923.*

One of the keys to scaling the business was getting control over the supply and production chain. In its new, state-of-the-art factory, Hall Brothers now produced most of the products it sold. This gave the company freedom to expand its offerings as it saw fit, respond to customer demand, and experiment with new products. Even more important to J.C. Hall was the idea that in producing their own products, they never had to compromise on quality.

In the early 1920s, Hall Brothers had started labeling its shipping cartons with the word "Hallmade." It was a nice, tidy way to incorporate the name of the business onto its packaging—nice, but not quite perfect. It would be a few years later, in 1925, before J.C. Hall would have the idea of changing a few letters and substituting the word "Hallmark." By 1928, "Hallmark" began appearing on the back of the company's greeting cards.

From his earliest days as a publisher of greeting cards, J.C. Hall understood the importance of a strong, recognizable brand—what is referred to today as "brand identity." Printing the word "Hallmark" on the back of each card reflected that belief. And while the company was selling its greeting cards throughout the country by the late 1920s, Hall wanted more than merely the receipts for product sold—he wanted a presence in the marketplace. He strove to sell a product that customers associated with the highest quality and asked for by name.

A Very Merry Christmas: *Hall Brothers shipped $60,000 in orders for Christmas 1925. In 1924, the company had shipped only $6,000.*

Hall Brothers
INCORPORATED

MANUFACTURERS OF

Fine Greeting Cards

GRAND AVE. AND WALNUT AT TWENTY-SIXTH STREET

KANSAS CITY, MISSOURI

November 25, 1931.

Mr. Walter E. Disney
2719 Hyperion
Hollywood, California

Dear Mr. Disney:

I am enclosing a photograph, accidentally torn in the mail, which shows what our dealer in Appleton, Wisconsin did in conjunction with the local theatre for Mickey Mouse card publicity.

While this is very crude, it shows the sort of interest some of the dealers are taking in Mickey Mouse cards. We have been discussing the possibility of working up some sort of a tie-up or display, which could of course be much more artistically done than this, to use in exploiting Mickey Mouse cards in the theatre lobbies. In return, I am sure the dealers would be glad to make window displays featuring the cards just at the time Mickey Mouse pictures were being shown.

We were also considering the advisability of making some Mickey Mouse slides for dealers to have run in the smaller picture houses where this sort of advertising is still used.

Our salesmen are all Mickey Mouse enthusiasts and I am sure they would heartily cooperate with us on any plans or ideas we could work out. They will all be here in about thirty days for our annual sales conference and it would be an opportune time for us to stir up some additional Mickey Mouse enthusiasm.

Our experience along the publicity line has been rather limited and I felt that you or your publicity man might have some ideas or suggestions that would be helpful and particularly timely just now.

---

*Hall Brothers
INCORPORATED
SHEET*

2.

One thing you mentioned when you were here was the autographing of originals for the better buyers. I am sure this would be helpful and I would be glad to hear how extensively you would be willing to go into it. By the way, I would be very glad to have one of them for my own office wall.

The retail buyers' reaction to Mickey Mouse is continuing to improve and we intend to make a more extensive line for the coming seasons. These numbers are now being worked on and some of the proof samples will be available in a few weeks.

The family, including our three-year old boy, had a very enjoyable evening last night watching the "Beach Party." The boy has some suggestions that he would like to have passed on to you. He thinks that the Mickey Mouse film should be a little longer and two or three of them included in each program.

I hope that the trip to Florida got you to feeling tip top again.

With kindest regards for yourself and brother, I am

Sincerely yours,

J. C. Hall

JCH:HPS

A star was born in 1928 when Walt Disney's Mickey Mouse made his film debut in the sound cartoon, Steamboat Willie. *Disney, who grew up and had his first studio in Kansas City, attended the same grade school as Elizabeth Dilday Hall. In 1932, Hallmark made one of its first licensing deals to put Disney characters on greeting cards.*

LEFT: *Letter from J.C. Hall to Walt Disney discussing marketing ideas for Mickey Mouse.*

BELOW: *Some of the early cards produced by Hallmark using Mickey and Minnie.*

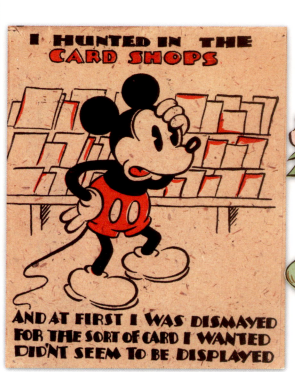

TOP: *J.C. Hall personally wrote the copy for Hall Brothers' first national print ad, which appeared in the December 1928 issue of* Ladies' Home Journal. *The ad included Edgar Guest's popular poem "A Friend's Greeting" and an impressive New York branch office listing.*

ABOVE: *A holiday card sold during the Great Depression acknowledged the tough economic climate of the day.*

Part of his strategy for achieving this goal was national advertising. In 1928, Hall personally wrote the company's first national print advertisement—a full-page ad, which ran in the December 1928 issue of *Ladies' Home Journal*. Though the company was still officially called Hall Brothers, the ad featured the firm's torch and shield logo, which included the words "Hallmark Cards."

With a burgeoning product offering and a growing national presence, Hall Brothers was flying high in the late 1920s. A second shift kept presses rolling into the night. The number of employees, though it fluctuated with the seasons, had nearly doubled in four years—from about 150 at the beginning of 1926 to more than 300 at the end of 1929. Sales records were broken with each passing year. The company's successes were reported in a new internal publication scripted by Charlie Stevenson, the *Hall-Mark News*. Like many of the country's businesses, Hall Brothers had thrived through the Jazz Age.

But in October of that year, when the stock market tumbled and the nation slid into the Great Depression, the cloud that hung over the nation cast a shadow over Hall Brothers as well.

"No one had any experience with what happened to greeting cards in bad times. Almost everyone decided that people would stop buying greeting cards. But I wasn't sure this would be the case. I felt there might even be a greater demand. Perhaps people would be even more concerned about communicating with one another."

Though frightened by the economic collapse, Hall didn't panic. Against the advice of nearly everyone concerned, he refused to lay off a single employee. This despite a national unemployment rate that reached nearly 25 percent at the height of the Depression in 1932. Charlie Stevenson, serving as general manager, remembered how Hall leaned on his sales force to keep revenue flowing:

"Mr. Hall kept those salesmen working. He checked on them, called on them, told them what to do, how to do it. It was magnificent the way he did it."

Such efforts kept the company growing, if ever so slightly, during the Depression years, and Hall Brothers did occasionally have job openings—a rarity for the times. Stevenson remembered how heart-wrenching filling those jobs could be. "I would run an ad for five people and get 200 applications. The hardest thing I ever had to do was pick five people out of 200. You can't do it."

For the most part, Hall's instincts about the effects of the Depression would be borne out over its long course. Business grew in every year except 1933—the first year of negative financial performance in the company's history.

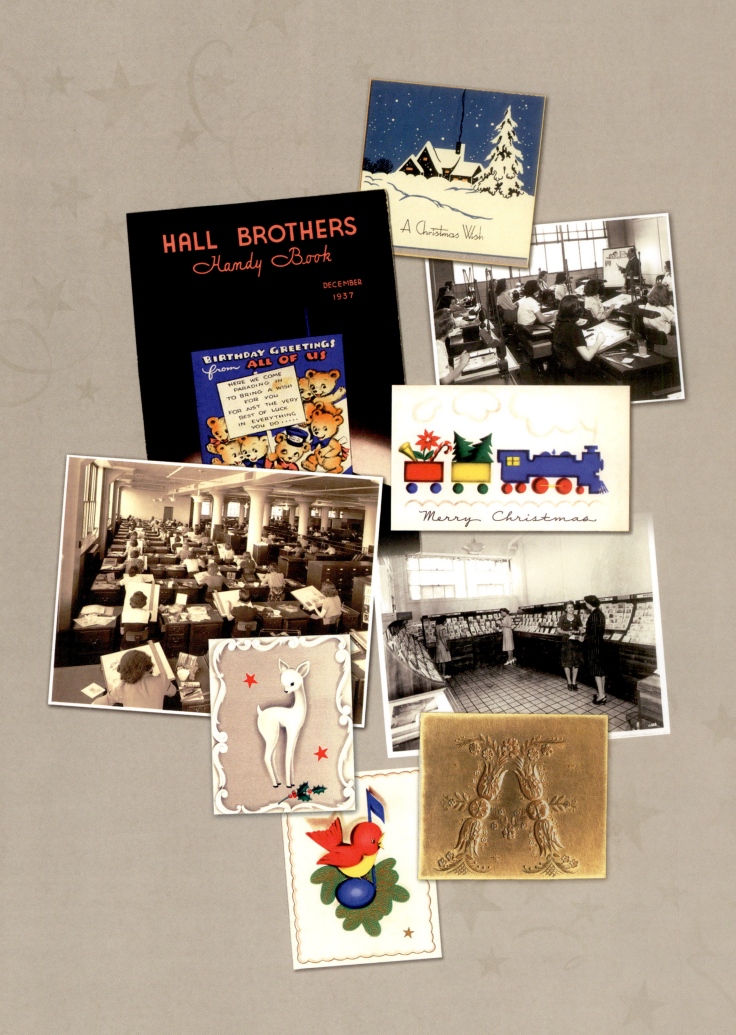

A Christmas Wish

HALL BROTHERS
Handy Book

DECEMBER
1937

BIRTHDAY GREETINGS
from ALL OF US

HERE WE COME
PARADING IN
TO BRING A WISH
FOR JUST THE VERY
BEST OF LUCK
IN EVERYTHING
YOU DO.....

Merry Christmas

CHAPTER FOUR

Hanging Tough in Hard Times

(1933–1951)

*"There is a mysterious cycle in human events.
To some generations much is given.
Of other generations much is expected.
This generation of Americans has
a rendezvous with destiny."*

— *Franklin Delano Roosevelt, June 27, 1936*

IN THE PRESIDENTIAL ELECTION OF 1932, FRANK-LIN D. ROOSEVELT CAMPAIGNED ON A PLATFORM OF REFORM AND RECOVERY—WHAT HE TERMED "A NEW DEAL FOR THE COMMON MAN." HE DEFEATED INCUMBENT HERBERT HOOVER by a staggering 472–59 electoral vote margin. His prize was a nation in the grip of the worst financial depression in modern history.

The stock market crash of 1929 had brought the Roaring Twenties to an abrupt halt and spread misery far beyond Wall Street. The prosperous decade leading up to the crash had brought unprecedented numbers of novice investors into the market. Warnings about overspeculation were widely dismissed as newcomers and veteran traders alike poured more and more money into stocks. Many bought shares on margin as low as 10 percent—meaning brokerage firms would lend nine dollars for every one dollar an investor deposited. After the month-long economic collapse in the fall of 1929, hundreds of thousands of people found themselves owing far more money than they ever had in the first place.

But the number who lost money directly as a result of the great crash was only a fraction of those that would suffer because of the Great Depression that followed. The decline in stock prices caused mass bankruptcies, business closures, and a commensurate loss of jobs. Heavy industry, capital investment, and construction practically froze. Bank failures became epidemic as more than a third of the nation's banks—about 9,000—closed their doors during the 1930s. With no federal deposit guarantees, unfortunate patrons often lost their entire savings. By 1934, two out of every five homeowners were in default on their mortgages. In rural areas, it was even worse. As crop prices fell by 60 percent, fully one-third of America's farms were foreclosed upon between 1929 and 1932. And that was before the worst of the Dust Bowl years in the middle part of the decade. If the great crash hit Wall Street, the Great Depression hit every street in America—and the dirt roads, too.

ABOVE: *A political cartoon from 1932, indicating the challenges FDR faced upon taking office.*

OPPOSITE PAGE: *The Farm Security Administration (FSA) was famous for its photography program that portrayed the challenges of rural poverty during the Great Depression. Many of the most famous photographers of the era were fostered by the FSA project. Walker Evans, Dorothea Lange, and Gordon Parks were three of the best known.*

THE DUST BOWL

By 1934, a 150,000-square-mile stretch of Midwestern farmland was turning to desert, the topsoil blowing off in monstrous dust storms. They were triggered by drought, but the origins lay in the excesses of the 1920s. Spurred on by increased postwar grain prices, farmers had plowed up vast tracts of land that had been held down by native grasses. When the drought came, there was nothing to keep the prairie wind from stripping away the land.

The so-called Dust Bowl caused major ecological and agricultural damage to American and Canadian prairie lands. From 1930 to 1936 the soil dried, turned to dust, and blew away east and south in large dark clouds. At times the clouds blackened the sky, reaching all the way to East Coast cities such as New York and Washington, D.C. Much of the soil ended up deposited in the Atlantic Ocean.

Degradation of the land claimed peoples' cultural heritage and livelihoods. Thousands of penniless families fled the affected regions, traveling to California and other states, where they found conditions little better than those they had left. Many traveled from farm to farm picking fruit and other crops. This exodus was later captured in John Steinbeck's Pulitzer Prize-winning novel *The Grapes of Wrath*.

ABOVE: *Dorothea Lange's famous 1936 portrait of 32-year-old Florence Thompson with three of her seven children, destitute in a pea pickers' camp because of the failure of the early pea crop in California.*

TOP LEFT: *Dust storm approaching Stratford, Texas, in 1935. The storms of the Dust Bowl were given names such as "Black Blizzard" and "Black Roller" because visibility was reduced to a few feet.*

TOP RIGHT: *Walker Evans' 1936 portrait of Floyd Burroughs, an Alabama sharecropper. Evans' photographs and James Agee's moving prose detailing their stay with three tenant families in southern Alabama during the Great Depression was published in the groundbreaking book* Let Us Now Praise Famous Men.

RIGHT: *Family who left their Texas home in 1936, hoping to find work in the Arkansas cotton fields. Penniless with no food and three gallons of gas in the tank, the father is trying to repair a tire.*

Roosevelt's first New Deal began with the basics. Banking reform laws, emergency relief programs, agricultural programs, industrial reform, and a federal welfare state were among the first wave of bills that Roosevelt pushed through a compliant Congress in his first hundred days in office. By the spring of 1933, he had taken the nation off the gold standard and repealed Prohibition. A Second New Deal initiated in 1935 brought more progressive reforms including additional aid to farmers, the Social Security Act, and creation of the Works Progress Administration (WPA), a massive public works program designed to get unemployed Americans back to work.

It would take the manufacturing boom of World War II to fully shake the Great Depression, but by the mid-1930s, confidence was slowly returning to the American public.

Overall, the economic and employment situation in Kansas City was better than most places during the Depression. About one in ten Kansas City residents received some form of public relief in the mid-1930s. The number was twice as high in similar-sized cities of the region. The difference, by most accounts, was the active hand of political boss Tom Pendergast, known by all as "Boss Tom."

Through patronage, intimidation, and puppet-master control of city government, Pendergast kept the booze flowing during Prohibition and the city growing despite the nearly global economic downturn. Boss Tom brought his own version of the WPA to Kansas City, helping secure funding for a host of civic construction projects even as the Depression dragged on. Among many other projects, a new Jackson County courthouse, downtown's Municipal Auditorium, and the wholly unnecessary paving of a small city waterway called Brush Creek, provided construction jobs for thousands. As it happened, the government contracts for these projects also provided good business for Pendergast's own Ready-Mixed Concrete Company.

Just as Kansas City had weathered the Great Depression better than the average municipality, Hall Brothers greeting card company had pulled through the first half of the 1930s in remarkably good shape.

In 1935, the firm celebrated its first quarter-century in business. At 25, Hall Brothers was beginning to act like an industry leader, and company founder J.C. Hall was rising to prominence among the city's movers and shakers.

BELOW: *"Boss Tom" Pendergast (far right) conferring with lawyers during his trial for income tax evasion in 1939. His conviction resulted in a 15 month hitch in a federal penitentiary and brought the end of an era to Kansas City.*

ABOVE: *In 1935, Hall Brothers' 25th anniversary year, it opened an eastern sales office on the 13th floor of the Empire State Building in New York. Finished just four years earlier, the art deco structure would stand as the world's tallest building until 1972.*

CRAZY LITTLE WOMEN AND A WHOLE LOTTA JAZZ

Kansas City in the 1930s had a worldwide reputation as a "wide-open" town, where liquor laws were discreetly ignored and closing times never came. Political corruption and organized crime ran rampant, but in Kansas City's storied Jazz District—centered around the corner of 18th Street and Vine—the joints were always jumping. In clubs like the Hey-Hay, the Cherry Blossom, and Dante's Inferno, hometown heroes Charlie Parker, Count Basie, and Jay McShann mixed it up in all-night jam sessions with the likes of Coleman Hawkins, Lester Young, and Mary Lou Williams.

ABOVE: *Mary Lou Williams, who once said of Kansas City in the early 1930s: "You had to have a strong left hand in those days or they wouldn't pay any attention to you."*

ABOVE RIGHT: *Charlie Parker.*

RIGHT: *1940* Kansas City Jazz *album.*

BELOW: *Jay McShann.*

BELOW RIGHT: *1930s Kansas City hot spot, Dante's Inferno.*

"KANSAS CITY WAS DIFFERENT FROM ALL THE OTHER PLACES BECAUSE WE'D BE JAMMING ALL NIGHT. AND (IF) YOU COME UP HERE PLAYING THE WRONG THING, WE'D STRAIGHTEN YOU OUT."

—*Claude "Fiddler" Williams*

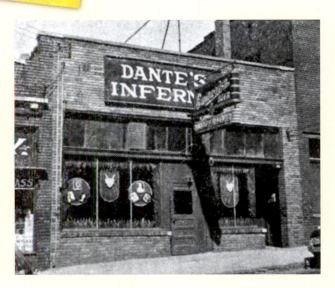

Hall had served on the governing board of the national Greeting Card Association for many years, serving as its president in 1931. Locally, he served as president of the Kansas City Rotary Club in 1933 and along with his brother, Rollie, was an active volunteer with the Boy Scouts of America.

Hall was also busy at home. He had steadily added to the wooded acreage he and Elizabeth owned south of Kansas City. By 1930 he had completed construction on a grand, Georgian-style home on the property—an ideal place to raise three children. By the time they moved into the new home, the oldest, Elizabeth (who by then had acquired the nickname "Jimmie") was eight years old, and her younger sister, Barbara, was seven. The youngest, son Donald Joyce Hall, was born just two years earlier, in 1928.

But the business at 26th and Grand was always first and foremost among Hall's priorities. And his tireless work there was paying off.

"It had always been such a fascinating business that it commanded all my time. It was my work and my hobby. I put in long hours at the office six days a week and carried a full briefcase home every night."

Hall Brothers in the mid-1930s was a company on fire with ideas and ambition. The next decade would be defined by innovations in product, marketing, and distribution, but even more so by people.

64

ABOVE: *The Hall home under construction in 1930. J.C. Hall purchased the original 41-acre property in 1927, but through a series of acquisitions the Hall farm grew to more than 700 acres by the mid-1930s.*

BELOW: *Conrad E. "Ed" Goodman, the first head of dealer services and developer of Hall Brothers' Eye-Vision greeting card display.*

LEFT: *Donald, Jimmie, and Barbara Hall, with father J.C. around 1932. Jimmie and Don shared their mother's deep love of the outdoors, but sister Barbara could more often be found playing with dolls inside. It's a passion she never quite shook. In adulthood, Barbara Hall Marshall would become a founder of The Toy and Miniature Museum of Kansas City.*

A great many men and women who would prove instrumental in leading the company in the decades to come began their tenures during this era. Their names read like a *Who's Who* of Hallmark for the middle decades of the 20th century: Jeannette Lee, Bill Harsh, Ed Goodman, and Hans Archenhold. After steering his company with minimal executive help for 25 years (with the notable exception of Charles Stevenson), J.C. Hall knew that he could no longer do it alone. With this group of talented people, he wouldn't have to.

From 1935 to 1945, much of the Hallmark chronicle can be told through the stories of these remarkable individuals.

The first of the group to join the company was Conrad E. "Ed" Goodman. Ed Goodman was just 17 when he took a part-time job working nights at the Hall's downtown retail store. He had hoped to make some money for college and go on to become an architect, but a few months after being hired on, he was offered a full-time position in the purchasing department. It was 1932—no time to be quitting a perfectly good job.

In a few years, Goodman became the assistant to Charlie Stevenson, a rather amorphous job that included, among other things, occasionally driving J.C. Hall's car to pickup his children from school. On one of those pick-ups, Goodman had the misfortune of sideswiping a passing streetcar. "That's when I met Mr. Hall for the first time," Goodman would recall many years later. "He was very nice about it. I continued driving his children and started driving him to meetings downtown occasionally."

Goodman found Hall an easy man to talk to. In one of their conversations, Hall lamented the state of dealer merchandising for greeting cards. It had long bothered Hall that many stores kept greeting cards in boxes stored under the counter. Customers first had to ask to see them and then file through one-by-one to find a suitable choice.

Soon, Goodman was appointed to a new department, Dealer Services. It was a department of two—Goodman himself and an architect named Herb Duncan. Charged with the job of coming up with a better way to merchandise cards, the two set to work. After a series of prototypes, they presented their solution. Built out of walnut wood, the free-standing fixture consisted of several rows of long, shallow shelves built along a concave curving backboard. These shelves sat on a base that elevated the cards to a customer's eye level, and each row was slanted at a slightly different angle to hold all the cards at a natural reading position. Integrated lighting made the cards even easier to see.

The new fixture was patented and dubbed the Eye-Vision display, and within a few years it would forever change the way greeting cards were sold. But first it had to be sold to dealers.

ABOVE: *In 1935, J.C. Hall purchased a herd of 38 Jersey dairy cows from the estate of a prominent Kansas City lumberman, R.A. Long. Soon faced with a daily surplus of rich Jersey milk, Hall started daily delivery to the plant to give employees a glass "to renew their energies." Tea and coffee were quickly added to the offering, resulting in what some consider the original office "coffee break."*

Hall Brothers' salesmen were supplied with photos to show their accounts, and the displays were offered at cost. But few were willing to make the capital outlay based on a promise and a black-and-white glossy.

J.C. Hall knew in his gut that the new display would revolutionize greeting card merchandising. But short of dragging the fixture around the country to show retailers how it worked, he wasn't sure how to convince them.

So he decided that dragging it around the country was just what he would do. He installed an Eye-Vision display—fully stocked with cards—in a custom-built trailer and tapped Ed Goodman to take his show on the road. Goodman started visiting greeting card retailers across the Midwest, pulling the model card shop behind his car. The results were immediate. Dealers who installed them reported card sales doubling or even tripling. Within a few months, a fleet of trailers was dispatched around the country. Within a few years, the trailers were no longer needed— the fixtures were selling themselves. Competitors naturally rushed to create their own customer-friendly displays, but for several years, the patented Eye-Vision display gave Hall Brothers a significant competitive advantage.

If the greeting card displays were eye-catching in 1935, the product that filled them was also capturing the public's attention. The creative department was cranking out new products as quickly as the public could absorb them.

ABOVE: *The patented Eye-Vision display. The modular displays could be combined and configured to suit available retail floor space.*

RIGHT: *Yet another innovative sales tool, the* Hall Brothers Handy Book *began in 1935 as part of J.C. Hall's aggressive dealer service strategy. These monthly publications were filled with ideas, promotions, and programs that dealers could use to help sell Hall Brothers products.*

RIGHT: *In the late 1930s, Hall Brothers dispatched a fleet of house trailers around the country to promote its Eye-Vision displays to retailers. Inside each trailer was a model card shop outfitted with the new displays.*

Hall Brothers pioneered processes like metallete (greeting card add-ons stamped out of thin metal), pop-up paper engineering, gold foil stamping, mirror cards, billfold cards, and cards bearing glued-on "everlasting flowers," actual flowers that had been treated with a preservative to retain their natural appearance.

Licensing deals brought even more excitement and timeliness to the lines. Popeye, Wimpy, and Donald Duck joined Mickey Mouse in the company's card displays, as did NBC radio star Jimmy Durante. And when the St. Louis Cardinals baseball team won the World Series in 1934, Hall Brothers rushed to market a line of cards featuring the "Gashouse Gang's" "Dizzy" and "Daffy" Dean. The products coming out of the Hall Brothers plant increasingly reflected what was currently captivating the American public.

The firm's creative division was gaining more structure and specialization by the mid-1930s as well. An editorial department was first formed in 1934—and the company's first full-time writer came on board in 1935. Other new departments included retouch, lettering, photography, and lithography.

The end of the 1930s brought two people to Hall Brothers who would prove to be true giants in their field. They would work the two sides of the design process—one on the creative side and one in prepress and printing. Their tenures would span several decades, and the impact of their accomplishments is still felt at Hallmark to this day.

Jeannette Lee was hired in 1939 as an artist but was almost immediately promoted to assistant to the firm's design director, Ethelynn Hills. Lee would quickly establish herself as a keen talent and an indispensable advisor to J.C. Hall. Her career—spanning seven decades—broke new ground for women not just at Hallmark, but in all of corporate America.

Hans Archenhold's story is perhaps even more remarkable. A German Jew from Munich who was briefly imprisoned at the Dachau concentration camp, Archenhold escaped Germany and found his way to Hall Brothers in 1940. He brought with him a knowledge of lithography possessed by only a handful of people in the world. Within the span of a few years, he would have the company at the leading edge of printing technology.

AROUND THE WORLD IN 1935

◆ On January 11, Atchison, Kansas, native Amelia Earhart becomes the first person to fly solo from Hawaii to California.

◆ The Social Security Act is voted into law on August 14.

◆ Former Jackson County, Missouri, judge Harry Truman—hand-picked and supported by political boss Tom Pendergast—serves his first year in the U.S. Senate.

◆ Coopers Inc.—later to become Jockey International—sells the first pair of men's briefs at Marshall Field's in Chicago, during the worst blizzard of the year.

◆ Kansas City bandleader Bennie Moten dies of a heart attack. His piano player, William "Count" Basie, forms his own band.

◆ Popular songs: "Begin the Beguine," "I Got Plenty o' Nuthin," "It Ain't Necessarily So," and "Just One of Those Things."

◆ Porky Pig debuts in *I Haven't Got a Hat* by Looney Tunes.

◆ Spring brings the return of dust storms that ravage North America's Great Plains states, which become collectively known as the Dust Bowl.

◆ On May 24, the first Major League Baseball game is played at night under the lights at Crosley Field in Cincinnati between the Reds and the Philadelphia Phillies.

◆ The world's first parking meters are installed in Oklahoma City.

◆ The Hughes H-1 Racer, piloted by Howard Hughes, sets a new airspeed record of 352 mph.

◆ The board game Monopoly is introduced by Parker Brothers.

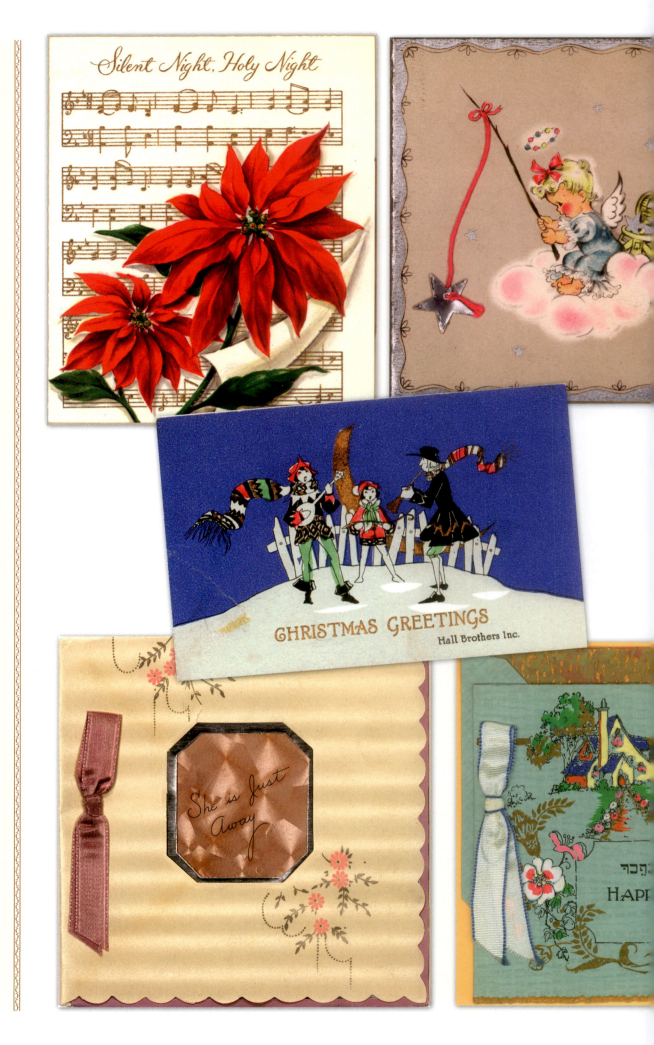

and I say SO

"Daffy" Dean Says So

So . . . you sure ought to have A HAPPY Birthday

Merry Christmas To A Dear Little Granddaughter

TO MY VALENTINE WITH JOY ON VALENTINE'S DAY

EW YEAR, ER

If you'd say you'd be MY VALENTINE... It sure would be Sweet Music to my ears

During the 1920s and 1930s, most Hall Brothers' greeting cards were produced using the techniques of airbrush, silk screen, and steel die engraving, while an army of handworkers and a host of special processes added an array of elegant features. Besides its ribbon attachment, the sympathy card (bottom far left) uses specialty paper—a coated, textured stock that is diecut into a scalloped shape. The angel sitting on a cloud (center top) has a fishing line made of yarn, and the die cut valentine card (center) has hand-attached brads that let the car's wheels roll. Also during the 1930s, several licensed characters joined the Hallmark family. These included Disney's Mickey Mouse, the real-life baseball stars Dizzy and Daffy Dean, and Shirley Temple (top right), whose skirt is made of real fabric.

JEANNETTE LEE: A CREATIVE FORCE FOR HALF A CENTURY

Jeannette Lee had planned to be a teacher. While completing her degree in art education from the University of Kansas City (now University of Missouri—Kansas City), she student-taught at Center High School and had been offered a full-time job upon graduation. But, before the deal was finalized, the principal asked Lee if she was planning to get married. She answered "yes," she did plan on marrying though she had no immediate plans. "That was the end of that," Lee remembers. "They didn't hire married women or women who were going to get married." The year was 1939. The winds of war were swirling, and many employers were reticent to hire a woman who might soon be displaced by her husband's service obligations. "Hallmark," Lee recalls, "was really one of the only places you had much chance of getting a job."

Jeannette Lee's tenure at Hallmark (as a full time employee) spanned 43 years, and along the way she forged a new leadership path for women. Hired on as an artist, she steadily moved through the ranks of the creative department, becoming assistant to the design director, then design director, art director, vice president, and ultimately the first woman elected to the board of directors.

It might come as a surprise, then, to know that Lee seriously considered quitting the company two weeks into the job.

To get the job, she had interviewed with J.C. Hall himself—a somewhat harrowing experience. Nearly 70 years later, she vividly remembers him bluntly asking, "How do we know that you won't just work long enough to pay off your student loan and then leave?"

Lee found the question particularly unsettling as that was essentially what she had planned to do. Still, she survived the interview and accepted a job offer. The first two weeks consisted of hand-folding greeting cards and filing work. "By the end of the two weeks," she recalls, "I was about ready to call it quits." But then her luck changed. The assistant to the design director was forced to quit when her military husband was reassigned. The vicissitudes of war that cost Lee a teaching job now opened up another path. Lee was offered the job. She accepted it and never looked back.

Jeannette Lee did it all in her time at Hallmark. In addition to guiding the professional development of countless artists, she contributed to the design effort on everything from individual greeting cards to the Crown Center retail and hotel

Jeannette Lee (standing) with artist Margaret Montgomery, early 1950s.

development. She personally worked with a list of artists and creative thinkers that includes Saul Steinberg, Norman Rockwell, Gloria Vanderbilt, I.M. Pei, and Henry Dreyfuss.

In 1963, Lee spent a memorable day working with Jacqueline Kennedy on her painting technique. The first lady was creating two paintings that would be printed on Hallmark cards and sold as a benefit for the soon-to-be-built Kennedy Center. She would also work closely with the Kennedys on their presidential Christmas cards—as she did with the Eisenhowers before and the Johnsons after.

In the 1960s, Lee traveled the world scouting creative talent for the company, hiring many foreign artists who would bring even more diversity and perspective to the firm's creative output.

"You need to provide an environment that makes them feel creative. For some artists, that's nothing—a total lack of stimulation. For others, it's constant stimulation. You don't want to put a creative person to a routine."

—Jeannette Lee

For more than three decades, Jeannette Lee was, in essence, the creative go-to person at Hallmark no matter what the job—a woman with the ability to retain her keen creative senses even as she moved through the halls of power within the corporation. Yet, despite her pioneering career path and long list of lofty accomplishments, Lee remains most proud of her work training, counseling, and mentoring the generations of young artists she directed over the decades. "I guess it's the teacher in me," she says. "This was just like a big classroom."

On February 28, 1983, Hallmark's daily *Noon News* employee newsletter carried the following item:

"What comes to an end today after forty-three years, eight months, and nine days, Jeannette Lee's career as a Hallmarker—a career unequalled in the annals of the creative division, with the exception of that of the late Joyce C. Hall, founder of the company with whom she worked so closely for so many years."

It was an appropriate sentiment—but it didn't turn out to be precisely true. Lee would continue to serve the company, in a consulting role, all the way through the 1990s. Some people are just too valuable to let go.

Hans Archenhold: New Life in the New World

On a cold, gray day in February 1940, a young, serious-looking man walked into J.C. Hall's office without an appointment and asked for a job. Hans Archenhold had just escaped Adolf Hitler's Germany with his wife and small daughter. All that he possessed of value was a brilliant mind and an expertise in lithography.

J.C. Hall, though stern and unsmiling at the interruption, knew brilliance when he saw it. After a conversation that stretched on for hours, he offered the Jewish refugee a job. It would prove one of his wisest decisions.

"His arrival—within a few years—really changed the way cards were produced."
—Jeannette Lee, on Hans Archenhold

During his 30-year association with Hallmark, Archenhold would advance the art and science of color reproduction like few other men in history. In 1940, however, Archenhold's personal journey was the mirror opposite of his new boss's rags-to-riches story.

Born in 1905 in Germany's Rhineland to a cultured family of wealth and influence, Archenhold was a university graduate with a background in engineering and art history. He'd become a creative force at Berger & Röckel in Munich, Europe's largest greeting card manfucturer, a company owned by his wife's family. He was one of Germany's top lithographers when Germany was the world leader in fine lithography.

Everything changed with the rise of Hitler's Nazi party. The printing plant was seized by the government and converted to build Messerschmitt fighter planes. Archenhold and other men of his family were sent to Dachau concentration camp.

But Archenhold had made powerful friends around the world. Foreign clients who owed money to Berger & Röckel refused to pay until Archenhold was released. Though he spent only 10 days in Dachau, the horrors he witnessed there never left him. By the time he and his immediate family escaped to England, on visas arranged by Josiah Wedgwood of the famed English china company, all their possessions had been looted.

The Archenholds immigrated to an America still in the grip of a long economic depression. Unable to find a job in the big eastern cities or Chicago, Archenhold continued west to Kansas City. He'd seen Hallmark cards at a department store in London. Desperately needing a job and a home for his family, he intruded into J.C. Hall's office.

"You have to realize," he said years later, "that I had been in Dachau, having been deprived of everything I ever owned. Joyce Hall's office looked to me like heaven."

Today, lithography is the primary reproduction process for greeting cards at Hallmark. But in 1940 colors were still applied by hand by hundreds of women in long rows using outdated silk screening methods and airbrush guns, which produced beautiful but temporary results, because the colors faded over time.

Though Hallmark leaders knew a change was needed, the cost and technical difficulties held them back. It took all of Archenhold's ingenuity to show them how to make the shift to a more efficient, mechanized system to meet the growing demand for greeting cards.

During the war years—when surging demand for cards ran up against materials rationing and manpower shortages—J.C. Hall charged Archenhold with making sure product quality didn't suffer. Archenhold responded by imposing a strictly disciplined quality control system. After the war, he kept Hallmark on the leading edge as American printing technology began to outpace Europe's.

Hans Archenhold officially retired from Hallmark in 1970 but continued to serve as a trusted advisor for many years after.

When Archenhold died at age 93 in 1998, Don Hall Jr. summed up his importance: "Hans' contribution to our company cannot be overestimated. He brought Hallmark into the forefront of American lithography and never stopped striving to make our products the very best."

Airbrush Department in 1938 before Archenhold's methods were adopted.

A Grand New Home

The success of the Eye-Vision fixtures, coupled with a much-improved stock control and reorder system that went along with it, brought even more growth to Hall Brothers. With nearly 800 employees, the company's facilities were bursting at the seams by the mid-1930s.

J.C. Hall increasingly found himself staring out his office window at the mammoth Overland Building that stood just north of the Hall Brothers' headquarters. The six-story behemoth, built in 1916, covered an entire city block. Hall dreamed of moving the company one more time. He made some inquires about the building to a local banker, sure that nothing would come of it.

The owners of the 240,000-square-foot building were interested in talking. Within a few weeks, a deal was struck. It would take nearly a year to refurbish the building, but by Christmas Eve 1936, the last of the employees were moved in. It was the eighth location for Hall Brothers in 25 years, and it nearly doubled the size of the company's operations. Still, J.C. Hall had learned not to underestimate his company's capacity for growth. As soon as the deal was completed, he turned his attention to buying 24,000 square feet of vacant land to the south of the new building for a parking lot.

Helping to coordinate the 1936 move was a young man who had joined the company that same year. William P. Harsh was hired as an assistant to Charlie Stevenson, the general manager of the firm and J.C. Hall's right-hand man. Both Hall and Stevenson must have seen something special in the University of Missouri

graduate from the beginning. They quickly implemented a management training program and made Harsh its first participant.

At the time, Charlie Stevenson was responsible for multiple divisions of the company, including filing, shipping, manufacturing, and warehousing. Harsh assisted Stevenson in all areas, but he found a natural affinity and talent for working with the personnel department. He would become director of the department in 1947, but long before then, he was instrumental in helping Stevenson bring industry-leading benefits to Hallmark employees.

"(HALL BROTHERS') NEW HOME WILL BE THE LARGEST IN THE WORLD TO BE OCCUPIED BY ITS TYPE OF BUSINESS. ...
THE KANSAS CITY PROPERTY, WHOSE NORTH WINDOWS AFFORD BLOCK-LONG STRETCHES OF NORTH LIGHT DESIRED BY ARTISTS AND COLOR WORKERS, WILL BE OVERHAULED AND REMODELED DURING THE NEXT FOUR MONTHS."

—The *Kansas City Star*, 1936

LEFT: *The Overland Building at 25th and Grand, before renovation by the Hall Brothers. The nearly quarter-million-square-foot structure had been built in 1916 by the Willys-Overland automobile manufacturing company—at the time one of the nation's largest car manufacturers.*

ABOVE: *The new Hall Brothers administrative offices on opening day December 24, 1936.*

RIGHT: *The Shipping Department.*

BELOW: *The Art Department.*

ARCHENHOLD'S COLOR SEPARATION PROCESS

In offset lithography an image is reproduced from a flat stone surface, with each color applied by a separate stone. In Hans Archenhold's method, a metal plate and large cameras replaced the stone.

• The process began in the art studio with an artist painting the card's design.

• The design then went to Archenhold's color separation department. There an artist created a key drawing in black ink that carried all the detail of the original design with open areas for color to show through.

• The key drawing was laid on a light table with semi-transparent paper over it, and the artist sketched in color areas, making a separate gray-tone drawing to represent each color.

• Each drawing would be photographed separately to make a printing plate. The process usually used six or seven colors, though as many as 12 colors could be required.

Black plate — *Blue plate* — *Dark Red plate*

Pink plate — *Red plate* — *Yellow plate*

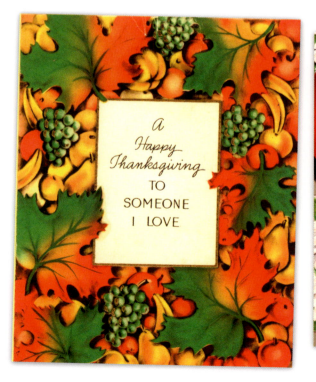

LEFT: *Hall Brothers greeting cards produced after 1941 using Hans Archenhold's hand separation process could be printed more efficiently and showed color tones with more depth and variation.*

ARE YUH LISTENIN'?

Ever since he was a boy poring over magazine ads in the family store, J.C. Hall had been fascinated by advertising. And despite conventional wisdom in the 1930s, he was convinced that advertising could help strengthen the brand awareness and even the sales of Hall Brothers' greeting cards.

Despite the fact that Hall Brothers would represent a sizable account, several advertising agencies turned Hall down flat when he approached them about putting together an advertising program. Their reasoning was always the same: greeting cards can't be sold by brand name. No one cares about the brand.

Hall persisted, and he finally found an agency willing to take on the business. Together, they decided to take Hallmark to the airwaves. This was the golden age of radio. In 1938, no medium was more powerful. The nationwide panic caused by Orson Welles' *War of the Worlds* radio play that very same year was proof enough of that.

The ad agency recommended sponsorship of a program being broadcast in Chicago, *Tony's Scrapbook.* Wons was an established radio host whose program included chatty observations and recitation of poetry and quotations. A 1932 *TIME* magazine article offered a mixed review of the radio talker:

> *"Wons is regarded by a shuddering minority as the most offensive broadcaster on the air. To his enormous radio following, principally in rural regions, he is a comforter of rare understanding who drops in for a friendly chat…. Wons puts (the poems) through a microphone in a voice hushed, saponaceous, insinuatingly folksy, with an ingratiating 'Are yuh listenin'?' or 'Isn't that pretty?'"*
>
> —TIME *magazine, February 8, 1932*

For Hall Brothers, Wons would read sentiments from greeting cards and encourage his listeners to "look on the back for the identifying mark—a Hallmark card."

Despite the faint praise of *TIME* magazine, Tony Wons' show went to network radio in 1940, reaching a national audience—and Hallmark's sponsorship went with it.

The response from Wons' instruction to "look on the back of the card" exceeded even J.C. Hall's expectations. He recalled: "Customers turned cards over, looking for the Hallmark emblem. Cards displayed on cardboard mountings were pulled loose to check the back of them. I even received homemade cards from children, who would fold a piece of paper, inscribe a message on the front and draw a Hallmark crown on the back. The entire industry benefited—the sale of greeting cards increased."

ABOVE: *Orson Welles and the Mercury Theater broadcast a radio dramatization of H.G. Wells' famous tale* War of the Worlds *that chronicled the Martian invasion of Earth, on Halloween night in 1938. Thousands of Americans tuned into CBS radio stations and heard what seemed to be panicked news coverage of a gory Martian invasion. Many listeners believed they were under attack; some even fled their homes, and police stations were swamped with frantic inquiries from concerned citizens.*

BELOW: *Tony Wons, whose radio show* Tony's Scrapbook *was the first radio program sponsored by Hall Brothers. He encouraged listeners to "look on the back for the identifying mark—a Hallmark card."*

BILL HARSH: A MAN OF THE PEOPLE

Over its 100 year history, Hallmark has earned countless accolades for its generous benefits, innovative employee outreach, and supportive work environment. "Caring enough," after all, applies to employees as well as customers.

This tradition of going the extra mile for employees was already established when William P. Harsh joined Hall Brothers in 1936, but according to J.C. Hall, Harsh was "the man who did the most in setting the standards for our personnel practices."

Harsh was a freshly minted graduate of the University of Missouri when he was hired as assistant to operations manager, Charles Stevenson. Just the year before, J.C. Hall and Stevenson had put in place a virtually unheard of benefit package for employees that included retirement pension, medical aid, life insurance, and vacation pay—all at a time when getting a job at all was difficult for millions of Americans.

Watching the boss, Harsh was amazed—and inspired—by what he saw. "Mr. Hall was exceedingly close to everybody. He always was. Even after we got bigger he stayed that way. He knew everyone. He knew their families and all about them."

Harsh made an immediate impression on J.C. Hall as well. "Bill Harsh makes more friends in less time than anyone I've ever known," Hall was fond of saying. "He is a man who perfectly combines ability and affability."

Harsh served in the navy during WWII, and shortly after returning he was named personnel director of the company whose employment rolls then totaled about 2,000 people. Surely no one in the company's long history was better suited to his job.

Harsh's career spanned 40 years, meaning that he worked under both J.C. Hall and his son, Donald J. Hall. Don Hall was, in fact, assigned to Harsh for training when he joined the company full time in 1953. He too singles out Harsh as one of the true greats in the company's long history.

"Bill Harsh was probably the finest mover of doing good things for employees. He was and is the 'it' for our employee relations."

—Don Hall

When Hallmark moved into its new building in 1956, Harsh thought the benefits package offered to employees was due to be upgraded as well. Working closely with Don Hall, he developed and proposed a broad extension of benefits including an ambitious Career Rewards Program that included enhanced insurance benefits, profit sharing, an employee savings program, a retirement plan, and extensive educational assistance. So rich was the plan that at the time *Fortune* magazine called it, "the country's most liberal employee-benefit and profit-sharing plan."

Bill Harsh retired from Hallmark in 1976 as executive vice president and a member of the board of directors. But his legacy is still felt by every employee who walks through the door. And if he were still there, standing by the door, he would likely greet each of them by name.

"He was a very unusual man. In 1954, there were close to a thousand people working here. He would walk around and greet everyone by name, and on the appropriate day wish them happy birthday. I think if I were to say who was the biggest, single contributor to the growth of Hallmark, it was the dynamic character of Joyce Hall. But Bill Harsh was able to surround him with the right people. That is an amazing quality to be able to select the kind of people that will do the best job for the company. He wasn't just personnel. He was a people person."

—Jack Jonathan, former director of new product development, on Bill Harsh

ABOVE: *With the Great Depression dragging on, the small but vigorous Hall Brothers company encouraged employee leisure activities to keep up morale. Operations manager Charles Stevenson was usually at the center of these events, organizing company picnics, ice skating parties, and weekly baseball games that drew as many as 300 employees to cheer on the company team. In Stevenson's words, the May 1938 Hallmark Amateur Follies—a musical comedy in three acts, written and acted by Hall Brothers employees—was "one of the best-accepted personnel relations projects."*

LEFT: *Charles Stevenson (center, with hat and flowers) donned ice skates and posed with co-workers at a Hall Brothers skating party on a Thursday night after work in 1938.*

OK JC: Gaining the Stamp of Approval

"We would bring all of the artwork that was done for that day. Sometimes it would be a rough painted sketch or drawing, sometimes it would be completed and ready for approval. Each one would be looked at carefully and have the sentiment read. If the cost looked okay and everything else met quality and taste standards, Mr. Hall would give the final OK by writing 'JC' on the back. This happened every day, and those meetings would last however long it took to get through the cards."

From the mid-1930s through the 1950s, an evening ritual took place in J.C. Hall's office. At 5:15 p.m.—after the official end of the workday—a small cadre of executives and managers assembled to review that day's output of greeting cards. The group was known as the OK Committee, and at the center of it was J.C. Hall himself.

In addition to Hall, the group included at least one representative from the editorial and design departments, cost accounting, and lithography and production. Two other committee members—Hall's secretary June Shikles and his younger daughter, Barbara—were included to supply "everywoman" commentary and judgments on taste.

Jeannette Lee, who became a fixture on the committee after joining the company in the late 1930s, provides a first-hand account of a typical meeting:

TOP: *The OK Committee at work, 1947. Clockwise starting with J.C. Hall, Jeannette Lee, Joe Kipp, Luther Scheffy, Hans Archenhold, June Shikles, Mary Barrett, and Francis Rogers.*

LEFT: *Hallmark's pansy cart greeting card carries the distinction of being America's best-selling greeting card ever. Painted by artist Dorothy Kelly Mainschien and debuting on Mother's Day, 1939, the design—in various forms—has sold about 30 million total cards since 1942. (Sales prior to that year are unrecorded.)*

ABOVE: *Art classes and sentiment review were staples for Hallmark artists and writers.*

RIGHT: *Mirror study was a common practice that helped artists capture realistic facial expressions for their card characters.*

BELOW: *Mary Dorman, hired in 1935 as Hallmark's first full-time writer, not only penned the verse but often dreamed up the design concepts for hundreds of successful greeting cards like this husband anniversary card from 1935.*

Hallmark in the War Years

As it did to so many, World War II came suddenly to the Hallmark family.

Ted Hall, a 24 year old navy seaman—and until just a few months earlier, a Hall Brothers employee—was killed in action on December 7, 1941, at Pearl Harbor, Hawaii.

Hall, who was unrelated to the J.C. Hall family, was the first, but would by no means be the last, of Hall Brothers employees lost in the war.

On Monday, December 8, Franklin Roosevelt declared war on Japan. And within a few days, the U.S. would officially join the Allied battle by reciprocating Germany's declaration of war.

Hall Brothers was open for business on December 8th, but it was far from an ordinary workday. Jeannette Lee, employed by the firm for just over two years, remembers, "The war was something everyone was worried about. We knew it was coming, but we didn't know what it meant to any of us."

No one, J.C. Hall included, knew what effect the war would have upon business or life.

The first indications were not encouraging. Just a few weeks before the Pearl Harbor attack, the *New York Times* reported that the British Ministry of Supply had banned production and sales of Christmas cards in the United Kingdom due to restrictions on paper use.

On the home front, the challenge came from the U.S. War Production Board. In 1942, the newly formed government agency was created to regulate production and allocation of materials including fuel, metals, rubber, and paper.

Early in 1942, the board announced plans to limit production of printers and publishers. From the outset, it gave short shrift to the greeting card industry. The agency categorized greeting cards as nonessential luxuries, in the same category as pool halls and beer parlors. So undisguised was the disdain of the board chairman that he was quoted as saying he hoped greeting cards would go the way of the English tea dumped in the Boston Harbor.

J.C. Hall, who had been appointed to the board's advisory committee representing the commercial printing industry, argued vehemently against the board's nonessential designation. With the help of a public relations firm and other greeting card industry representatives, he set about making the point that greeting cards were, in wartime, more necessary than ever. The PR firm came up with a slogan: "Keep 'em happy with mail." As J.C. said later:

> *"They soon found out that next to food and bullets,*
> *mail from home was the most important product of all.*
> *The troops needed them to keep up morale. It wasn't long*
> *before greeting cards got their paper allotment, and*
> *the board chairman got removed from the board."*

"THE POST OFFICE, WAR, AND NAVY DEPARTMENTS REALIZE FULLY THAT FREQUENT AND RAPID COMMUNICATION WITH PARENTS, ASSOCIATES, AND OTHER LOVED ONES STRENGTHENS FORTITUDE, ENLIVENS PATRIOTISM, MAKES LONELINESS ENDURABLE, AND INSPIRES TO EVEN GREATER DEVOTION THE MEN AND WOMEN WHO ARE CARRYING ON OUR FIGHT FAR FROM HOME AND FRIENDS. WE KNOW THAT THE GOOD EFFECT OF EXPEDITIOUS MAIL SERVICE ON THOSE OF US AT HOME IS IMMEASURABLE."

—*Annual report to the Postmaster General, 1942*

ABOVE: *The massive explosion of the destroyer USS SHAW when her magazine exploded after being bombed by Japanese aircraft in the sneak attack on Pearl Harbor.*

BELOW: *Ted Hall, the first Hallmark employee killed in action. He died in the attack on Pearl Harbor on December 7, 1941.*

The Greeting Card Industry Organization offered up its own voluntary conservation program in hope of securing a reasonable and workable federal one. Ultimately, the industry was assigned a 10 percent decrease in resources from the previous year, 1941. As the war continued, paper restrictions became increasingly severe, resulting in additional cuts of 10 percent and 15 percent in the two subsequent years.

Despite the rationing, Hall Brothers was actually able to boost its sales during the war years. A few factors are likely responsible. First, greeting cards sent to military bases were exempt from the quota, and Hall Brothers got into this market with gusto. The company also found ways to make more product with less material. "Before the war, we produced a lot of multifold cards," explains Don Hall. "We cut down on that quite a bit. And we also produced lots of cards on a very thin, lightweight paper stock."

Having dealt with the problem of material resources the struggle at Hall Brothers' headquarters turned to human resources. According to Bill Harsh, who served as personnel director after the war, an estimated 500 employees enlisted or were called into service during the course of the war—a number that represented more than a third of the company's workforce. Harsh himself was among their ranks. He served as a naval officer from 1943 through the end of the war.

On April 26, 1942, the Kansas City Star *reported on an increasingly frequent ceremony observed at Hall Brothers' headquarters when another of its young men left the firm to report for duty. The article reported six other "leave-takings" in the most recent week alone and explained that in addition to the companywide announcement, "the young men about to enter service are handed vacation checks of two weeks pay and a diary, in which friends soon are scribbling messages and admonitions."*

An even greater staffing challenge came courtesy of the fact that national employment levels reached as high as 98 percent during the war. Competition for workers kept even the best companies scrambling to fill jobs. With roughly 40 percent of the national economy tied to national defense, the more closely tied a city was to the war economy, the keener the competition to attract workers. And few cities experienced the war boom more intensely than Kansas City.

Kansas City's economy was transformed by the war. Tens of thousands of civilians from throughout the Midwest flooded into the metropolitan area to take jobs at newly built or converted defense factories. Just east of Independence, Missouri, the huge

Lake City Ordnance Plant, built by Remington Arms Company, produced 200 million rounds of ammunition monthly. Twenty miles west, at the B-25 bomber plant in the Fairfax district of Kansas City, Kansas, employment topped 26,000 people at the height of the war. Meanwhile, in south Kansas City, the new Pratt & Whitney aircraft engine plant employed another 24,000. The massive P&W facility was like a city unto itself—its roof covering three million square feet of factory floor.

The intense competition for workers, coupled with the very real possibility that the War Department could at any point commandeer their main manufacturing plant for the war effort, led J.C. Hall and Charlie Stevenson to a creative idea. Hall Brothers' solution to the employee shortage was to take the jobs to the people, literally. The company began setting up small plants in neighborhoods around the city, and in outlying towns, and staffing them almost exclusively with women who were not already working outside the home.

Most of their duty consisted of handwork: finishing specialty cards that required hand-folding, gluing, or similar finishing. Neighborhood women could walk to work and work a flexible schedule. In all, the company set up 32 of these branch facilities. According to Bill Harsh, "Those small in-town plants and out-of-town plants are the things that kept the production end of this company going during the war."

Three larger cities with satellite plants were Topeka, Lawrence, and Leavenworth, Kansas. As Hall Brothers production boomed during the war and in postwar years, large manufacturing facilities would be built in each of these cities. The Topeka Production Center, the first full-service, out-of-town manufacturing facility, was opened in 1943.

At the dawn of World War II, no one knew how the greeting card industry would be affected by the uncertainties of global war. But by the end of 1945, it was certainly clear. Hall's argument to the War Production Board years earlier had been borne out in the marketplace. Families torn apart by the war—separated by military deployments or out-of-state employment—turned to greeting cards to keep in touch like never before.

The increase in Hall Brothers' sales during the war years is nothing short of staggering. Annual sales rose from just under $4 million in 1940 to nearly $14 million in 1945. Competitive comparisons are difficult with private companies, but by now, few would dispute that Hall Brothers was the largest manufacturer of greeting cards in the world.

By the time the war ended, Hallmark had solidified its standing, not just as a force in the greeting card business, but as an iconic American company.

ABOVE: *Women training to become welders. They played an important role in the war effort at home, taking jobs previously held by men.*

RIGHT AND BELOW: *Factory posters from the war years.*

OPPOSITE PAGE: *Cards published by Hall Brothers during World War II.*

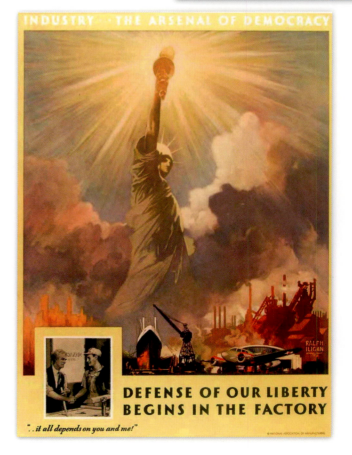

To My Sweetheart in The Service

SOLDIERS RECEIVE MAIL

Somebody said in the papers,
"When you write to the boys, be gay!
And tell 'em what fun you're having
While all of them are away!"

At the dance we had
one night last week,
The girl with her
little brother
Had lots more fun
than all the rest—
Who danced with
one another.

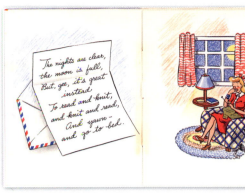

The nights are clear,
the moon is full,
But, gee, it's great
instead
To read and knit,
and knit and read,
And yawn—
and go to bed.

And, oh, we're having
such grand hikes!
A mile or two inspires.
A person to be healthier
And saves on gas
and tires.

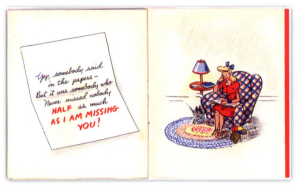

Yep, somebody said
in the papers—
But it was somebody who
Never missed nobody
HALF as much
AS I AM MISSING
YOU!

Christmas Greetings to an
A-1 MARINE

Hi, Soldier

Hello, SAILOR

PRAISE THE LORD,
AND PASS THE
AMMUNITION!

GREETINGS FROM "OUR CAMP"

WHENEVER
MAIL'S PASSED OUT
IN CAMP
I ALWAYS HOPE I'LL FIND
A BIG, FAT LETTER
WAITING
FROM "THE FOLKS I LEFT BEHIND,"
AND THIS JUST COMES TO
LET YOU KNOW
I OFTEN THINK OF YOU,
AND SAY I SURE DO WISH YOU'D
WRITE
A LOT MORE THAN YOU DO!

The Hallmark MILITARY NEWS

VOL. IV   KANSAS CITY, MISSOURI, AUGUST, 1944   No. 8

Afton Reports on D-Day

One of the best stories of D-Day, one which has attracted crowds around the service bulletin boards, comes from LT. AFTON TAYLOR, who is an M.P. in France. Although lack of space prevents its being printed in full, the following exerpts describe Afton's channel-crossing and the following twenty-four hours:

"As we moved through the mine fields into the open water of the channel, we saw more troop ships and escorts as far as the eye could reach. There was in each of our minds that most reassuring feeling that at least we had a lot of company. Planes buzzed overhead in clusters, bombers to continue the terrific hammering of the French coast and fighters to escort them and to harass German troop concentrations.

LT. AFTON TAYLOR

"No German planes were sighted until we were within a mile or so of the beach. Even then we were one of the fortunate ships neglected by the enemy airmen. However, our ship was now within range of their 88mm guns. Passing our own battleships and nearing the beach it was fascinating to watch those shells send up geysers of water. The blast of our big naval guns behind us was almost deafening. What a pounding that area took!. . .While still off-shore large fires on the beach testified as to the accuracy of enemy artillery.

"Approaching the beach, threading our way through a thick curtain of artillery fire, we transferred to LCVP's and buzzed through a quarter of a mile of water to the shore. The boat grounded fifty yards out and the end opened for us to go out. The water was chest-deep and I remember struggling to keep my feet in the choppy surf. . . The next thing I remember is lying flat on my stomach next to the sea wall a hundred yards away, trying to make myself as small as possible. When you hear that high-pitched whine of a heavy artillery shell you wish you were a turtle under that steel helmet and could hide yourself completely in it.

(Continued Col. 2)

Evert Wampler's Son Killed

We were all sorry to hear of the death of LT. CHESTER WAMPLER, son of Topeka Manager Evert Wampler. Chester, a pilot, was killed in the crash of a B-17 Flying Fortress at Gander, Newfoundland, on August 3. He received his wings last February at Pecos, Texas; and shortly after that he visited 2505 with his father before reporting to Kingman, Arizona, for further training. Besides his parents, Chester leaves his wife and a daughter, Sharon Kay.

LT. CHESTER WAMPLER

(Continued from Col. 1)
"Between artillery bursts I dug my first foxhole with my helmet. We were to report to a pre-arranged traffic headquarters as soon as we landed; and following a German communications trench we worked our way away from the beach while we watched our first tanks grind their way up from the sandy beach. What a welcome sight that was!

"The first tank was the victim of a direct hit from an 88 when half a mile inland. We went back to the beach and reported to the Provost Marshall at traffic headquarters, who was plotting traffic routes, setting up prisoner-of-war inclosures and doing a thousand-and-one jobs."

The rest of Afton's letter tells about his reconnaissance of the area of which he was to be in charge for the next few weeks; about his meeting a paratrooper group and their skirmishs with enemy snipers and about an encounter with a German tank and the return to the beach. "This concludes my first twenty-four hours in France," writes Afton, "And as one of the paratroopers said to me, 'If anyone ever cracks wise about an M.P. never seeing combat duty, tell him this little story'!"

ABOVE: *Started early in the war and written by Charles Stevenson, the* Hallmark Military News *carried welcome news from home to Hall Brothers' employees serving in the military ranks. One of the editors of the newsletter was a Hall Brothers' employee, Betsy Maxwell, who would later become Mrs. Walter Cronkite.*

TOP: *American soldiers, leaving the ramp of a Coast Guard landing boat on D-Day under heavy Nazi machine gun fire, June 6, 1944.*

RIGHT: *Anti-aircraft gunners watch dogfights over Normandy.*

LEFT MIDDLE: *Day five on the beaches of the Normandy invasion. D-Day was in reference to the day of actual landing—June 6, 1944.*

ABOVE: *Gen. Dwight D. Eisenhower gives the order of the day, "Full victory—nothing else," to paratroopers in England, just before they board their airplanes to participate in the first assault.*

LEFT: *A marine after two days and nights of hell on the beach of Eniwetok in the Marshall Islands.*

BELOW: *A Hallmark card that pays tribute to a fallen soldier.*

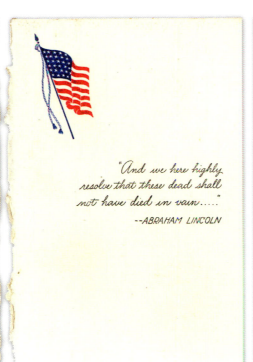

A
Message in Tribute
To the Memory
Of Your Loved One

"And we here highly resolve that these dead shall not have died in vain....."
--ABRAHAM LINCOLN

He gave his last full measure
of devotion
And though, of course,
his passing brings you pain
Still may it bring you surcease
from your sorrow
To know his sacrifice was not
in vain;
For as he lives forever in your memory
As one who died, that mankind
might be free,
So he will long be honored
by his country---
A hero in the cause of Liberty.

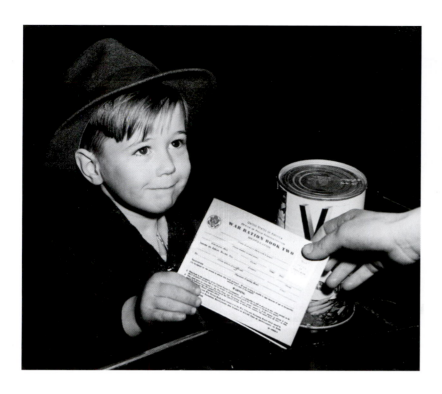

ABOVE: *A young boy has his first experience with a rationing card.*

BELOW RIGHT: *A Hall Brothers greeting card celebrating victory.*

BELOW: *In 1942, Hallmark began sponsorship of the nationally broadcast radio program,* Meet Your Navy. *The show featured talent from within the military ranks and popularized the slogan, "Keep 'em happy with mail." The campaign is given much credit for strengthening the public's habit of sending greeting cards.*

Alfred Eisenstaedt/Time & Life Pictures/Getty Images

"IT WAS REALLY THE WAR WHICH OPENED UP THE GREETING CARD BUSINESS. IT GAVE MILLIONS OF PEOPLE THE NEED TO KEEP IN TOUCH. A LOT OF THEM DID IT THROUGH GREETING CARDS. THEN, WHEN THE WAR WAS OVER, THEY'D GOTTEN IN THE HABIT OF DOING THOSE THINGS AND THEY KEPT IT UP."

—*J.C. Hall*

LEFT: *Alfred Eisenstaedt's famous photograph of a sailor kissing a young nurse on V-J Day in Times Square (August 14, 1945), which was originally published in* LIFE *magazine.*

RIGHT: *American servicemen and women gather in front of the Rainbow Corner Red Cross Club in Paris to celebrate the unconditional surrender of the Japanese.*

RIGHT: *Ed Clark took one of the most famous domestic photographs of the war years at the funeral of President Franklin D. Roosevelt. Although he had been unwell for many months, his death on April 12, 1945, in Warm Springs, Georgia, shocked the nation. Elected four times to the presidency, the beloved FDR had guided the country through 12 tumultuous years of depression and war. Now, with the end of the conflict clearly in sight, he was gone. On the following day, as Roosevelt's body was solemnly carried away, Clark recorded Navy officer Graham Jackson weeping openly as he played the mournful tune "Going Home" on his accordion.*

A Slogan Worthy of the Very Best

The tremendous population shifts brought about by World War II meant a commensurate need to keep in touch— surely a big reason for the phenomenal growth experienced by Hall Brothers in the 1940s. But it wasn't the only reason.

Even as the war dragged on, J.C. Hall, Charlie Stevenson, Ed Goodman, and other company leaders were looking for creative ways to move the company forward. Product, processes, and distribution all made great strides forward in these years. Advertising advanced, too. Hall continued to believe in strong promotion of the Hallmark brand, and relied most heavily on radio sponsorships and advertising. After the success of the Tony Wons program and the wartime programming of *Meet Your Navy*, the company forged a new relationship with comedic host Charlotte Greenwood on the ABC radio network in 1944 and 1945. Sponsorship of radio plays and digests would continue throughout the decade.

Regardless of the program, the primary goal was essentially the same—to establish and distinguish the Hallmark brand and to persuade customers to ask for it by name.

The company had long sought a slogan to accurately position the brand. Ed Goodman, who was head of advertising and sales in the 1940s, remembered that for several years the company used the line, "Hallmark cards best express your perfect taste, your thoughtfulness." "But," he admitted, "we were the only ones that seemed to know about it."

Goodman continued to tinker with slogans and promotional lines on the 3 x 5 index cards that were so ubiquitous at Hallmark. On one of these cards, he had written a random assortment of lines that read like the radio promotions typical of the era:

> *Three little words that mean so much...*
> *—A Hallmark Card*
> *—They tell your friends you cared enough to send the very best.*
> *—They best reflect your perfect taste... your thoughtfulness.*
> *... So... Before you buy—look on the back*
> *For those three identifying words...*
> *—A Hallmark Card*

As Goodman tells the story, he looked at the card every day, occasionally changing a word here or there.

"One time, Mr. Hall came out and I was just idly playing with the cards without thinking about it, and he picked up the card and looked at it. He said, 'Where'd you get this?' I said, 'Oh, I've just been playing around with it.'"

One line on the card jumped out at Hall. He had always been keen on emphasizing the quality of the firm's products. Goodman,

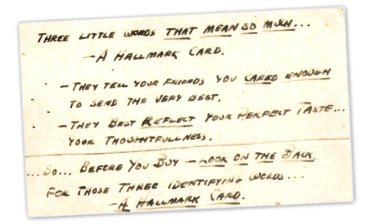

ABOVE: *Hallmark's eventual slogan, "When you care enough to send the very best," was tucked in among other lines written on a 3 x 5 index card by Hall Brothers' executive Ed Goodman in 1944.*

BELOW: *An ad from 1949 that uses the phrase "When you care enough to send the very best" and the new company logo.*

Why did you hire a receptionist with a friendly smile?

Undoubtedly because you knew her friendly smile would be an asset to your business, serving as a company welcome to all who call.

Just as her smile creates an atmosphere of friendliness for your company, so can the Christmas cards you send. And this year with the new Hallmark Christmas Cards designed especially for men and business firms, you'll find it takes but little time.

Simply visit the store that features Hallmark Cards. Ask to see the Hallmark Album for Men containing Christmas cards for men and business firms. In a matter of minutes you can select the card you want imprinted with your name. Select from a wide variety of Christmas cards designed with dignity and good taste— confident in the knowledge that to everyone, everywhere, the Hallmark on the back of a card means, "You cared enough to send the very best!"

"When you care enough to send the very best"

RIGHT: *The evolution of the Hallmark corporate logo can be traced back to 1911 when Hall Brothers, named after founder Joyce C. Hall and his brothers, was formed. The word Hallmark first appeared on products in 1925. At various times, the name was incorporated into the torch and shield logo from the 1920s (second from top) and the simpler version from the 1930s (fourth from top). The Hall Brothers logo from 1923 (third from top) was never actually used on products. In 1949, the Hallmark signature and crown logo, first appeared. The Hallmark logo became a registered trademark in 1950, though the company did not officially change its name to Hallmark Cards until 1954.*

he knew, was intent on finding a slogan that emphasized caring. And there, in the middle of that hastily composed index card, was a single phrase that accomplished both: "...you cared enough to send the very best."

The company started using the slogan immediately and quickly realized that it was more than just a promotional statement. Central to the slogan was a promise—one that Hall, Goodman, and everyone associated with the company from that day forward has taken very seriously. J.C. Hall explained:

"While we thought we had only established a good advertising slogan, we soon found out we had made a business commitment as well. The slogan constantly put pressure on us to make Hallmark cards 'the very best.' I somehow feel that without the slogan our products would not have been as good."

Just a few years later, in 1949, a new logo, featuring the now familiar Hallmark crown and signature, was designed by graphic designer Andrew Szoeke. The company's name would not officially be changed from Hall Brothers to Hallmark Cards, Inc. until 1954, but the firm that had long been referred to colloquially as "Hallmark" now had a logo that put its eventual name into clear focus.

RIGHT: *By 1947, nine Hallmark employees (including J.C. Hall) had served the company for at least 25 years. Pictured, from left, are Rollie Hall, Charles Sefranka, A.F. Morrison, Charles Stevenson, Dorothy Smith, J.C. Hall, Evert Wampler, O.E. Brown, and William Hall.*

The Trademarks of Hallmark Cards

What's in a name? When the name is the Hallmark and Crown trademark of Hallmark Cards, it means years of advertising effort — effort that has resulted in immediate brand recognition and product respect on the part of nine out of ten social expression customers. The Hallmark advertising slogan, "When you care enough to send the very best," is one of the three best-remembered slogans of any American product.

Surprisingly enough, the fame of these familiar Hallmark trademarks has been established in only a few short years. The slogan was first used on the Charlotte Greenwood radio show in 1944. The Hallmark and Crown has been a registered product trademark only since 1949.

But though the Hallmark trademark and slogan are relatively young, the traditions of trademarks have been around several thousand years.

From the beginning of civilization, proud workers have identified the products they made. Archeologists have uncovered loaves of bread from the ruins of ancient cities bearing the seal of the baker who made them. They have found wine jars in the Mediterranean imprinted with the marks of Roman wine merchants.

Such marks, whether symbol or signature, served the same purpose as a trademark. They identified the goods of the manufacturer who made them, and signified that he was sure enough of their quality to identify them as his own.

SYMBOL OF QUALITY. A manufacturer shows his pride of workmanship by identifying his products. And identification protects his enterprise and distinguishes it from that of others.

In 14th century England, craftsmen who fashioned products of gold, silver, wood, and other decorative materials were members of

6   CONTINUED 7

9

"HALL BROTHERS HAD BEEN THE NAME OF OUR COMPANY ALMOST FROM ITS START IN 1910. SOMEHOW IT HAD NEVER BEEN SATISFACTORY TO ME. IT SOUNDED OLD FASHIONED. ONE NAME HAD BEEN ON MY MIND SINCE THE EARLY '20S, WHEN I READ A STORY ABOUT THE GOLDSMITHS OF 14TH CENTURY LONDON. A MARK HAD BEEN ADOPTED FOR EACH MEMBER OF GOLDSMITHS HALL GUARANTEEING THE PURITY OF EVERY GOLD AND SILVER ARTICLE MADE. IT WAS CALLED A "HALL MARK." THE WORD FASCINATED ME. IT NOT ONLY SAID QUALITY IN AN AUTHORITATIVE WAY, BUT IT ALSO INCORPORATED OUR FAMILY NAME."

—*J.C. Hall*

ANDREW SZOEKE'S CROWNING ACHIEVEMENT

Andrew Szoeke was never an employee of Hallmark Cards. He visited the company's headquarters in Kansas City only once in his life. But for more than 60 years, every person who has looked at a Hallmark card, advertisement, or envelope has seen his work.

The story of Hallmark and Andrew Szoeke is an unlikely one. It began on a busy sidewalk in New York City in 1948. Jeannette Lee and J.C. Hall were visiting the city on business. Lee, Hallmark's design director at the time, vividly recalls the moment they saw Szoeke's work:

> *"We were looking in a window display at Bergdorf Goodman when we saw a small display card. The lettering on the card was so refined and beautiful, we had to find out who was responsible."*

A bit of inquiry led them to Andrew Szoeke, a Viennese émigré who, despite being somewhat reclusive, had become a highly sought-after calligrapher, working for companies such as Revlon, Saks Fifth Avenue, Macy's, and American Airlines. He was equally accomplished in the ancient art of wood marquetry, which involves designing with wood veneers.

Hall, Lee, and artist Vivian Smith met with Szoeke in his New York studio, and soon the designer's exquisite lettering was appearing on Hallmark Christmas cards, gift wrap, and albums.

A higher profile assignment quickly followed. J.C. Hall had long desired an updated corporate logo and asked Szoeke to take on the job. Lee remembers that it didn't take long for the designer to bring forth a few variations on the now-familiar crown logo. The effect was immediate. "He hit it right on the nose," recalls Lee. "It was so beautiful. So perfectly proportioned. And it still seems fresh after all these years."

Soon the logo was everywhere—on packaging, advertising, store signs, and eventually on the *Hallmark Hall of Fame*. In 1949, Hallmark officially trademarked the logo, and in time it became a classic in corporate identity.

Though he made his most prominent contribution in his first year of association with the company, Szoeke continued to work with Jeannette Lee and the greeting card designers for two decades. He worked with the lettering group, welcoming artists to his studio in New York for master classes. He was also an expert at deep embossing, the raising and lowering of a paper surface to enhance a design. "We did embossing at the time," explains Lee, "but not nearly as well as he did."

Szoeke consulted for the company until his death in 1969 at the age of 76. He had created his graceful lettering for an impressive list of clients over his long career, but his obituary in the *New York Times* mentioned only one by name: Hallmark.

ABOVE: *Szoeke's final design for the Hallmark logo, which was later adapted from his sketches by two Hallmark artists, Jim Sturdivan and Audrey Wilkinson, who refined the image and standardized the logo for its many uses.*

LEFT: *One of the very early logo designs that incorporated the crown and an early Hallmark typeface.*

VIVIAN TRILLOW SMITH

Thousands of artists have worked at Hallmark over its 100 year history, and each has contributed something uniquely his or her own to the company's creative legacy. But every generation of Hallmark artists seems to produce its star. One of the first break-out talents to emerge from the long rows of drawing tables that filled the company's art department was a high-spirited woman named Vivian Trillow Smith.

Smith's career began in a rather unextraordinary way. She was hired in 1924 as a color girl, responsible for adding color to other artists' designs. But not long after, she won a contest to become Hallmark's first artist trainee. Her first assignment was as a lettering artist, and it would be four more years before she was allowed to start contributing original artwork. Still, by the time she retired in 1970, Smith had attained the title of stylist—the highest available in the creative division. She also holds the distinction of being the first Hallmark artist allowed to add a signature, "VIV," to her work.

Smith could do it all, from cute children and light-hearted animals to stylish couples and jolly Santa Clauses. Her lettering—always a strong suit—placed her name forever in the Hallmark vernacular when a typeface named *Vivian* was added to the font library available to artists.

But what really moved Vivian Smith to the pantheon of Hallmark artists was a series of paper doll greeting cards that she began creating in 1947. The dolls, lavishly designed front and back and topped with a feather plume, were a smash. The first series, called "Dolls from the Land of Make-Believe," featured 16 storybook characters including Little Red Riding Hood, Cinderella, and Little Bo Beep. The storybook series was followed by an international series called "Dolls of the Nations" and by a set of dolls depicting the main characters from Louisa May Alcott's *Little Women*.

J.C. Hall was one of Smith's biggest fans and, along with Jeannette Lee, called upon her creative insight and opinions on regular research trips to Chicago and New York City. Lee, who served as Smith's design director for decades, counted Smith as one of the most talented artists she ever managed. "She was a positive, curious, happy spirit," Lee recalled fondly. "Her life was an expression of affection for the product and for her art."

HELLO THERE, **Two** YEAR OLD

A hat is to wear,

"HER PHILOSOPHY WAS
TO CREATE A LIVING SITU-
ATION FOR EVERY CARD.
MAD WAS MAD, GLAD
WAS GLAD—CONVEYED
TO THE GREATEST DEGREE
IN THE MOST MINUTE
DETAIL."
—Jeannette Lee

Little Bo-Peep

Polly, Put the Kettle On!

COWBOY JOE

J.C. Hall loved Vivian Smith's
highly decorated paper dolls—
and buyers did, too. The dolls
were an unexpected hit in the
late 1940s. "I am so excited
about the doll project," Smith
wrote in a 1948 letter to Hall.
"I have tried to make them
detailed and still not fussy."

93

CHAPTER FIVE

The Power of Association

"Tell me what company you keep and I'll tell you what you are."

—*Miguel de Cervantes Saavedra*

I N 1910, WHEN 18-YEAR-OLD JOYCE C. HALL WAS NAVIGATING HIS FIRST YEAR ALONE IN KANSAS CITY, HE WOULD SPEND HALF HIS WEEK RUNNING OFFICE AFFAIRS AND THE OTHER HALF ON SHORT SALES TRIPS AROUND the Midwest. On one such trip, working towns on the Hannibal and St. Joseph Railroad line, he found himself waiting for a train in Troy, Kansas. He was bound for Hiawatha, the next town down the line, but the train was late and he grew restless. He recounted the story in his 1979 memoir, *When You Care Enough*:

> *"I started walking up the tracks to pass the time when I saw the outline of a man in a long dark coat and a black hat coming toward me. It couldn't have been anybody else except the man I had seen at a Chautauqua when I was a small boy—William Jennings Bryan."*

The two men stood facing each other on the train tracks—a lean, hustling, 10th grade-educated, young entrepreneur and one of the political and cultural giants of the age. Bryan, a populist known as "The Great Commoner," was a lawyer, a three-time Democratic Party presidential nominee, and one of the most illustrious orators in U.S. history. The hero of the working man had just met one of his constituents.

Hall goes on to recount how he overcame his initial intimidation to strike up conversation with the larger-than-life Bryan. They talked, he said, "for a good part of the afternoon." When the train arrived, the two boarded together, continuing their conversation all the way to Hiawatha. Once there, Bryan invited Hall to have supper with him. "I was scared all the time," said Hall, "but tried to remember that he was 'The Great Commoner.'" "Bryan," he would say, "was probably the most important person who had ever set foot in that town."

From his earliest days as a young clerk, reading profiles of great men of arts, politics, and business in *American Magazine* while minding the family bookstore, Hall had harbored a naked admiration for high achievers and a fascination with the famous. Meeting William Jennings Bryan impressed him deeply. The politician was certainly the most important person J.C. Hall had ever met in his first 18 years of life, but in the coming decades, he would encounter and befriend some of the 20th century's most

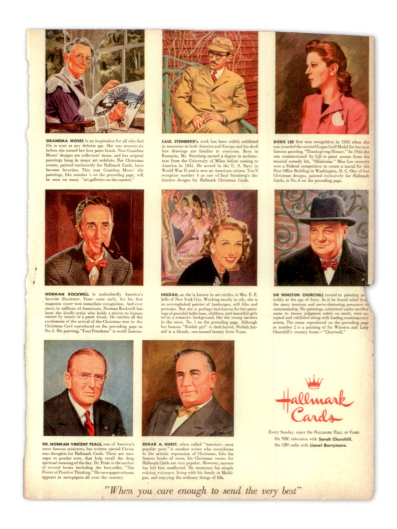

> "MR. HALL MADE FRIENDS WITH ALL OF THESE INVENTIVE, CREATIVE PEOPLE. HE ALWAYS LIKED PEOPLE LIKE HENRY (DREYFUS) AND (SAUL) STEINBERG AND INDIVIDUALS WHO WERE INTELLIGENT AND GIVING, AND HE WAS ALWAYS ON THE LOOK-OUT FOR PEOPLE WHO HAD THAT SPECIAL QUALITY."
>
> —*Jeannette Lee*

ABOVE: *A magazine advertisement from the early 1950s showcased prominent people and artists who contributed work for Hallmark cards.*

RIGHT: *After sketching a new piece, Rockwell would send the drawing to J.C. Hall for approval. Rockwell then made a tightly rendered pencil drawing the exact size of the final piece in order to work out the details. He used the smaller format watercolor and oil sketches to devise his color scheme.*

notable people—many of whom with his effort—would be woven into the history of Hallmark Cards.

By the mid-20th century, Hallmark's cultural relevance—as well as its sheer size—made it an attractive creative partner for plenty of high-profile artists. The name *Hallmark* had the ability to open doors, and J.C. Hall wasn't shy about using it to go after the artists he admired. In the early 1950s, the company created cards featuring the artwork of Grandma Moses, Saul Steinberg, Andrew Wyeth, Salvador Dali, and Norman Rockwell. There were others, not famous for their artwork, who also saw their work published on Hallmark cards. Actors Fred MacMurray, Henry Fonda, Lionel Barrymore, actress Jane Wyman, and comedian Groucho Marx were among those whose artistic aspirations were indulged by Hall. On the editorial side, inspirational writer Norman Vincent Peale and humorist Ogden Nash both penned sentiments for the company. The Dali connection never amounted to much. The Spanish painter's surrealist take on Christmas proved a bit too avant garde for the average greeting card buyer. But Rockwell was another story.

Thanks in large part to his long association with the *Saturday Evening Post*—a magazine for which he created more than 300 cover paintings—Norman Rockwell was the most prominent American illustrator of the 20th century. In the late 1940s, J.C. Hall approached Rockwell about creating a series of Christmas cards for the company. As was often the case when Hall got acquainted with artists, the assignment grew into a long professional and personal relationship. Between 1948 and 1957, Rockwell created 32 Christmas designs for Hallmark. During those years,

RIGHT: *Hallmark's Fine Art Collection includes 32 Norman Rockwell Christmas-themed paintings and 21 preliminary drawings.*

THE KANSAS CITY SPIRIT AND THE FLOOD OF '51

"Measured in terms of human suffering, tremendous losses in property, and extensive disruption of business activities throughout the flooded area, it was the greatest catastrophe within the history of the region."
—N.T. Veach, 1952, founding partner of the Blash and Vele engineering firm

The spring and early summer of 1951 had already been exceedingly wet in eastern Kansas with triple the average rainfall. The ground was saturated and rivers ran high. And on Friday, July 13th, the fifth day of a torrential storm that dropped 16 inches of rain in parts of the Kaw River watershed, the floodwalls broke—literally. Kansas City's West Bottoms—home to its expansive meat-packing facilities and the first part of town that J.C. Hall had laid eyes on some 40 years earlier—was engulfed in the waters. Trucks, railroad cars, and thousands of animals were swept downstream. The raging waters continued to rise, and the next day thousands of homes in the Armourdale and Argentine neighborhoods and hundreds of businesses, including the Trasworld Airlines overhaul base were flooded out.

While Hallmark's headquarters sat on high ground a safe distance from the river, the company had product and materials stored in three large West Bottoms warehouses. Up to eight feet of water poured through them, washing away around a half-million dollars' worth of paper stock and Christmas cards.

"By the time I got to the scene, our supplies were rolling down the river like confetti."

—J.C. Hall

ARLINGTON
VERMONT

August 10, 1951

Mr. Joyce C. Hall, President
Hall Brothers, Inc.
Twenty fifth and Grand Ave.
Kansas City, Mo.

Dear Joyce:

You have already received two extremely temperamental telegrams from me, but I do want to write and tell you how really stimulating and inspiring my visit to Kansas City was.

The idea of this picture depicting the spirit of a city—Kansas City—is truly a great challenge, and I am going to give it every thing I have. It may be a short time before I send on the sketches, but I don't want to hurry it, and I know you will agree that it will be worthwhile to do it in this way.

I am sending Ed Goodman the transportation cancellations, etc. When I arrived in St. Louis I didn't have the heart to take that early plane out again, so I stayed with Jerry until midnight.

Thanks again, Joyce, for your many courtesies, and I can't tell you how happy I am to be doing this picture. The whole idea is so inspiring that I can't wait to get started on it.

Sincerely,

Norman

When Hall's friend Norman Rockwell heard the news about the devastating flood, he called from his home in Vermont to ask if there was anything he could do. After giving it a little thought, Hall asked the painter if he would come to Kansas City and create a painting that showed the city rebuilding after the flood. Rockwell agreed.

The painter arrived in the city and literally waded in, donning rubber boots and trudging through the sodden debris. He observed and sketched, and then he returned to his studio to produce a nearly life-sized oil painting of a man with his sleeves rolled up, holding blueprints, and surveying the city.

The can-do spirit of the painting no doubt put Hall in mind of another inspiring Kansas City story—the one told to him by a traveling cigar salesman back in 1909 about the rapid rebuilding of the city's convention hall after a horrendous fire. It was that story, and its embodiment of the Kansas City spirit, that helped persuade J.C. Hall to move there in the first place. And now, 40 years after arriving, he witnessed that never-say-die attitude first hand. This time, because of his friend Norman Rockwell, that fighting spirit was captured on canvas. The painting, called *The Spirit of Kansas City*, was presented to Hall in 1951 and has proudly hung in the Hallmark headquarters ever since.

Rockwell's face—not just his work—would become a familiar sight around the company as he came to town to hold painting clinics with Hallmark artists. According to Jeannette Lee, Rockwell the man had the same genial manner that came through in his work. "He loved to visit us," she recalls. "And we loved to have him visit."

In addition to holiday cards, Rockwell's Christmas paintings have adorned ornaments, plates, gift wrap, and a host of other products in the decades since J.C. Hall sought out the contribution of the extraordinary illustrator. The two men saw each other as kindred spirits, united in their love of traditional values and respect for the common person. In a 1952 letter to Hall, Rockwell expressed his regard for their relationship, writing: "There is nobody else that I enjoy working for so much, personally and professionally."

ABOVE: *Norman Rockwell in Kansas City doing preliminary sketches for* The Spirit of Kansas City.

RIGHT: *The finished painting was a collaborative work done by Rockwell and John Atherten that became a civic symbol for Kansas City.*

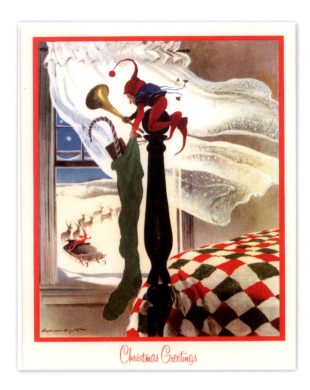

Christmas Greetings

Busy Day

Grandma Moses

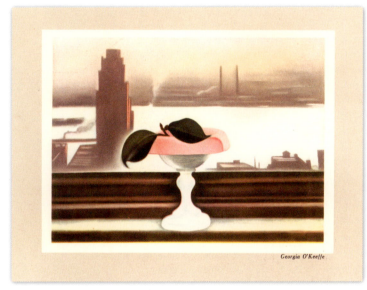

Georgia O'Keeffe

MOSES.

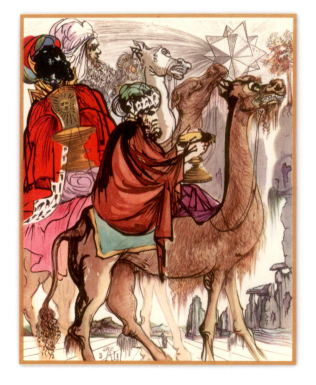

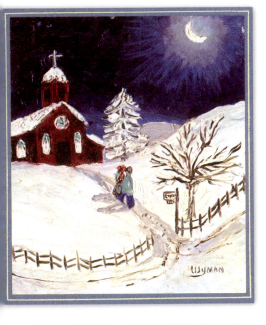

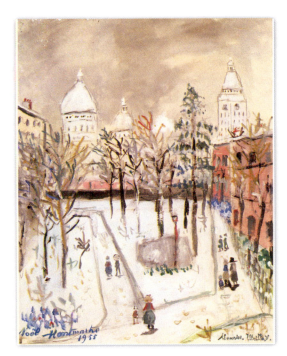

Max Weber

Fred Mac Murray

GROUCHO MARX

Pictured on these two pages are Hallmark cards bearing artwork created by celebrities and published in the 1940s, '50s and '60s.

TOP ROW FROM THE LEFT: *Andrew Wyeth, Grandma Moses, Jane Wyman, Salvador Dali, Maurice Utrillo.*

MIDDLE ROW: *Georgia O'Keeffe, Henry Fonda, Lionel Barrymore, Max Weber.*

BOTTOM ROW: *Grandma Moses, Salvador Dali, Fred MacMurray, Groucho Marx.*

A Small World. Very Big Ideas.

There are some striking parallels between the lives of Joyce C. Hall and Walter Elias (Walt) Disney. Coming of age in the early part of the 20th century, each man essentially redefined the industry he chose to work within—the greeting card industry for Hall and the animated motion picture industry for Disney. Each would build his business from humble beginnings into a brand recognized the world over.

But long before Hall and Disney became legends of American business, each was an ambitious young man trying to make a go of it in Kansas City, Missouri. Joyce Hall arrived alone in Kansas City in 1910. Walt Disney came to town with his family the very next year. Though they didn't know each other then, and Hall was 10 years Disney's senior, at times the two lived only about a mile apart.

Walt Disney was a paperboy in his primary school years in Kansas City and delivered daily to the home of Hall's future wife, Elizabeth Dilday. Elizabeth knew Walt from school, too. She remembered him as the boy who was always drawing.

But Disney and Hall never crossed paths in Kansas City—not directly. Their first meeting wouldn't happen until 1932—four years after the former had introduced a new character, Mickey Mouse, forever into the public consciousness. By then, Disney was nurturing his animation business in Burbank, California. Hall had stayed in Kansas City, of course. By the early 1930s, he, too, had established himself as a man to watch. His vision and hustle had helped build a thriving greeting card business. In 1928, the same year that Mickey Mouse made his first on-screen appearance, the word "Hallmark" started appearing on the back of Hall Brothers greeting cards.

Walt Disney's brother and business partner, Roy, made the first official connection between the two companies. He visited Hall in 1932 to propose putting Walt's characters on greeting cards. "We were charmed by the cartoons and agreed on a contract," J.C. Hall wrote in his 1979 book, *When You Care Enough*. It was one of the first licensing ventures for both of the young companies. It would also be the longest. More than 75 years later, Disney greeting cards are still among Hallmark's most consistent sellers.

Hall and Disney cultivated a genuine friendship over the years, often consulting each other on new ventures. When Hall began dreaming up development plans for the parcel of land that would become Crown Center, one of the first persons he asked for advice was Disney. Who better, after all, to help him dream a new world than the man who had just created Disneyland.

Don Hall remembers many meetings between the two men.

In some of the early ones, the two discussed the possibility of opening a Disney theme park on the property—an idea that was fairly quickly dismissed as unfeasible.

In the late 1950s, Don Hall sat in on a memorable meeting held in Malibu, California, with his father, Disney, and James Rouse, a pioneering developer of planned communities. "It was one of the most fascinating meetings I've ever been involved in," recalls Hall. "Disney had just purchased most of the land that would be home to EPCOT, so he was talking about that. Rouse was talking about the planned community he wanted to build outside of Baltimore, and Dad was talking about our plans. Each was envisioning his own way to build a new community, and they were all interested in telling their story."

Remarkably enough, over the next few decades each man would see a version of his plan take shape. In the 1960s and '70s, Rouse did go on to develop the entirely new city of Columbia, Maryland, between Baltimore and Washington, D.C. Disney's EPCOT Center (short for Experimental Prototype Community of Tomorrow) opened at the Disney World resort in 1982. Crown Center, was opened as an 85 acre mixed-use development in the center of Kansas City in the 1970s.

The vision for such ambitious projects isn't often summoned and is even less often realized. But J.C. Hall knew one of the great keys to high achievement—surround yourself with people who aren't afraid to dream big.

Walt Disney and his wife Lillian, c. 1931.

WALT DISNEY

July 2, 1954

Dear Joyce:

I have your note regarding DISNEYLAND and am
happy to know of your interest. Although I do
so with all modesty, I must say it's going to be
one Hell of a show!

I think it would be a mistake, if you don't come
over and get some first-hand knowledge about
DISNEYLAND the next time you're out this way.
I definitely feel you will want a spot somewhere
in the setup.

We have some big important concerns, who are
very excited about it, and we are "booking" them
in as they come.

Thanks for your expressed good wishes, and with
kindest regards,

Sincerely,

Joyce C. Hall
Hall Brothers Incorporated
25th and Grand Avenue
Kansas City, Missouri

WD:es

"EVERYTHING HE DID
APPEALED TO CHILDREN
AND ADULTS ALIKE.
HE WAS FULLY AWARE
OF JUST HOW BRIGHT
TODAY'S CHILDREN ARE.
AND I WONDER IF ANY
MAN WAS EVER KNOWN
AND LOVED BY MORE
PEOPLE."

—J.C. Hall on Walt Disney

TOP LEFT: In 1954 Walt Disney wrote to his old friend J.C. Hall, hoping to interest him in a store lease at Disneyland, then under construction in Anaheim, California. Disneyland opened in July of 1955.

TOP RIGHT: When J.C. Hall opened the Hallmark Communication Center on Disneyland's Main Street, USA in 1960, it was the renewal of a 30-year association and friendship with Walt Disney.

LEFT AND ABOVE: The Hallmark Communication Center sold greeting cards, of course, but put an emphasis on non-card products such as books, albums, puzzles, and gift trims made especially for Disneyland visitors.

Uncommon Men, Common Interests

Throughout the 1950s, J.C. Hall forged and cultivated friendships with a group of men widely recognized as historical giants. Among these were two American presidents who played key roles in World War II.

Hall met Dwight D. Eisenhower in 1950 through mutual acquaintances. The general, who grew up in nearby Abilene, Kansas, had given the town permission to build a museum to house his war trophies. Hall was asked to serve on the museum committee. Before the museum was completed, Eisenhower announced his candidacy to run for the Republican nomination for president, and in 1953 he took the oath of office. By that time, Hall and Eisenhower's acquaintance had grown into a genuine friendship, and it was with Eisenhower that Hallmark began the long tradition of creating the personal and official Christmas cards for U.S. presidents.

In 1956, Eisenhower founded People To People International, an organization dedicated to international understanding and friendship through educational, cultural, and humanitarian activities. He asked J.C. Hall to be chairman of the executive committee, and over the course of the next decade, the two would work closely on the organization's development. Their warm personal relationship continued until the Eisenhower's death in 1969.

Though their political leanings differed, Hall also had great respect for and a friendly relationship with President Harry Truman, who returned home to nearby Independence, Missouri, after leaving the presidency in 1952. "I was a Kansas Republican and he was a Missouri Democrat," Hall noted in his memoir, "but I was impressed by his humble approach to the presidency and found little to criticize his performance. President Truman was frank and fearless. What a good thing it would be if everyone in public life was as honest and decisive."

LEFT & ABOVE: *In 1962, J.C. Hall and Dwight D. Eisenhower crossed the Atlantic en route to a global teaching conference that the former president addressed in Sweden. After the ship docked at Cherbourg, France, they took a private train through the river valley route of the Normandy invasion as Eisenhower told personal stories of the historic conflict. It was the first time the general had been back to the region since the war.*

TOP: *General Eisenhower took up painting in 1951 while serving as the U.S. commander of occupied forces in Bavaria. He was encouraged in the hobby by another avid amateur painter and friend of J.C. Hall, Sir Winston Churchill.*

ABOVE LEFT: *In 1958, Hallmark reproduced an Eisenhower painting of a barn that President Eisenhower sent as a Christmas gift.*

ABOVE RIGHT: *Eisenhower's painting* Church in Bavaria *was a gift to his staff in 1960.*

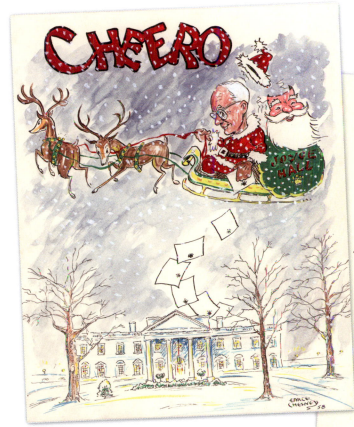

RIGHT: *President Eisenhower commissioned Hallmark artist Earl Chesney to create this personal holiday greeting for his friend J.C. Hall in 1958.*

Merry Christmas
and
Happy New Year

"WHEN WE CARE ENOUGH
TO SEND THE VERY BEST"

SAUL STEINBERG

By the time J.C. Hall met Saul Steinberg in the early 1950s, the Romanian-born artist and illustrator was already renowned for his brilliant and often barbed cartoons that regularly graced the cover of the *New Yorker* magazine. In 1945, Steinberg had begun designing annual Christmas cards exclusively for the Museum of Modern Art (MOMA) in New York City—many featuring his distinctive loose-lined Santa Claus engaged in a whimsical activity, like riding reindeer bareback or gracefully skating a figure eight. The MOMA cards were immensely popular, but sales were limited by the museum's relatively small distribution. In 1952, Hall offered Steinberg a retainer contract that ensured the artist's holiday cards would reach a much wider audience. Steinberg produced holiday cards for the company until 1959. When Hallmark entered the calendar business in 1960, Steinberg was among the prized licensed artists the company signed on. He produced his Sketchbooks calendars for the company until 1969.

"No one could take a line out for a walk quite like Saul Steinberg."

—Maureen Mullarkey,
contributing editor at *Artcritical*

Merry Christmas

MORE THAN A SUNDAY PAINTER

Through the course of his remarkable life, J.C. Hall made acquaintances with U.S. presidents, titans of business, artists, actors, and celebrities of every type. But it was his friendship with a man of a very different type that Hall would count among the most meaningful of his life.

J.C. Hall first met Sir Winston Churchill on March 5, 1946, just nine months after the statesman failed to be reelected as Britain's prime minister. The occasion would prove to be historic, for it was on this date, at Westminster College in the small town of Fulton, Missouri, that Churchill delivered his most famous postwar oratory, a lecture now known as The Iron Curtain speech. Along with other Kansas City civic leaders, J.C. Hall and Don Hall had been invited to the reception afterward.

Two years after the Westminster College speech, Churchill published—and J.C. Hall read—a book of essays titled *Painting as a Pastime*. Hall's wheels started turning immediately as he started dreaming of reproducing Churchill's oils on Hallmark cards. It was an unlikely possibility as Churchill tended to keep his paintings private, only occasionally giving one to a close friend. Hall was surprised and delighted to hear of Churchill's reply to an offer made through his solicitor: "That's a good firm," he told his man. "Make a deal with them."

A contract was immediately drawn up and sent to Churchill.

Shortly after, J.C. Hall received a cable that read: "I am delighted at the opportunity of having my paintings exhibited through the medium of Christmas cards—Winston Churchill." The *New York Times* reported the deal on August 13, 1950, calling it "the Churchill coup." Hallmark ultimately requested and was granted the right to reproduce 12 paintings from Churchill's collection.

The Association of Art Museum Directors happened to be meeting in Kansas City at the same time the original paintings arrived to be photographed and reproduced. Hall invited the group of prominent curators to his home for a private showing of paintings but didn't reveal the artist's identity.

"We simply told the curators that we were thinking of using the paintings on greeting cards and wanted their opinions. Among the group was the man who directed one of the largest museums in the country. After carefully examining each painting, he was the first to speak up: 'Well, one thing is certain. Whoever the artist is, he's more than a Sunday painter.'"

—*J.C. Hall*

The Churchill coup turned out to be a great commercial success in 1950 and the following two Christmas seasons. But for J.C. Hall, the real triumph was in introducing Americans to a lesser-known facet of the statesman he so admired.

"I HAD GREAT ANXIETY AND NO MEANS OF RELIEVING IT.... AND IT WAS THEN THAT THE MUSE OF PAINTING CAME TO MY RESCUE— OUT OF CHARITY AND OUT OF CHIVALRY, BECAUSE AFTER ALL SHE HAD NOTHING TO DO WITH ME—AND SAID, 'ARE THESE TOYS ANY GOOD TO YOU? THEY AMUSE SOME PEOPLE.'"

—*Sir Winston Churchill, on taking up painting as a palliative after being dismissed from his post as First Lord of the Admiralty following the disastrous failure of the Dardanelles campaign in 1915. (Excerpted from* Painting as a Pastime.*)*

AN INVITATION TO CHARTWELL

Standing: Don Hall, Anthony Moir, (Churchill's Solicitor), J.C. Hall.
Sitting: Elizabeth Hall, Sir Winston Churchill.

Don Hall graduated from Dartmouth College in the spring of 1950. A few weeks later, he would begin a summer of selling Hallmark products throughout the Midwest. But first, he accompanied his parents on an extraordinary trip across the Atlantic. They had accepted an invitation to visit Sir Winston and Lady Clementine Churchill for an afternoon at Chartwell, the Churchill estate in Kent, England. Though J.C. Hall and Winston Churchill had corresponded over the previous months, the two had only met briefly once.

Arriving for lunch at the country estate, they were greeted "rather brusquely," J.C. Hall would recall. "He asked me, 'Do you want Scotch or tomato juice?' I said tomato juice, and he poured a large glass. As I was about to reach for it, he drank it himself. I poured my own." Both Hall men quickly realized that the statesman was considerably more attentive toward Elizabeth Hall than to either of them. As he escorted Mrs. Hall to the dining room, her husband wondered whether the old bulldog would speak to him and his son at all.

> *"By his stature he was intimidating, but he was actually a very warm person. He was great with women. He loved my mother—they got along beautifully."*
> —Don Hall, on meeting Winston Churchill

But as the first course was served, Churchill warmed to his guests—all his guests—and the conversation started to flow easily. Turning to Elizabeth, he said, "I've found that the best way to get my energy is in whiskey." Then, looking to 21 year-old Don, added, "That is in the case of older men. It doesn't apply to young people who are getting regular exercise and have good appetites."

When the meal was over, Churchill led the group on a tour of Chartwell House and its grounds. Striding briskly up and down the property's sloping lawns, he kept up a lively travelogue, stopping along the way to greet his "darlings"—Golden Orfe fish in a pond he had built himself, a flock of black swans, and a yearling colt in a small paddock. The Halls were touched by the affection he showed the animals and amazed by the 75 year-old's vigor.

After touring the grounds, the once and future prime minister (he would be reelected in 1951) led the Halls into his painting studio—a small building facing the pond. As Don Hall recalls, it was a small, rather messy room with paintings covering nearly every inch of wall and floor space. An adjoining room held even more canvases, unframed and stacked, filling a 20 foot-long wooden rack. "I thought how much it would mean to me to own even the worst of the lot," recalled J.C. Hall, "But I had been told Churchill would part with a painting about as readily as he would with a child."

By then, the afternoon was growing late. There was time for tea—naturally—and then Churchill promptly announced that it was time for his physician-prescribed afternoon nap. He gave the group a warm goodbye and invited them to visit again someday. J.C. Hall left with mixed feelings of "being thrilled to have spent the afternoon with Winston Churchill and let down to think that I probably would never see him again."

Hall didn't realize two things on that bright spring day. The two would have many more meetings over the next 15 years—and he would also someday own several of Churchill's paintings. *Jamaica Beach* (below) was given to J.C. Hall by Churchill in 1954.

The Halls' relationship with Sir Winston deepened when, in 1951, his daughter, Sarah Churchill, began hosting a Hallmark-produced weekly television interview program called *Hallmark Presents Sarah Churchill.* In the show, Sarah Churchill, an experienced stage actress, interviewed prominent celebrities "in the theatre, fashion, science, sports, and the arts." Her first guest was former first lady Eleanor Roosevelt. The following year, Hallmark began a new program called *Hallmark Television Playhouse,* also hosted by Churchill. A few weeks after it began, its name was changed to *Hallmark Hall of Fame,* and a new chapter in television history began.

Sarah Churchill became a great friend of the Hall family, visiting frequently and once spending a memorable summer week at the Hall summer house at Grand Lake, Colorado. In 1954, in appreciation for the Halls' kindness to his daughter, Sir Winston Churchill gave J.C. Hall one of his original paintings—a gift Hall wrote "that I value as much as anything I've ever received."

J.C. Hall was proud to have introduced Winston Churchill's paintings to the American public through their reproduction on Christmas cards and equally proud to exhibit one of the statesman's original works in his private collection. But he longed to bring Churchill's original work to a broader audience. He first broached the idea of a traveling exhibit on a return trip to Chartwell in 1953. The prime minister flatly refused saying that his paintings weren't good enough to be exhibited.

Hall wasn't easily dissuaded. It would take nearly five years and the persuasive help of President Eisenhower, but Churchill ultimately did grant permission for an exhibition. In 1958, a touring exhibit of 35 Churchill paintings opened at Kansas City's own Nelson Gallery of Art. Over the next year, the exhibit was hosted by some of the most prestigious art galleries and museums in the country, including the Smithsonian Institution in Washington D.C. and the Metropolitan Museum of Art in New York City. The exhibit broke attendance records at nearly every venue where it was shown. It was Churchill's first one-man show.

Two years after the exhibit, during a visit to London, J.C. Hall had a brief meeting with Churchill and his secretary, Anthony Montague-Brown. The 86-year-old Churchill spoke sincerely of how much the exhibit of his paintings had meant to him. Later, Montague-Brown privately expressed the same to Hall, saying, "Sir Winston was grateful for bringing this new adventure into his life at such an advanced age."

Hall would see Churchill several more times over the next few years, both at Chartwell and in the U.S. Their last visit was at Churchill's Hyde Park home in 1964, the year before the venerable former prime minister died. Hall recounted the memory in his 1979 book, *When You Care Enough*:

"When I arrived, he was sitting in the library leaning on a cane. He seemed to remember old times but was terribly weary. I soon excused myself and joined Anthony (Montague-Brown) in an anteroom where I could still look in on Sir Winston. In a few minutes, Lady Churchill entered the library. She approached him from behind, gently put her hands on his shoulders, leaned over, and kissed him on top of his head. It was the last sight I had of Sir Winston Churchill. I try to forget. I try to remember the robust figure who bounded into the living room that noon at Chartwell the first time we visited. And I can."

Tapestries at Blenheim

Cork Trees Near Mimizan

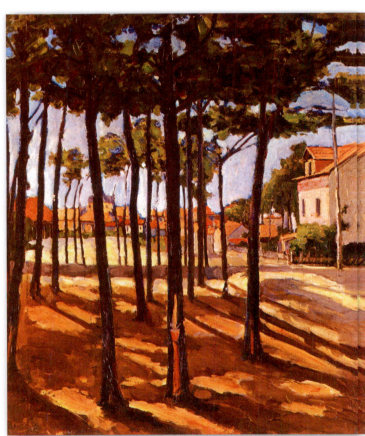

Mimizan

Bottlescape

FAR LEFT: *Sarah Churchill at the Hall summer house in Grand Lake, Colorado, in 1954.*

MIDDLE: *Sarah Churchill going over scripts for* Hallmark Television Playhouse.

LEFT: *Crowds queue for the Churchill exhibit at Kansas City's Nelson-Atkins Museum in 1958.*

ABOVE AND RIGHT: *A few of the paintings by Sir Winston Churchill that were reproduced on Hallmark cards.*

Venice

When you care enough to send the very best *Hallmark Cards*

ah!

It is nice to Remember — and to be Remembered with *Hallmark Cards* that say, "You cared enough to send the very best"

happy easter

TO POP ON FATHER'S DAY

CHAPTER SIX

Coming of Age

(1951–1966)

O N December 1, 1950, Hall Brothers opened a thoroughly modern retail store at 1114 Grand Avenue in the heart of downtown Kansas City. The store, designed by one of the nation's most progressive architecture firms, was new in every way, but the address was familiar. The three-story building at 1114 Grand had been the home of Hall Brothers' entire operation 30 years earlier.

But what a difference 30 years had made—not just in the company, but in the country, and, in fact, the entire world. After the Roaring Twenties, the Great Depression, and the second World War, the United States may have seemed relatively placid at the dawn of the 1950s—its citizens intent on getting back to everyday life. But just below the surface, dramatic changes in the way that Americans live were taking shape. Over the next decade, these changes would affect virtually every American company in profound ways. Hall Brothers was no exception.

Following World War II, America experienced the greatest economic boom in its history—a period often called the golden age of American capitalism. Rising wages swelled the ranks of the middle class. At long last, working-class people had the means and the confidence to buy—cars, appliances, furniture, and most exhilarating of all, televisions! After 10 years of depression and five years of war, pent-up demand for consumer goods exploded.

But the most remarkable boom of the era involved babies. As GIs returned home to marry sweethearts or resume family life, the U.S. birth rate skyrocketed, jumping from 2.8 million in 1945 to nearly 3.5 million in 1946. It would continue to grow until peaking in 1957 at over 4 million.

As wages rose and families grew, one of the first indicators of newfound prosperity was a new house in the suburbs. In 1950 alone, 1.4 million houses were built in the U.S.—the vast majority of them in new subdivisions. As families moved into these freshly developed communities, commerce quickly followed. Soon the hottest concept in shopping was the retail mall—indoor, outdoor, strips, and plazas. As downtowns saw downturns, suburban shopping centers thrived.

So even as the Halls' downtown store opened in 1950, the migration of people away from urban areas had taken hold. J.C. Hall was

"Our retail stores have always been a source of new ideas. To do the right kind of job as a manufacturer, you can never lose touch with the retailer and the consumer."

—*J.C. Hall*

ABOVE: *Hall Brothers opened a modern retail store in December 1950 in downtown Kansas City.*

RIGHT: *Magazine ads from the 1950s for Zenith televisions and a Cadillac Eldorado.*

no doubt aware of these changes in consumer shopping habits, but to Hall, opening the downtown store still made sense. He simply loved the retail side of the business, and he was determined to maintain a store that reflected his commitment to the highest quality in products and retail enviroment. But Hall saw also the store more as a place to observe customer behavior and experiment with his card lines. He knew that demographically balanced Kansas City was a perfect test market for Hallmark products. And throughout the 1950s and early 1960s, new product development would be *the* big story at what was now America's biggest greeting card manufacturer.

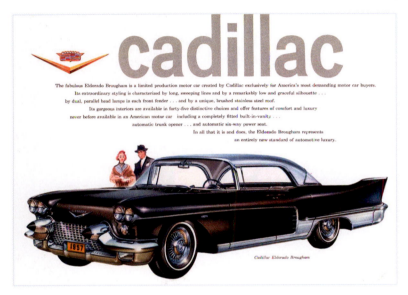

J.C. Hall was not a man who liked to get away from the office. Not only did his work follow him home every evening, his home often became a practical extension of the office. Meetings with out-of-town associates were often held on a sun porch at the back of the house, and national sales conferences—until they got too large—were annually held on the third floor of the Halls' large country house. "Living in the house, we were involved in the company at all times," remembers Don Hall.

To J.C. and Elizabeth Hall's three children, there was nothing particularly unusual or noteworthy about a large contingent of dark-suited men showing up en masse once a year for the big sales meeting. It was simply business as usual. Besides, from a child's point of view, the unfinished crawlspaces in the eaves of the big house's third floor were far more interesting than the meetings being held on the finished side of the wall.

The house itself was unusual. It was constructed entirely of steel and concrete—a method of residential construction that was virtually unheard of at the time, but one that J.C. Hall had insisted upon for fire prevention purposes.

Don Hall recalls a small playhouse in the backyard, but he left that mostly to his sisters. The real house held plenty of fascination for a spirited and imaginative young boy. There were cubbies and crannies, secret closets, and a three-story laundry chute that Hall says he's lucky he didn't end up at the bottom of. But best of all was a tunnel that ran all the way from the house's basement to a small pasture a few hundred feet away. "It took all the drainage and services under the driveway and away from the house," Hall explains. "They always told me that it had snakes in it—and actually it did—but that didn't bother me."

Even better than the house was the pasture and woodland that surrounded it. Striking out with one of the family dogs or in league with a visiting friend or cousin, Don Hall would roam the woods and track up and down (and in and out of) the two creeks that ran through the property. Just the right amount of mystery and danger loomed, too. Barbara Hall Marshall remembers that as children they would hear the coyotes howl at night and were sometimes warned of gypsies that camped down by the creek.

Though J.C. Hall was a "gentleman farmer," there were still plenty of chores to do on the farm—especially after he bought a herd of Jersey cows in 1936. "On Saturdays and summer vacation days, Dad would leave a long list for me," Don remembers. "There was yard work, ground to plow, manure to spread, and hay to bale." Then he adds with pride, "I drove mules when I was 10 years old and a tractor when I was 12."

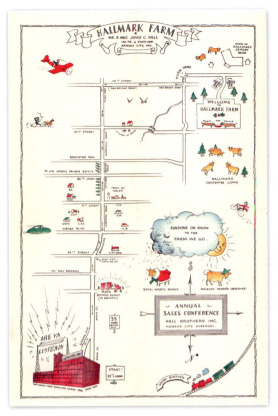

THE HOME OF HALLMARK JERSEY CREAMLINE MILK

TOP LEFT: *Map showing directions from Hallmark headquarters in downtown Kansas City to the Hall family farm about 16 miles way, for an annual sales meeting.*

TOP RIGHT: *Spouses were welcome at sales meetings for socializing and tours of the farmstead.*

RIGHT: *The Hall farm dairy barn housed J.C. Hall's prized Jersey cows until it burned down in 1937.*

FAR RIGHT: *Don Hall with one of his loyal companions.*

MIDDLE RIGHT: *J.C. Hall at the farm with a mare and her new foal.*

RIGHT: *J.C. Hall with daughters Barbara (left) and "Jimmie."*

LEFT: *The Hall family poses for a photo in front of a fountain at their newly built home in 1931. Pictured fom left are Elizabeth Hall's sister, Mae, Barbara Hall, J.C., Jimmie Hall, Elizabeth Hall, (with Donald on her lap) and Elizabeth's other sister Lucy. The dogs are Masco and Silverbell.*

Although J.C. Hall put in long hours at the office and worked virtually every weekend, he was home for dinner most evenings. Inevitably, the conversation around the table was of business. "Dad loved to tell stories about people at the company," Don Hall recalls, "but there was always a purpose to the story and a lesson he was trying to get across."

After dinner came another evening ritual. J.C. Hall would sit in his chair by the fireplace and pull up a small table stacked with work. The night's work might include sales tabulations, reports, or correspondence, and as Hall read, he would jot notes on three-by-five index cards—messages that would be delivered the following morning at the plant. But the bulk of the pile was typically greeting card designs in various stages of completion. Hall liked to review these in the calm of his home—and he frequently asked his wife and children to add their own commentary.

Of the three children, Barbara Hall Marshall took the most interest in the creative review, and her father found her critiques particularly insightful. "I believe I was the only one who actually sat by him and looked at them," she recalls. "I think with the others, he'd call them over and ask them. Daddy always wanted to know what everyone thought. If we had company and he was looking at a card, he'd ask whoever was there what they thought about it, because he figured they represented the consumer."

Marshall's early exposure to greeting card design and composition served her—and the company—well in later years. After graduating from college, she would become a fixture on the OK Committee meetings held in her father's office every afternoon.

J.C. Hall also introduced his children to the concept of "working vacations" at an early age. "We took trips every year—the whole family—and during spring vacation we'd visit retailers. That's all we did," remembers Don Hall. "Now, it'd be an interesting part of the country, but that was our vacation, visiting retailers."

Growing up the child of J.C. Hall meant growing up in the business. "Dad's business and his family were his life," explains Barbara Hall Marshall. "One fit into the other." But Marshall admits that from the beginning, the situation was different for her five-years-younger brother. "Women didn't go into business back then," she explains, "but I don't think it ever occurred to Dad that Don could or would do anything else."

By the late 1930s, when Don Hall was around 10 years old, his father had begun taking him along on occasional sales trips and to business meetings. "I don't know what he thought about my future within the company," Don says, "because he never talked about my future, but he was always teaching."

ABOVE: *J.C. Hall's younger sister, Marie, was beloved Aunta Ree to his three children. Barbara Hall Marshall thinks of her aunt as an unsung hero of the early days of Hall Brothers, because their young sister did much of the cooking and housekeeping in the home she shared with her sickly mother and brothers. "She made their work a lot easier, because they had a home to come to at the end of the day."*

As a grown woman, Aunta Ree took on part-time caretaking duties for Don, Barbara, and Jimmie Hall. Their aunt lived near the school the children attended, so when the school day ended, they would often stay with their Aunta Ree until their father finished work for the day. "We were always very close to her," Barbara Hall Marshall remembers.

ABOVE: *Don Hall with parents Elizabeth and J.C. Hall, while traveling in Europe.*

BELOW: *While attending Dartmouth College, Don Hall maintained a small sales territory, regularly lugging heavy sample cases of Hall Brothers products on calls to area retailers.*

"From the time he was born, I was hopeful he would come into the business and even succeed me. But I didn't want to encourage him unless he was sure it was what he wanted."

—*J.C. Hall, speaking of his son, Donald J. Hall*

J.C. Hall may not have known what the long-term future held for his son, but when Don graduated from Pembroke-Country Day School in the spring of 1946, he did know how the young man would be spending his summer. He'd asked his top sales trainer, Frank Cozad, to take the boy out and show him the ropes.

Cozad recalls, "J.C. arranged the timing and left no leisure time. Don's high school graduation was on Friday. We left on the following Monday and were gone all summer. We returned a week before he was due at college. Elizabeth (Hall) demanded the week so Don could get clothes arranged."

The trip took them west through Kansas, eastern Colorado and Wyoming, and then back across Nebraska, Iowa, and Missouri. It covered much of the same territory, in fact, that Hall's father had worked when the company was in its infancy. "I think dad wanted Don to have the experience that he'd had with Uncle Rollie," his sister Barbara speculates. "I didn't hear Dad ever mention that, but I think that was his feeling."

The two men logged thousands of miles in a car with no air conditioning. The summer was a scorcher. Don Hall loved it.

"I always did enjoy calling on accounts," he remembers. "I liked the interface with people and enjoyed being out on my own."

During the summer of their extended sales trip, Hall Brothers was debuting a new rotating sign it was making available to select retailers. The two men had a little routine they performed on their calls. When they entered a store, Don would set up and plug in the sign, keeping it covered with a cloth. Then, after sufficient dramatic build-up, he would whip off the cloth and demonstrate the state-of-the-art accessory.

Cozad liked what he saw in his protégé. "I always appreciated that summer I got to spend with Don. He impressed me as a very thoughtful and well-disciplined individual."

In accordance with the schedule, a week after the trip ended, Hall took a train to Hanover, N.H. to begin classes at Dartmouth College.

The choice of Dartmouth allowed Hall to continue with his practical sales education. While in school, he sold and serviced a small sales territory in and around Hanover. Back in Kansas City for summers, he'd hit the road again, calling on midwestern accounts.

At Dartmouth, Hall majored in economics. "An absolutely worthless degree," he jokingly points out, "because economic theories change every five years." Still, as graduation approached in

1950, he considered enrolling in the college's prestigious Tuck School of Business.

"It was sometime in college, when you start to think about something beyond the next Friday night, that I started to get deeply ingrained into what the company was all about and really grew to love it. I came to work at Hallmark because I wanted to work at Hallmark, not because I felt as though somebody expected me to."

—*Donald J. Hall*

That plan was scrapped on the frank recommendation of a friendly professor who happened to be dean of the Tuck School. Hall recalls, "One day, I was sitting with him talking about enrolling and he said, 'Don, you know what you're going to do. Why don't you go do it?'"

Hall took his professor's advice and passed on business school, but he wouldn't be starting full time at the company just yet. Instead, he reported for basic training at the U.S. Army's Fort Riley in Kansas. The draft was still on in 1950, but Hall decided to enlist rather than wait around for his number to come up. If he was going into the service, he would do it on his terms. He applied and was accepted into Officer Candidate School (OCS).

Looking back on the decision, he has no doubt that he learned more about business in the army than he would have in another two years of college. He was a top student in his OCS class and after graduation was sent to Fort Benjamin Harrison in Indianapolis for training in the army's Finance Corps.

With his officer and finance training complete, Hall shipped out for Japan in early 1952. The Korean War had begun just three months before his enlistment and was raging on as he sailed to Tokyo on a troop ship. "I thought I was going to Korea," Hall remembers, "but when I got to Tokyo, I got new orders to report to a post in Gifu, Japan, which I didn't mind at all." Gifu was a support and training base, and Hall was to be the fiscal officer.

The young officer found his first overseas deployment endlessly interesting—and busy too. His responsibilities soon expanded well beyond the finance officer role. In quick succession, he was put in charge of a training program that hired and trained Japanese civilians working on the base. That assignment expanded to include command of the base's labor office. One of Don Hall's favorite maxims is, "If you want to get a job done, give it to the busiest person you know." His commanding officers in Gifu had obviously learned that lesson themselves. They didn't hesitate to pile it on the capable and industrious young man.

"There was a general there most of the time and two or three colonels, so I wasn't a big dog, but I did have quite a bit of authority

at that base," recalls Hall. "I took the job seriously. I took my whole army experience seriously."

Hall looks back on his years of service with pride and a realization that he learned lessons during his enlistment that would serve him well in the private sector. "I think I gained more than at any other time in my life," he says. "First of all, I learned to work with almost any kind of person. You encounter a myriad of people going through basic training and leadership school and OCS, and you learn to get along with them. There is no other experience in life, I think, where you are forced to do that. But I also found it fun, and I generally got along with everybody."

Something else Hall took away from his army experience was a deep interest in and appreciation for Japanese people and culture. Because of his leadership of the base's training and labor programs, he had daily and intensive contact with hundreds of Japanese citizens. He picked up some of the language, "enough to get around the country fine," he says. And he forged friendships—real friendships that lasted well beyond his service assignment.

"Once you were a friend, you were a close friend," Hall continues. "I knew a number of families there quite well. I've gone back to Japan several times for reunions with the people I worked with, and it always amazed me that they've told me I'm the only military person ever to come back and visit with them again."

As much as he enjoyed his army training and the service in Japan, at the end of his three-year commitment, Don Hall was ready to get home. Two compelling motivators were waiting for him back in the states: a job at the family company and a certain young woman from Lincoln, Nebraska. He got his discharge papers in September of 1953. A few days later, he drove to Lincoln and proposed to Ms. Adele Coryell. They were married a month later in Lincoln and moved into a duplex apartment in Kansas City. But naturally, there's a bit of back story to this romance...

OPPOSITE PAGE, TOP: *Lt. Hall shortly before shipping out to Japan in 1952.*

OPPOSITE PAGE BOTTOM: *Don Hall poses with one of his employees at the army base in Gifu, Japan.*

RIGHT: *Don and Adele Coryell enjoy a quiet moment at the Hall family farm.*

TOP: *Don Hall and Shiguro Nashino. Shiguro was Hall's office manager during his assignment in Gifu and remained a lifelong friend.*

ABOVE: *Don Hall poses with his staff in front of the Gifu fiscal office.*

Don and Adele Hall: A Partnership Begins

It all started with a seasick dog.

Early one August morning in 1934, six-year-old Donald Hall and his father left the family's cabin on Colorado's Grand Lake to go for a boat ride. They brought along the family dog, but a few minutes into the cruise, the animal had lost its sea legs. Sympathetic to the woozy pooch, they pulled up to the nearest dock to let it run up on the grass to recover.

The dock, as fate would have it, belonged to the Coryell family of Lincoln, Nebraska. Within a few minutes, Mrs. Margaret "Peg" Coryell came hustling down the path to ascertain the situation. Scooting right behind with long curls bobbing was her daughter, Adele, a few months shy of three years old.

What the two young ones thought when their eyes met for the first time (or whether their eyes met at all) is lost to the lapping waves of time. But the repercussions of that first, chance meeting are a love story that would take 10 books of this size to document and a philanthropic legacy the likes of which Kansas City won't likely see again.

Needless to say, the courtship was a long one. The Halls and Coryells became fast friends. Both families spent several weeks at the lake each summer, and they always made a point of spending time together. Adele, an only child, was enthralled by the two Hall sisters—eight and ten years her senior—and Barbara and Jimmie Hall were delighted to have a pint-sized blonde doll to fuss over. "They were so nice to me," Adele Hall recalls. "They let me comb their hair, and we'd go to movies together—and that was a pretty big deal in Grand Lake."

Their brother Donald she remembers mostly as a tag-along but also as "the nicest boy I'd ever met."

"It was probably about the fifth or sixth grade that I can remember noticing Donald and thinking, 'He's a nice boy.' So many of the boys that I knew in Lincoln would tease girls…and Donald was different. He was so nice and so polite. He'd open the door to the theater for me and let me go down the aisle first. He took me on the aquaplane, taught me how to water ski, and showed me how to canoe."

—Adele Hall

Throughout those childhood summers, the children grew up together in the rustic environs of the historic and genteel resort community on the west side of Rocky Mountain National Park. Days were filled with beach play, boating, water skiing, hiking, card games, and some fiercely competitive badminton. Evenings often included cookouts and campfire sing-a-longs, the latter of which Adele enjoyed more than Don ever did. There were other families in the little collective of

summer friends and a small knot of kids to play with. But more often than not, there was Adele and Donnie (as he was called), one generally found in close proximity to the other. "We seemed to always be on the same side of the badminton net," recalls Adele.

LEFT: *Adele Coryell, Donald Hall and Helen Peak— an early rival for Don's affection—in Grand Lake, Colorado.*

ABOVE: *Adele Coryell shows off the Kirkpatrick Cup, won in a model boat regatta at Grand Lake.*

LEFT: *Don Hall estimates that he was about 16 years old when this photo was taken of him in uniform for the Pembroke-Country Day varsity football team.*

RIGHT: *Adele Coryell was 12 years old when this portrait was taken before a piano recital.*

BELOW LEFT: *Don, Adele, and Barbara Hall ski at Grand Lake.*

BELOW RIGHT: *The Coryell family in their boat "La Pegadele," named for Earl Coryell's wife and daughter.*

At the end of each summer break, the families decamped for Lincoln and Kansas City with the implicit assumption that they'd see each other again next year. Through the balance of the year, the children kept in touch with occasional letters and, naturally, greeting cards.

When Jimmie Hall announced plans to marry in the spring of 1944, she asked Adele—then 12 years old—to be a junior bridesmaid. "I was thrilled," remembers Adele. "I adored Jimmie and wanted to grow up to be just like her." By then, Don was a strapping high school football player, "a big, mean guard," he jokes. "one hundred forty-five pounds soaking wet." Adele's family stayed at the Hall farm during the festivities. On the night of the bridal dinner, Donald walked her upstairs to her room, told her to sleep well, and, quite to her surprise, planted a kiss on her forehead.

Beaming at the memory some 65 years later, Adele recalls, "He was the first boy who ever kissed me."

Through ensuing years, the summer friendship continued. Group activities were still the order of the day at Grand Lake, but Donald and Adele grabbed any chance at time alone together. They would spend long hours at the boathouse, washing the Halls' Chris-Craft speedboat—drudgery made delightful by the company. And after an evening of family activities, Don was always quick to offer Adele a boat ride back to her family's cabin. They would hold hands under the stars as Don drove the boat across the black lake. "Those were our first 'dates,'" Adele recalls, "washing the boat and going back and forth from each other's cabins. I would call it, at that point, an unconditional friendship. That's what happened first. The love part came later."

They each dated others and were upfront about it. Adele had no shortage of suitors at NU, but she was clear with all of them that any engagement was subject to cancellation at short notice. "I don't know why anyone ever took me out," she laughs, "because I would always let these guys know that I had this summertime friend that was in OCS at Fort Riley, and if he could come to town, I would break the date."

When Don graduated from Officer Candidate School in 1951, he asked Adele to be his guest at the ceremony. She was flattered and intensely proud of her newly commissioned officer and gentleman. A favorite Hall family story was born on that day when Adele was introduced to base commanders in a long reception line. When the first officer asked the young woman's name, she pertly replied, "I'm Adele Coryell." To which he replied, "Pleased to meet you, Imadelle," and introduced her to the next officer in line by

Neither Don nor Adele can pinpoint the moment when this lifelong friendship grew into something more, but both agree that his years in the army deepened and illuminated their devotion to each other.

Long handwritten letters flew back and forth between Lincoln, where Adele was studying education at University of Nebraska, and the locations where Don was posted—first Fort Riley, Kansas, then Indianapolis, and finally Gifu, Japan. While stationed at Fort Riley, Don would drive up to Lincoln to see Adele whenever he could secure a weekend furlough. Army rules dictated that soldiers on leave could go no farther than 150 miles from base. Fort Riley to Lincoln was 152. Don made up for the difference by driving a little bit faster.

her new appellation. The Fort Riley brass handed "Imadelle" off, in turn, all the way down the line to the general standing at the end.

While Don was stationed in Japan, the correspondence between the two escalated in frequency and affection. Still, no plans for a future together were set. Adele would graduate in the spring of 1953 and fully intended to begin teaching that fall, most likely in Lincoln. Don would muster out of the service around the same time and join the family business in Kansas City.

Don Hall completed his service in Japan in August of 1953 and boarded an aircraft carrier bound for California. The Halls and Coryells were vacationing at Grand Lake at the time. J.C. and Elizabeth Hall announced plans to make the 16-hour drive to Oakland to meet the ship, and they asked Adele if she'd like to come along.

When the USS Windham Bay made port, Adele Coryell was waiting on the dock. And at this dockside meeting—19 years after their first—we can be assured that the eyes of Don and Adele did meet. The sweethearts had just enough time for a welcome-home kiss before 1st Lt. Hall fell back into ranks to board a train to Colorado Springs to finalize his decommissioning. Adele Coryell and Don Hall's parents drove back to Grand Lake—proud of their soldier and curious, each in their own way, about what the future might hold.

As it turns out, that question would be answered sooner than later. Back in Kansas City in September, Don called Adele to inquire about her plans for the fall. When she informed him that she had recently signed a contract to teach at third grade, he said, "I might like to break that contract." The very next weekend, he was in Lincoln with a ring.

On November 28, 1953, just two months after Don Hall returned to the States, the two were married in Lincoln's Holy Trinity Cathedral. Adele Coryell Hall was 22 years old. Her husband was 25. Nineteen years after meeting on a dock in a crystalline alpine lake in Colorado, their ship had come in.

OPPOSITE PAGE
TOP: *The Hall family at Grand Lake. From left: J.C., Barbara, Elizabeth, Jimmie, and Don.*

MIDDLE: *Adele and Don, c. 1944*

BOTTOM: *For the first 15 years of their acquaintance, Don Hall and Adele Coryell saw each other mostly at Grand Lake, Colorado, where their families had summer cabins.*

THIS PAGE: *Don and Adele maintained frequent correspondence while he was stationed in Japan in 1952 and 1953. Just two months after he returned home, the two were married in her hometown of Lincoln, Nebraska.*

HALLMARK INTERNATIONAL ART AWARDS

When Hallmark sponsored the first International Art Award in 1949 no one guessed that it would mark the beginning of one of the nation's great corporate art collections. Today the Hallmark Fine Art Collection contains approximately 3,800 objects, representing leading artists from nearly every major contemporary art movement, from Grandma Moses and Norman Rockwell to Jasper Johns and Andy Warhol.

Sixty years since the first of the awards were announced, many of the most important and valuable pieces of the Hallmark collection—by famed painters such as Edward Hopper, Charles Sheeler, Andrew Wyeth, and Maurice Utrillo—come from the 250 works that Hallmark purchased from the five International Art Award programs held between 1949 and 1960, according to Joe Houston, the collection's curator.

As it happened, the late 1940s were an auspicious time for J.C. Hall to concentrate on the fine arts, which long had been an interest and inspiration of his. Postwar America was emerging as a world leader in the arts. Hallmark, meanwhile, had become the leading manufacturer of greeting cards in the U.S., exerting an influence on popular culture through its products and its sponsorship of national radio broadcasting. The Hallmark Gallery Artists card line had debuted in 1948, and J.C. Hall had taken pleasure in bringing the work of the great masters to the public through the supposedly "unsophisticated" medium of greeting cards. That same year, with the encouragement of his advertising agency, Foote, Cone and Belding, Hall decided to sponsor an international art competition which would attract the attention and participation of artists and museums around the world. Instituted in 1948, the art awards took place the following year, under the direction of Vladimir Visson of the Wildenstein Gallery in New York City. Each of the programs was juried by a panel of distinguished experts, who selected the winners.

In the catalogue to the fifth and final International Art Awards in 1960, J.C. Hall laid out his reasons for sponsoring the awards: "We wanted in effect to sponsor a 'laboratory of fine art' in which artists would give their imaginations free rein and from which would come ideas to stimulate and inspire the world of design. Thus we could express the deep gratitude of Hallmark Cards to living painters everywhere for their constant elevation of the public's taste."

That final phrase—"elevation of the public's taste"—echoed a theme that J.C. Hall had promoted from almost the beginning of his career. His hard-scrabble background had engendered an appreciation for life's finer things. From his oft-quoted phrase "I'm hell-bent on quality," to his observation that "people always reach up for a social custom, never down," he'd championed good taste and refined design. And though he never spoke of the awards as an image-building endeavor for Hallmark, it was inevitable that his company could only gain prestige by its association with the world of fine arts.

Writing of Hallmark's sponsorship following the Fourth International Art Awards in 1957, Jean Lipman, editor of *Art in America* magazine, noted that in the 20th century "American business as a patron of the arts seems about to rival in impact and influence the great patrons of the Renaissance."

Of course, there was a product-related benefit for Hallmark in sponsoring the art awards. The works from the first four award programs were acquired for potential use on Hallmark product. The fifth art awards, however, were judged strictly on the basis of merit, with no thematic limitation, and these paintings were distinguished by a larger prevalence of abstract paintings.

Large touring exhibitions were mounted following each of the five awards programs. By the time the final exhibition was concluded in 1960, a total of 357 artists from 27 countries had been represented in 100 exhibitions throughout the U.S. and abroad, with 12 canvases later exhibited at the 1965 New York World's Fair. An estimated 2 million people saw these paintings—at a time when gallery space for contemporary art was much more limited than today. And what they saw represented the finest painters of the day.

"The Hallmark International Art Awards were a major outlet for contemporary art at that time, and the top artists wanted to be involved," Houston says. With commercial galleries being relatively few, the financial incentives were important too. For a top-tier painter such as Edward Hopper, whose work today commands millions, the $2,000 first-place prize for his painting *California Hills* was a whopping sum in 1957.

So the Hallmark art awards had at least some impact on one of J.C. Hall's more ambitious goals for his art awards—"to build a mass audience for fine painting." As he put it:

"A painting can make just as important a contribution to everyday living as a book, play, or movie—provided enough people see it."

THE FIVE HALLMARK INTERNATIONAL ART AWARDS

1st: 1949 Open to French and American artists, with the subject limited to a Christmas theme, with nearly 10,000 works submitted.

2nd: 1952 Open to artists in the Americas and Western Europe; limited to watercolors on a Christmas theme, with about 4,500 works submitted.

3rd: 1955 By invitation only for 50 artists from the U.S., Canada, England, Ireland, France, and Italy; on a Christmas theme.

4th: 1957 By invitation only to 50 artists from the Americas and Europe without limitations on medium or theme.

5th: 1960 Titled "Fifty Painters of Promise—The Question of the Future," with invited artists selected by an international jury of distinguished critics.

PRIZE-WINNING PAINTINGS FROM HALLMARK'S INTERNATIONAL ART AWARDS APPEAR BELOW AND ON THE TWO FOLLOWING PAGES.

California Hills   Edward Hopper

Greek Islet   Sergio de Castro

Mother and Child   FRED CONWAYT

Two Against White   Charles Sheeler

The Christmas Tree   Anton Refregier

Village in Normandy   Maurice Vlaminck

128

Mother and Child   Jean-Marie Carzou

Christmas Coach   Maria Massimiani

Homage to Ensor   Pierre Alechinsky

Rain Over the Potato Fields   Jane Frellicher

Coming Home to Hallmark

By the close of 1953, Don Hall was back in Kansas City with a new bride, a new home, and a new job at the company he had known all his life. But in the seven years he had been living away from his hometown, the company had changed in remarkable ways. By any measure, it was larger—much larger. Sales of greeting cards had boomed right along with the nation's postwar economy. A populace that seemed to have acquired a greeting-card habit during the war years now found sending cards an established behavior. The firm's sales and market share had steadily increased, and by 1953, the full-time employee count had reached 2,500. By the end of the year, ground had already been broken on a 6-million-dollar expansion of the company's headquarters. Square footage was no longer a sufficient way to describe Hallmark's facilities. The new building would add 25 acres of floor space.

Thanks to its increasing television presence, its high-profile licensing partnerships, and programs like the International Art Awards, the company's profile had been steadily raised in the first few years of the 1950s. In 1953, the company's highly successful series of television specials was officially christened the *Hallmark Hall of Fame.* And though everyone but the contract lawyers had been calling the firm Hallmark for years, the old Hall Brothers name was finally retired on April 1, 1954. Change seemed to come from every angle.

In the first several months of his full-time employment, Don Hall did a grand tour of work rotations. He worked turns in purchasing, warehousing, graphic arts, and nearly every other department of the company. His sales experience had given him an outside perspective of the company. Now he was getting acquainted with the inner workings. He closed out his familiarization tour with a stint assisting a systems wiz named Del Lofsted, tabulating and analyzing sales numbers. "His system used tab cards," explains Don, "and it worked so well we had trouble improving on it when we started bringing in computers."

In 1954, Don Hall was named assistant to the president. When asked what that means, he jokes, "I have no idea," but even if the job description lacked exactitude, the recently decommissioned army officer set about his wide-ranging assignments with conviction and earnestness. By this time, Don Hall had developed a pretty fair picture of the company his father had built. Now he was curious to find out what he could learn from other firms.

With J.C. Hall's encouragement, Don and Bill Harsh went to school on other corporations—some creative companies like advertising agencies and some large family-owned companies.

LEFT: *Three years after the Hallmark Hall of Fame was first aired, Hallmark's national advertising was doing double duty—promoting new products and plugging upcoming Hallmark Hall of Fame productions. This 1955 ad announces the new Hallmark Christmas Album card lines, as well as the television performance of George Bernard Shaw's play* The Devil's Disciple, *with star Maurice Evans.*

ABOVE AND LEFT: *During the boom years of the 1950s, consumers learned of Hallmark's rush of new product offerings through regular advertising in popular national publications. In 1954 sales were bolstered for the latest Hallmark Dolls line (center) and ready-to-make Hallmark May baskets with full-page ads (left) in the colorful general interest magazine,* LIFE.

DREAMING OF A WHITE (HOUSE) CHRISTMAS

Although no company is more closely associated with official White House Christmas cards, the tradition of presidential holiday cards did not begin with Hallmark. As far back as 1927, President Calvin Coolidge issued a brief, hand-written message addressed "To the American People" in honor of the holidays. The text was carried in newspapers across the country on Christmas day.

Among the presidents that followed, many gave small gifts and Christmas cards to members of their staff, friends, and associates. Franklin D. Roosevelt's gifts included letter openers (1936); paperweights (1938); a savings stamp album which when full could be redeemed for a savings bond (1942); and in his last Christmas in office, a reproduction of the prayer he had read on the radio on the evening of D-Day, June 6, 1944.

Hallmark produced its first presidential holiday card for President Dwight D. Eisenhower in 1953. By then, J.C. Hall and Eisenhower had forged a strong personal friendship—and Ike took full advantage of his friend's line of work. In addition to the official White House holiday cards, Hallmark produced prints of the president's own paintings, which were given as gifts to staff. The signed gift print has become a popular presidential staff present ever since.

Over the ensuing decades, Hallmark has produced at least one official Christmas card for Presidents Kennedy, Johnson, Nixon, Ford, Carter, Reagan, George H.W. Bush, and George W. Bush.

ABOVE: *Christmas greetings from the White House is a time-honored tradition. Calvin Coolidge, the 30th president, sent the first one in 1927 (top center), but it wasn't a Hall Brothers card. Hallmark has enjoyed its share of business with recent presidents, however, beginning with President Dwight D. Eisenhower in 1954 (top left). Others using Hallmark cards were presidents John Kennedy, 1962; (upper right, clockwise); George W. Bush, 2004; George H. W. Bush, 1992; and Ronald Reagan, 1985.*

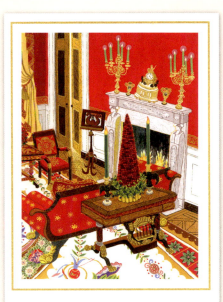

The more they saw, the more they were convinced that in order to attract and keep the best employees, their company needed the richest possible benefit package. The two worked on the plan throughout 1954 and 1955, and it was enacted for all employees—from executives to maintenance workers—in 1956. Among multiple other benefits, the package, called the Career Rewards Program, introduced Hallmark's profit sharing program, ensuring that as the company grew every one of its associates would share in the prosperity.

Don Hall's wide exposure to the company had engaged and excited him. But certain aspects of its operation also worried him. As he came to learn the inner workings of the corporate structure, he realized that even though the firm had grown exponentially in the past decade, it was, in certain ways, being run by entrepreneurial principles. The information flow was strictly top-down, with nearly all activities of the firm somehow dependent on his father. J.C. Hall, as he always had, took a preeminent interest in the creative side of the business. Operations, too, under the trusted hand of Charlie Stevenson, got plenty of attention. But Don Hall was alarmed to see how little attention and respect was paid to the financial aspects of the business. "Dad didn't believe in budgets," Don Hall explains. "He just didn't care for financial people at all."

But it was more than just finance. The younger Hall noticed that the members of the management group rarely, if ever, communicated with each other, nor were they encouraged to. "Dad would get them together and talk to them, but he didn't want them meeting with each other. He wanted to be the voice, the only voice, which is natural because that's the way it had always been. But in the '50s, it just wasn't working anymore. The whole managerial system was lacking. They were professionals. They worked hard and did some good things in the early years, but something had to be done."

"I've been accused of running a one-man show—perhaps because I don't particularly believe in running a business by meetings and committees. More often they just complicate the decision-making process. I'm a firm believer in the idea that there is a simpler and better way to do almost anything."

—J.C. Hall

Though it would have been tempting to avoid confrontation, Don Hall did not shy away from what he saw as his most critical responsibility—to bring modern management principles to the nearly 50 year-old company. He knew that some of his ideas would likely meet resistance from his father, but he didn't see any way around it.

Don Hall was elected to the board of directors in 1956. Two years later, he became administrative vice president. "I got into the administrative end of the business pretty quickly because nobody

BELOW: *Don Hall grew up with Hallmark and learned the company's workings from the ground up. But after returning to Kansas City from military service he quickly perceived a need to modernize the company's administrative and management operations.*

else wanted it," he explains with typical modesty and dry humor. But the young executive knew he had serious work to do. "I fashioned my role in the company to convert from Dad's more hip-pocket operation to more professional management."

In 1958, Don Hall led the push for a management-training program. Two of its first participants were Robert (Bob) Stark, a future executive vice president of the company, and David Hughes, who from 1983 to 1986 served as president and chief operating officer.

Stark, who still speaks of J.C. Hall with a sense of awe, calling him "a towering individual," remembers that there was a definite sense of transition in the air when he joined the company.

> *I think its fairly certain that J.C. knew that the future wasn't going to be like the past and that this company, this operation, was going to get a lot bigger than he had planned, and that he couldn't do it the way he had done it in the past. J.C. was taking every design out to the farm to look at them and writing, 'OK' and "not 'OK.' I think he sensed we were getting to a point where he wasn't going to be able to do that anymore. I think he also knew there wasn't any one person here who could do that. There had to be an organization to allow that."*
>
> *—Bob Stark*

Through the '50s and '60s, Don Hall worked hard to implement the management organization that he saw lacking. He was also open to new ideas and eager to embrace the latest technologies. In 1959, he oversaw the implementation of a large-scale computing system used to streamline merchandise ordering. And in 1961, Hallmark would install an IBM 7070 computer to manage retailer information.

Though not directly involved on the creative side of the business, Don Hall strongly supported the advances being made in high-speed, offset lithography by Hans Archenhold and his proteges, Ken West and Harold Rice. Such advances in technology were invisible to the company's customers—and many of the company's employees were likewise unaware of the quiet revolutions taking place at the plant. But the impact these advances would have over the coming decades was immeasurable.

In many ways, such technological advances had the same net effect as the management advances championed by Don Hall. By implementing a more collegial management structure, where ideas were freely shared and managers were given more autonomy, Don Hall was bringing scalability to the venerable company—allowing it to get out of its own way and grow. As David Hughes explains, "Don was taking us from being a relatively small, successful company to being a large, relatively successful company."

EVOLUTION OF PRINTING TECHNOLOGY AT HALLMARK

Steel die engraving

Hallmark's first greeting cards in 1915 were printed text and line images made from steel die engravings. A hand-fed press would produce between 500-700 cards an hour. The images were then hand-painted, with each artist adding a color.

Silk screen

In silk-screening, color was applied to greeting cards by squeegees through silk stretched across wood frames. At first done completely by hand, the process could produce 200-300 cards per hour. Hallmark technicians later built silk-screening machines.

Airbrush

In the airbrush department, workers used spray guns to apply color to cards through stencils lowered by a foot-operated lever. Each color required a separate stencil.

Off-set lithography

In the 1940s, off-set lithography became Hallmark's major method of reproducing artwork. Lithography produces 95 percent of Hallmark products today. In lithography, printing plates are dampened first with water, then ink. Since water and ink do not mix, the ink adheres to the image area, the water to the non-image area. To prevent the image from being reversed, it is transferred to a rubber blanket cylinder, and from the rubber blanket to paper.

*Hand-color separation (See page 74)

Hallmark Colormaster Control

To control and standardize color printing, the Hallmark Colormaster Control was introduced in 1951. This involved printing color control strips, rows of small squares of colored ink of all colors along the end of each press sheet. These were read and calibrated by an electronic densitometer (first developed to read the color of fruit) to make sure each color was accurate and that all cards printed the same. Color balance was further standardized by requiring all outside lithographers doing work for Hallmark to purchase Hallmark-approved inks from a single company.

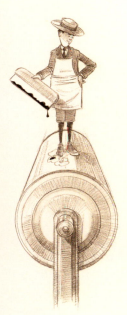

Gravure

Hallmark began using roto-gravure presses in the 1950s for printing at high speed on large rolls of paper. On a gravure press, an engraved cylinder is inked, then wiped off with a doctor blade, leaving ink in the engraved areas. The ink is transferred when the cylinder is rolled onto paper.

Photographic separation

In the early 1960s, Hallmark began using process cameras and photographic masking techniques for color separation and color correction for lithography. In this process, artwork was photographed through red, blue-violet and green filters. For example, a red filter would absorb the blue in the artwork and make it look black on the color separation negative, which would then be used for the cyan printing plate.

Six-Color System

The six-color system was introduced in 1962 to add greater color range to Hallmark's color reproduction. To the usual CYMK colors (cyan, yellow, magenta and black), a light magenta (pink) and a light cyan (light, clean blue) were added.

Rotary scanner

Scanners would eventually make separating colors on process cameras obsolete. In 1972, Hallmark purchased one of the first rotary scanners in the United States. On early rotary scanners, artwork was wrapped around a turning cylinder and scanned by a fixed sensor, which recorded the image on film. A separate scan was required for each color. Today, flatbed scanners are used.

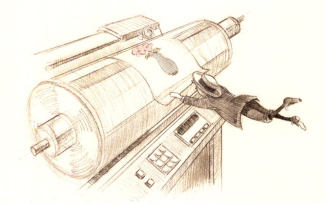

Digital Output

Today, an artist's work is either created digitally on a computer or later converted to a digital image. These digital files are assembled and sent electronically to a printer, who transfers it directly to a printing plate. The result is increased speed and efficiency, and better color reproduction.

MARY HAMILTON: KEEPING THE CUTE COMING

Over the company's long history, there have likely been hundreds of women named Mary employed by Hallmark. But if you had strolled through the art department at any time over the last 50 years and asked for Mary, you'd almost surely have been directed to just one woman. In the annals of Hallmark artists, there's really only one Mary.

Mary Hamilton was born in tiny Keytesville, Missouri, but her family moved to Kansas City when she was still a girl. The summer after high school graduation, she won a yearlong scholarship to the Kansas City Art Institute. She also applied for a job at Hallmark but was asked to come back after finishing her courses. On June 13, 1955, she returned to Hallmark with her slim portfolio of artwork. She was hired on the spot.

"Mary had it all. She could draw. She could paint. She could use color in very lovely ways. When an artist loves what she's doing as much as she does, it shows."

—Jeannette Lee

Mary began her career at Hallmark sketching flowers and finishing other people's art. But soon she was creating her own illustrations from start to finish. Though adept in a variety of media, Mary perfected a signature style of watercolor that is instantly recognizable. Often starting with a light pencil drawing, she paints over her sketch in light, "washy" watercolors, blending the subtle colors and adding darker tones that define each piece in just a few strokes.

"I try to put accents in each design to pop the little character or shape out of the background," she says. "It's important to help the customer focus."

Hallmark artists know that rendering emotion in brush strokes is tricky—and nearly impossible to explain. But Mary's colleagues recognize that her ability to produce an "aw" response with her innocent, sweet-faced waifs and little animals is what most endears her to fans—and generates the hundreds of fan letters she's received in her career. "I paint with a feeling in mind," Mary says. "I never have any set pattern. You learn to do it without quite realizing how."

Through the years, Mary has created hundreds of the whimsical characters for Hallmark greeting cards and gift products, but she has gained her greatest renown for her signature bears. In 1997, her artistic achievement was showcased in her own line of products. The "Mary's Bears" line included cards, stationery, albums, plush bears, a tea set, ceramic plates, mugs, books, a puzzle, gift wrap, and stickers.

Though she's become a Hallmark icon whose work remains in constant demand, Mary Hamilton is still the same dedicated, self-effacing artist who came to Hallmark, portfolio in hand, in 1955. And she still strives to grow and learn new techniques. When art directors ask for work that is looser, less detailed than her previous illustrations—in keeping with current trends—Mary delivers.

"I never want to say I've done it all," Mary Hamilton says. "I like the challenge of coming up with something different than the last time. As long as the emotion is there, I always want to try new things."

"SHE'S ALWAYS
CONDUCTED HERSELF
IN A WAY THAT INSPIRES
OTHER ARTISTS, BECAUSE
SHE DOES HER WORK
BEAUTIFULLY, PERFECTLY,
QUIETLY."
—*Don Hall*

A RETAIL REVOLUTION

In 1956, Hallmark Cards moved into its current headquarters. The building—built into the natural contour of a steep hillside—was a bold bit of architecture envisioned by J.C. Hall and executed by Welton Becket. A two-level enclosed bridge thirty feet over Kansas City's busy McGee Street connected the new structure with the old Overland Building. On moving day, employees crossed over from an inspiring past to a promising future. The building was comprised of eight stories with each floor having increased square footage as the terrain allowed. A ninth floor with a penthouse and guest apartment was later added.

The theme for the 1956 move was "Cross Over the Bridge." The phrase was inspired by a number two Billboard hit song recorded by Patti Page in 1954.

Up until the dawn of the 1950s, most greeting cards were sold through displays in department stores, drug stores, and bookstores. But in the early years of the decade, a transformation in the retail sales of greeting cards began to take hold. The main driver of this change was the popularity and profitability of greeting cards themselves. And the result was a great boom in dedicated card shops—many of them situated in new shopping malls springing up across the country.

Frank Cozad, Hallmark's longtime director of field sales, reflected on the rise of card shops in an interview conducted in 1992:

"The development of card shops wasn't the result of any plan. At the time, the average merchant had no dream he could sell nothing but cards and be profitable. The cards shops came about as a result of Hallmark's fixture program—and the stock control program that came with it. A bookstore or drugstore might start out with a 24-foot card department and the next year add another 20-feet, and the next year another 16, and so on. Then came the advent of party goods and stationery that added a great deal of volume to the stores. With the constant enlargement, it just pushed other products out. That was the evolution of the card shop."

As the number of card and gift specialty stores grew, Hallmark was faced with a substantial, albeit enviable, challenge—to produce a wide enough array of products to fill these dedicated stores. Thus, the 1950s and early 1960s became an era of tremendous growth in the breadth of the company's merchandise offering.

OPPOSITE PAGE TOP: *Beginning in 1956, Hallmark promoted its gift wrap line by sending young Kaye King (real name Sue Leist) around the country to give gift wrap demonstrations in stores, on television, and to women's groups and conventions. An estimated 200,000 viewers saw King performing her "pretty miracles" with paper and ribbon in "The Art of Gift Wrapping," a 23-minute Hallmark film in 1958. With the title of Hallmark Gift Stylist, King also taught classes and judged gift wrapping contests—traveling up to six months a year for about five years.*

The goal was not merely to provide commodity products to dealers but to help them establish full-line "social expression" shops. So, in the late 1950s when company leaders noticed a dearth of exciting party decorations on the market, Hallmark developed and introduced the "Plans-a-Party" line of paper party products. The years that immediately followed would see similar roll-outs of playing cards, stationery, calendars, and keepsake albums among other new products.

The dramatic expansion of its product lines necessitated newer and more sophisticated production and distribution facilities. To keep up with demand, Hallmark opened a ribbon production plant in Lawrence, Kansas, in 1958. At peak production, the facility was capable of turning out 2 million feet of ribbon per week. The very next year, to meet the production requirements of the Plans-a-Party line, the company opened a new plant in nearby Leavenworth, Kansas.

Hallmark's unqualified success with the specialty store strategy had validated one of J.C. Hall's most adamant contentions—that consumers did care about the brand name of the cards they sent and would select a high quality option over a lesser one, even if it cost a little more. Still, Don Hall, J.C. Hall, Ed Goodman, and other company leaders realized that a singular focus on specialty stores would not serve the company well over the long term. Throughout the 1950s, another major player—the mass-market discounter—was gaining prominence in America's retail environment. National or regional chain drug and variety stores—like Woolworth's, Kresge's, Newberry's, and Ben Franklin—catered to shoppers who were concerned with value and convenience. It was too big a market to ignore. So, in the fall of 1959, Hallmark developed a new brand to cater to them. Ambassador Cards was formed as a separate division within Hallmark, with its own sales force and marketing, design, and editorial staffs.

BELOW: *Starting on Valentine's Day 1960, Hallmark introduced a new concept—smartly-styled, coordinated party goods and decorations. "Plans-a-Party" included invitations, napkins, plates, paper cups, centerpieces, place mats, home decorations, and even a paper dress to match!*

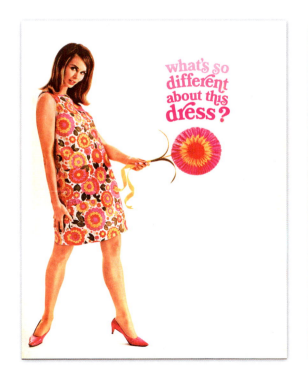

The launch of Ambassador was no trifling decision for Hallmark or J.C. Hall. At the time, most other large greeting card companies had more than one brand name. But in greeting card retail, no company had as much invested in its name as Hallmark. J.C. Hall agreed to the strategy, but held fast to his uncompromising position on quality, reminding the group, "We should be careful not to underestimate the taste of people who buy their cards in this type of outlet."

The group's solution to the challenge of providing a top-quality product to the mass-market retailers was to keep production values the same, but use creative work that had already been sold in the traditional Hallmark line. Much of the Ambassador line was comprised of designs that had appeared in Hallmark stores three to four years earlier.

The strategy worked. Ambassador launched in 1959 with a modest 350 designs. Sales increased substantially each year, and by 1969, the Ambassador line included more than 6,000 designs and was shipping 2 million cards per week to 12,000 accounts. More importantly, the Ambassador experiment proved that Hallmark could reach different market segments and not lose the brand stature that it had worked so hard to build over its first 50 years in business. The strategy would be repeated time and again—for the most part successfully—in the decades that followed.

Even as Hallmark was busy expanding its market reach and product breadth in the U.S., it was also—country-by-country—growing internationally. It made licensing deals with companies in Australia (1955) and New Zealand (1957) to produce and distribute its cards. In 1958, Hallmark acquired its longtime Canadian distributor, Coutts and Company. In 1959 it established Hallmark Cards Great Britain Ltd. and Hallmark Cards Ireland Ltd. Agreements to put Hallmark products into South Africa, Sweden, and France were established in the early years of the 1960s. By its 50th anniversary, the little company begun in a rented room at the YMCA was a global concern.

TOP: *Hallmark launched the Ambassador card line to better serve mass-market retailers in 1959.*

ABOVE: *In 1960, Hallmark introduced several new products within its new Plans-a-Party line of paper party goods. One of the earliest designs featured Charles Schulz's* Peanuts *gang. Hallmark began printing* Peanuts *greeting cards that same year.*

LEFT: *J.C. Hall and William Coutts. In 1958, Hallmark acquired the William E. Coutts Company, one of Canada's largest greeting card makers. But the relationship between the two companies actually dates all the way back to 1931 when J.C. Hall and William Coutts made a handshake deal to make the Coutts' company Hallmark's Canadian affiliate—Hallmark's first international venture. Hallmark purchased 40 percent interest in the Canadian company in 1948 and the remaining interest ten years later. It is now known simply as Hallmark Canada.*

IN 1960, HALLMARK CELEBRATED ITS 50TH ANNIVERSARY. AT THE TIME, THE COMPANY WAS PRODUCING 4 MILLION CARDS A DAY AND EMPLOYED MORE THAN 4,000 EMPLOYEES, INCLUDING 350 ARTISTS.

CARDS THAT PUSHED THE ENVELOPE

The pansy card and other gentle fare were still selling well, but by the mid-1950s a different breed of buyer was looking for a different kind of greeting card. To meet the demand for less traditional greetings, Hallmark launched Contemporary Cards in 1954. The Contemporary studio was run as an entirely separate creative group, headed by Bob McCloskey and staffed, in the words of Don Hall, by a group of "oddball artists." "They were brilliant people," he explains, "but they were hard to control."

With little respect for convention and a gleeful willingness to test Hallmark's long held taste guidelines, this group of oddball artists and writers churned out cards featuring simple, cartoonish characters that brought to mind late-night, bar-napkin doodles. The humor was quirky, quick, fresh, and occasionally bawdy— but also very funny. They created a sensation in the market. Asked once whether he liked the cards, J.C. Hall simply replied, "I like the way they sell."

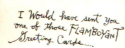

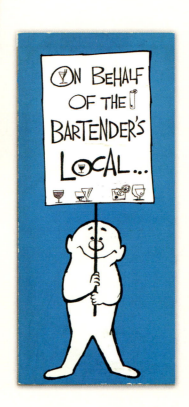

ABOVE: *In the late 1950s, the small staff of writers and cartoonists at Hallmark's Contemporay Cards—people such as Bob Harr, Dean Norman, Paul Coker, and Don Branham—were inspired by stand-up comics and captioned cartoons in publications like* Esquire, Playboy, *and* Mad *magazine. In fact, Coker and other Contemporary cartoonists published their work in* Mad, *while Branham did full-page cartoons for* Esquire. *Branham's style (above and left), with its shaky lines and intricately scrolled details, would influence a generation of cartoonists.*

BETSEY CLARK: THE WOMAN BEHIND THE WAIFS

"During my years at Hallmark, many people have sent work in saying they had been told their work should be on cards. This time it was for real."

—Jeannette Lee on Betsey Clark

No one at Hallmark Cards had ever heard of Betsey Clark when a friend of the Amarillo, Texas-based artist sent samples of her work to the company in 1962. But within a few years, Clark's illustrations would be recognizable to—and adored by—millions of people across the country and around the world.

The subjects of Clark's drawings were earnest-looking, ragamuffin children with big, soulful eyes, patchwork clothes, and large, often onion-shaped heads. And although they were entirely fresh to the greeting card market, Clark often said that she had been drawing her characters the same way since she was little girl. She called them her "waifs."

"I had no idea that my drawings would be so popular. I was kicked out of art classes for drawing exactly what I'm doing now."

—Betsey Clark

Greeting cards bearing Clark's waifs were an instant success and soon boasted sales numbers in the same league as the high-profile and top-selling *Peanuts* line. "Betsey Clark's designs simply leap across the generation gap," said George Parker, Director of Creative Services at Hallmark in the 1970s. "Teenagers, their mothers, and even their grandmothers find them equally appealing."

In 1968, an entire line of Clark's characters was launched across multiple platforms. Named the Charmers, the line-up grew to include nearly every category of Hallmark product, from cards to calendars, puzzles, partyware, figurines, candles, and books. In 1973, her painting *Musicians* appeared on one of the first four Christmas ornaments that later became the Keepsake Ornaments line. In 1976, Hallmark began to license out Betsey's artwork for a range of non-Hallmark products, such as dolls, watches, children's sportswear, and furniture.

The name Betsey Clark and her signature waifs are still internationally recognized. Her work has a loyal following of fans, and items featuring it are sought after at online auction sites and collector shows.

Clark continued to work up to her death in 1987, and her vast body of work stands as a legacy to her prolific talent. As recently as 2008, nearly 70 Hallmark products featured renderings of her artwork.

"When I was in college I was told a million times to be good at many things. True, it's not often you can be successful with one basic design. But when you can, why not?"

—Betsey Clark

A Meeting at Camp David

Hallmark had already created two presidential Christmas cards for the Kennedys when Jeannette Lee was called to Washington to discuss a different project—the development of two Jacqueline Kennedy-painted greeting cards to be sold as a benefit for the Kennedy Center. Along with longtime Hallmark artist Alice Ann Biggerstaff, Lee was driven from the White House to Camp David where she met with Mrs. Kennedy at the compound's main lodge.

"She couldn't have been nicer or more charming. And I was a Republican!"

The three talked about art and watercolor technique for several hours. "I remember that Jackie complained that her paint would always run," recalls Lee. " So Alice showed her how to use a sponge to put down a background. We found the sponge under the sink."

At four o'clock, the President was scheduled to deliver a speech in Germany.

"They turned on the television in the lodge, but it didn't work, so Jackie said, 'We'll watch it in the bedroom,' so we all went in to her bedroom—about six of us—and she jumped up on the bed and patted it and said, 'C'mon everybody!' So we all sat on the bed and watched his speech from Germany."

The date of this meeting was June 26, 1963. Kennedy's speech, delivered from West Berlin as a response to the newly erected Berlin Wall, would forever be remembered as the "Ich bin ein Berliner" speech—a defining moment of the Cold War. Jeannette Lee truly had a front-row seat to history that day. As she recalled some 45 years later, "It was quite an afternoon."

ABOVE: *The 1963 presidential Christmas card that was never sent.*

With our wishes
for a
Blessed Christmas
and a
Happy New Year

TOP: *The two cards painted by Jacqueline Kennedy printed by Halllmark to raise funds for the Kennedy Center.*

A Greeting Unsent

Just six months after Jeannette Lee's visit to Washington, President John F. Kennedy would fall to an assassin's bullet while riding in a motorcade in Dallas. Hallmark had delivered several hundred copies of the 1963 presidential Christmas card to the White House a few weeks before, but the President and Mrs. Kennedy had signed only about 30 of the cards before leaving for Dallas.

The 1963 card, which featured a color photo of a nativity scene in the East Room of the White House, was the first presidential Christmas card to feature a religious image. Of the 30 cards signed by both President and Mrs. Kennedy, less than two-dozen are known to exist today.

According to Mary Seeley, author of *Season's Greetings From the White House*, the dual-signed 1963 cards produced by Hallmark are "the most rare pieces of presidential Christmas memorabilia today."

In 1960, 10 years after making their debut in the nation's newspapers, Charles Schulz's Peanuts characters first appeared on Hallmark greeting cards. During what has been Hallmark's longest continual licensing agreement, Hallmark and United Media (the newspaper syndicate that controls licensing rights to Peanuts) have collaborated to produce more than 150 billion pieces of product.

But all that production starts with one-on-one relationships—and trust. Hallmark writing stylist Renee Daniels enjoyed a long working relationship with Schulz. "When I met Charles Schulz the first time, I was star-struck," she remembers. "That feeling quickly evaporated though because he's so humble. I was always amazed at how such a talented man could also be so approachable and kind."

Over 50 years of working together, Hallmark has gained infinite trust and respect from Charles Schulz and the Schulz family. So exacting and accurate are their depictions of Charlie Brown and friends that Hallmark designers were even asked to create a Peanuts style guide for worldwide licensing use.

Hallmark's Peanuts products are perennial top-sellers in the United States and in more than 100 countries around the world.

The Art (and Architecture) of Retail

When a company chooses to use the words "the very best" in its slogan—and actually holds itself to that standard—it sets the bar awfully high. In the early 1960s, J.C. Hall began to dream about building a showcase store worthy of the very best his company had to offer. The store he had in mind couldn't be just anywhere. In fact, by Hall's way of thinking, it really couldn't be anywhere other than what he considered the most prominent retail location in the country: New York City's Fifth Avenue. In early 1964, he signed a lease on a corner storefront at Fifty-sixth Street and Fifth Avenue.

But the very best location was only part of Hall's plan. He approached renowned modern architect Edward Durrell Stone with a proposition. He had been told that the highly sought-after architect—designer of award-winning art museums, embassies, and public buildings—would not bother with a "little retail store." But Hall was undaunted. "All I told him was I wanted him to make the best-looking shop on Fifth Avenue, and he liked the challenge."

For the Hallmark Gallery, Stone cut back the first floor 16 feet, exposing the main floor to the street through huge, arched windows. While the first floor served the retail needs of customers, the lower level space was used as a gallery to showcase the arts of everyday life. When it opened in 1964, the Hallmark Gallery was the first corporate art gallery in New York City.

Ultimately, the Hallmark Gallery would bring more to the company than just Fifth Avenue prestige. With its very first exhibit, it would impel Hallmark into a new realm of fine art collecting. That first exhibit was a one-man show of photographs by American photographer Harry Callahan. When Hallmark bought the entire exhibit of 141 Callahan prints, this collection became the genesis for its Hallmark Photographic Collection, which would grow to include 6,500 photographs by 2006—the year the entire collection was given as a gift to Kansas City's Nelson-Atkins Museum of Art.

Back in Kansas City, the company faced another retail challenge. In the 15 years since the Halls' department store had opened, the migration of businesses and shoppers out of the downtown core had continued unabated. In 1964, the store's president, Jack Kaiser, made a persuasive argument for a major new retail outlet in the city's favorite shopping area, the Country Club Plaza. "It seemed too ambitious to consider the same year we were opening the Gallery," recalled J.C. Hall, "but Jack had all the right answers at the tip of his tongue." The Halls Plaza store opened in 1965. Ambition is something J.C. Hall never lacked.

TOP LEFT & RIGHT: *The Hallmark Gallery graced the corner of New York City's Fifty-sixth Street and Fifth Avenue from June 1964 to January 1987. The corner storefront was designed by prominent modernist architect Edward Durrell Stone and won the Fifth Avenue Association's coveted architectural award. That same year, Stone had completed one of his most iconic and controversial commissions, a private gallery of modern art, which stood a few blocks away at Two Columbus Circle.*

RIGHT: *Hallmark chose Kansas City's most popular shopping area, the Country Club Plaza, as the location for its second Halls department store, which opened in 1965. The store's interiors were designed by Paul Laszlo and Associates, a leading modern architecture firm of the mid-twentieth century. Edward Durrell Stone designed the building's distinctive exterior.*

THE UNITED NATIONS OF HALLMARK

Fernando Casini   *Asterio Pascolini*

Hallmark's creative staff today can trace its roots to artistic traditions and cultures from around the globe. But in its first decades, the company was lucky to find artists with even basic art school training. Most early artists were Kansas City-area women with natural talent who learned their trade after being hired right out of high school. When the 1950s and '60s rolled around, however, J.C. Hall knew that his art staff needed new ideas and techniques to keep up with the increasing demand for greeting cards. To find it, he would reach across the oceans.

"Mr. Hall had a vision that Hallmark was going to be an artistic center," recalls retired artist Asterio Pascolini. "He wanted to integrate international talent and hope their technique would rub off on the homegrown talent."

Pascolini became one of a small-but-influential cadre of foreign artists who helped bring new skill and sophistication to Hallmark. He was recruited in 1958, after some American tourists sent J.C. Hall a sketchbook filled with drawings from a struggling Italian artist they'd met in Florence. Soon the young Florentine was in Kansas City, having accepted Hall's offer of a job and art school tuition.

Fernando Casini

"Art school is how they got me," Pascolini recalls wistfully, looking back half a century. "In Italy, I could not afford art school."

Jeannette Lee, the art director who oversaw the integration of foreign artists into Hallmark, remembers a 1962 recruiting trip that took her from England, through Scandinavia, France, and down the European continent, to Spain and Italy. A number of artists she met would go on to work for Hallmark, either as full-time employees or freelancers. In a Rome hotel room she interviewed Fernando Casini, a young university student working on his degree in costume and set design for the Italian opera. His enthusiasm for America and his art portfolio, filled with bright colors and intricate patterns, impressed Lee. Through an interpreter she asked if Casini would like to come work at Hallmark.

"Yes! Of course!" he remembers saying. "America had always been my dream."

Both Pascolini and Casini thought they knew what they'd find when they got to Kansas City—cowboys and Indians riding horses through the streets. "We weren't naive," Pascolini remembers, "but we did not expect that the Wild West would be completely gone. We expected at least a trace of it."

Asterio Pascolini

Nanae Ito

Nanae Ito

"Nanae was an outstanding example of this recruiting system working," says Lee. Casini agrees saying, "Nanae could paint in a western style. She was very successful."

Most foreign artists understood that they'd only stay at Hallmark for a year at most. For the few who made their careers and homes in Kansas City, the education process was a two-way street—they inspired with their old-world techniques but also learned to produce the kind of art that American consumers wanted.

"Successful artists were held in such esteem," Pascolini says. "Mr. Hall was so proud of us. But you had to know how to do it the American way."

Pascolini, who retired from Hallmark in 1997, went on to become an American citizen. Not only did he marry a Hallmark artist, but his daughter and two of his three sons work at the company.

Casini had a 33-year Hallmark career before retiring in 1999 and returning to Italy. Every few years he comes back to America to renew old friendships made at Hallmark.

Gradually, the influence of artists from countries such as Japan, Sweden, France, Germany, and Italy began to show up on Hallmark products. But through the 1970s, as American-born artists became more proficient and diverse in style, the campaign to recruit foreign artists waned. The venture had proven a success, however.

"We had wanted to bring in new ideas, new ways of working, and a broader way of thinking," Lee says. "And bringing in foreign artists really helped give us a more well-rounded creative staff."

What they found instead was a modern city and a growing company that had just settled into its new Kansas City headquarters, where artists were divided into many far-flung departments. The compartmentalized structure often meant foreign artists didn't socialize with other expatriates "We were separated by style," Pascolini says. "And we had a tendency to be friends with people with the same style too."

Casini remembers his American colleagues as warmhearted and welcoming. "I got to meet people like Mary Hamilton, Alice Ann Biggerstaff—incredible people who remained friends for life," he says.

It was a time of rapid learning for everyone. And for the foreign artists, learning English was paramount. "I thought I knew English," Pascolini says with a laugh. "But I did not know English. Jack Jonathan told me, 'Asterio, it's cute now, but two years from now they expect English!'"

Casini spoke no English at all. "I had to talk to my supervisor," he recalls. "She would look at me with big beautiful eyes, a wonderful smile, and she had no idea what I was talking about. Fortunately, you were judged for the work."

Casini still recalls his first Hallmark successes. "In my first month, Mr. Hall personally accepted three of my paintings, and they were printed on cards. I was so proud."

Europe wasn't the only source of foreign talent. Hallmark also recruited nearly a dozen Japanese artists through its connections to a California art gallery. Most would eventually return to their homeland, but Nanae Ito stayed for a long and successful Hallmark career, becoming one of Hallmark's most important artists.

Fernando Casini

Asterio Pascolini

149

CHAPTER SEVEN

The Hallmark Hall of Fame

"There has never been a TV signature as enduring as Hallmark Hall of Fame. As comparisons vividly show, nothing is even in its neighborhood.

— Howard Rosenberg, Los Angeles Times

O N AUGUST 21, 1951, JOYCE HALL ISSUED A MEMO TO HALLMARK'S NATIONAL SALES FORCE. NO ONE COULD HAVE KNOWN THEN THE HISTORIC IMPLICATIONS OF ITS OPENING LINE:

Dear Fellows:
We're going to try our hand at television.

The one-page announcement went on to detail a 15-minute weekly program that would be carried on a small collection of stations affiliated with the CBS network. It was a brief announcement of a modest plan, but with the memo Hall set in motion events that would—in relatively short order—bring a wholly new kind of program to a young medium that was still defining itself.

Like so many early television sponsors, Hallmark migrated from radio during the emergence of the new medium. Since as far back as 1938, Hallmark had sponsored radio programs, beginning with *Tony Wons' Radio Scrapbook*, a local Chicago show that was eventually syndicated nationwide. Other shows followed—like the wartime *Meet Your Navy* and *Radio Reader's Digest*, which dramatized stories from the popular magazine.

Neither of those shows bore much resemblance to what would become television's Hallmark Hall of Fame, but in 1948 the company launched, for the first time, its own dramatic radio anthology featuring adaptations of classic (and sometimes obscure) works of literature and drama. That program, carried on CBS radio, was called *Hallmark Playhouse*. In its first few years it featured big-name stars such as Ethel Barrymore, Gregory Peck, Joan Fontaine, Ronald Coleman, and Jane Wyman among others. Hosted by famed actor Lionel Barrymore, the show would continue until 1952.

But by the early 1950s the lure of television was impossible to ignore—for American families and for American companies. Corporate sponsorship of programs was the prevalent broadcast model, and in the decade following the end of World War II, no shortage of companies—like Texaco, Goodyear, Kraft, Philco, and Ford—rushed to link their products with new programs filling the airwaves. "Every program had a sponsor and everyone knew who that sponsor was," explains Brad Moore, president of Hallmark Hall

ABOVE: *Lionel Barrymore was the host of* Hallmark Playhouse, *which was carried on CBS radio until 1952.*

RIGHT: *J.C. Hall with Helen Hayes and Sarah Churchill, the host of Hallmark's first television program.*

Hotel Mediterraneo,
Blanes. (Costa Brava)

Mr. J.C. Hall,
Twenty-Fifth & Grand Avenue,
Kansas City,
Missouri.   12th May, 1952.

Dear Mr. Hall,

It is always a great pleasure to appear
at the Hallmark Playhouse radio program and
even a greater pleasure to receive your
letters of tribute afterwards.

I do want you to know how pleased and
touched I have been by your letters of kindness and interest.

I am at the present moment in Spain,
making a technicolor film entitled "Decameron
Nights". I should be through with the picture
by mid-September and look forward to returning
to our wonderful country and, I hope, to your
program in the fall.

With all good wishes to you.

Sincerely,

Joan Fontaine.

Hallmark's active role in broadcast sponsorship—first as a radio sponsor and ultimately with the Hall of Fame—provided J.C. Hall ample opportunity to meet Hollywood's biggest stars. Many of them became close friends. Joan Fontaine sent the letter above after starring in a Hallmark Playhouse radio production.

of Fame Productions. "You knew that *Dinah Shore* was sponsored by Chevrolet and the *Friday Night Fights* were Gillette—the sponsor and the program were pretty inseparable."

"In the early days of television, the big, powerful advertising agencies essentially controlled network programing," explains Moore. "The networks were just weak affiliations of local stations. All of these big ad agencies had production arms, and they actually produced the programs and delivered them to the networks, and then they'd fill them with their own commercials."

In the fall of 1951, just six weeks after Hall's memo, Hallmark went live on the air with *Hallmark Presents Sarah Churchill*, a short, weekly interview show hosted by Sir Winston's daughter. The program continued through the close of the year at which time it was restructured into a dramatic program with Churchill as host and renamed *Hallmark Television Playhouse*.

Hallmark's early experimentations in programming were typical of an era when nearly everything was new. Joyce Hall never doubted the power of television, but it took a little trial and error to harness that power. "When television first appeared, I was convinced it was the greatest educational and entertainment medium the world had ever known," Hall wrote in his 1979 book, *When You Care Enough*. "But we wanted shows that would not only be top entertainment but top quality as well. We wanted shows that would be appreciated by the entire family, and we wanted people to feel they had benefited from the time spent watching them."

Hall's was a lofty, if not entirely realistic, goal. It would be 10 years before then-FCC chairman Newton Minow would memorably refer to television as "a vast wasteland," but even in 1951 the majority of programming was disappointingly unintellectual and under-ambitious. Typical fare on television at the time ranged from western horse operas to game shows. But early in December of 1951, Hall saw what he thought was a rare opportunity. He learned from his trusted advertising partner, Fairfax Cone, that NBC Television was looking for a sponsor for an original opera written for television that it had commissioned for Christmas.

Hall knew that the planned Christmas Eve airdate would be too late to help as a holiday promotion of greeting cards. He also knew that opera wasn't exactly likely to be a top draw on television. At an hour long, it would also be expensive to sponsor. But he liked the idea nonetheless. It was quality programming—something that he felt was in short supply on television. He signed on for the sponsorship, considering it something of a Christmas gift to customers. "I felt we could use the show to thank all the people who bought Hallmark cards," he wrote. It was Hallmark's first sponsored television special and the first of hundreds of shows that would be presented under the name Hallmark Hall of Fame.

Broadcast live from New York City, the opera *Amahl and the Night Visitors* by Gian Carlo Menotti, was instantly hailed as a landmark achievement by critics and audiences alike. Hallmark received thousands of letters, cards, and telegrams of gratitude in the days following the broadcast. The *New Yorker* called it, "a lovely and wonderful thing to see and hear." *Daily Variety* lauded the ambitious production for "automatically lift(ing) the medium into a new sphere of cultural importance."

The live performance was so popular that Hallmark reprised it as an Easter special—just four months after its debut—and presented it a third time at Christmas. The following Christmas, 1953, the Hallmark Hall of Fame presented its fourth production of *Amahl*, but this time it was back to breaking new ground—the performance marked the first time a sponsored network show was broadcast in color. The program aired just two days after the FCC approved NBC's new "color in tint" process.

Amahl and the Night Visitors was just one show among more than two hundred that would follow over the ensuing half-century, but with this very first performance, the Hallmark Hall of Fame established two very important paradigms. First, it proved that a top-quality television broadcast could, and would, attract an audience. Second, it was evidence that Hall—and the Hallmark Hall of Fame—relished breaking new ground and pushing the medium to greater critical heights. The "firsts" claimed with *Amahl*—first original opera created for television, first commercially sponsored color broadcast—would be followed by many more.

The Hallmark Hall of Fame scored another first with its second production. In the spring of 1953, Hall decided to broadcast a live production of *Hamlet*. Again, it was a bold move. No one had presented a Shakespeare play on television before. No one had produced a show longer than an hour. And no single sponsor had supported two hours of TV time on one show.

> "HALLMARK HALL OF FAME WHEN IT STARTED WAS UNIQUE AMONG TELEVISION PROGRAMS IN THAT IT WAS FOCUSED ON VERY CLASSIC—I DON'T WANT TO USE THE WORD HIGHBROW—BUT ELEGANT, SOPHISTICATED PROGRAMMING, AS OPPOSED TO THE *FRIDAY NIGHT FIGHTS*."
>
> —*Brad Moore*

> "WE HAD BEEN CAUTIONED AGAINST SPONSORING SHOWS THAT WERE 'NOT IN THE POPULAR VEIN,' WHATEVER THAT MEANT. BUT FAX (FAIRFAX CONE) AND I WERE CONVINCED THAT THE AMERICAN PUBLIC WAS MORE INTERESTED IN QUALITY THAN SOME PEOPLE IN TELEVISION REALIZED."
>
> —*J.C. Hall*

Hamlet made television history. Like *Amahl*, it was lauded by critics. But even more importantly, it garnered a huge viewing audience. As Hall would later write, "*Hamlet* was seen that April Sunday by more people than had seen it in the 350 years since it had been written."

With *Hamlet*, the concept of a TV "special"—that is, a show that preempts regularly scheduled programming—was established. For Hallmark, it was a perfect model. The company could buy television time only when it needed it most—typically in advance of a major card-selling holiday like Christmas, Valentine's Day, or Mothers Day.

Over the next decade, more impressive "firsts" would follow. In 1954, Dame Judith Anderson received the Hallmark Hall of Fame's first Emmy for her performance in *Macbeth*. In 1958, the Hall of Fame presented its first original full-length play, *Little Moon of Alban* by James Costigan. That program garnered four Emmys, a Christopher Award, and a Peabody Award.

Year after year, the Emmy Awards piled up, and a cascade of critical praise followed virtually every new effort produced by the Hall of Fame. By its tenth year, in 1961, its impact on the television medium was recognized in unprecedented fashion. At that year's Emmy Awards, Joyce C. Hall received the prestigious Trustees' Award honoring Hallmark and the Hallmark Hall of Fame series for "uplifting the standards of television." True to the established pattern, it was the first time an Emmy had ever been awarded to a sponsor.

From its earliest years, Hall had taken a deep personal interest in the Hallmark Hall of Fame. As a sponsor, he didn't simply write the checks. A longtime fan of live theater, Hall was perhaps the show's most ardent booster. Joyce and Elizabeth Hall read every script before production began and reserved the right of approval.

In the early 1960s, the sponsorship of television programming underwent a radical change. Rather than offer single-company program sponsorship, networks opened up shows to multiple

ABOVE: *In 1961 Hallmark Cards received the first Emmy ever presented to a sponsor, with J.C. Hall accepting the honor.*

"WE WERE NOT UNIQUE IN 1951 IN BEING A FULLY SPONSORED PROGRAM. HOW WE WERE UNIQUE IS THAT OUR PROGRAMS WERE MORE SOPHISTICATED. IT WAS OPERAS. IT WAS SHAKESPEARE. IT WAS IBSEN."

—*Brad Moore*

advertisers. Within the span of just a few years, the "sponsorship model" was out, and the "advertising model" was in. By the mid-1960s, network television—with short advertisements from a wide variety of advertisers peppering its shows—looked much like it does today. Since that time, there has been one notable exception to that rule—the Hallmark Hall of Fame.

Hallmark sponsors its show from introduction to sign-off. Along the way, of course, there are commercials, and these commercials have become legendary in their own right. Far from the hard-sell, fast-talking fare typical of television, Hallmark Hall of Fame ads were, and are, like little movies within the movie. Most tell a small, finely crafted story about the ways in which we share our feelings and emotions with others—and how Hallmark cards are so often a part of the emotional connections we make. The commercials don't rush to make their point. The average length is two minutes.

Jan Parkinson, vice president of Hall of Fame Productions, has been a part of the team responsible for the Hallmark Hall of Fame since 1972—and he's the nearest anyone will ever come to being a Hallmark Hall of Fame historian. He recalls that the mold for the prototypical Hall of Fame commercial was likely struck as far back as the mid-1970s, perhaps with a spot called "What a Day."

Hallmark's "What a Day" spot was groundbreaking, both for the company and for television advertising in general. Previous Hallmark television ads had been product specific, consisting mostly of "table top" shots of the newest designs in seasonal cards and partyware. If there were people in the commercials, they were there as props—to hold a card and smile. They were all shot on a sound stage.

"What a Day" was the company's first "slice-of-life" commercial. It followed a young woman through an absolutely horrible day. She arrives late to the office to a disapproving look from her boss. She suffers through lunch with an overbearing co-worker and is caught in a torrential downpour. A stack of extra work keeps her late. Her posture and demeanor signal that, on this day, life has defeated her. But when she enters her apartment and goes through the mail, she sees an envelope embossed with the Hallmark logo. As she opens the card and reads the message, she smiles for the first time all day.

The commercial was shot at real locations in Chicago—not unusual today, but at that time such production values were rare. Remarkably, the viewer does not hear a single word of dialogue and doesn't get to read the inside of the card. But there's no mistaking the message—a Hallmark card can change someone's entire day.

"What a Day" garnered a lot of attention in the advertising community at the time. And for Hallmark, it became a prototype for dozens of Hallmark Hall of Fame commercials to follow.

In the mid-1970s, a Hallmark Hall of Fame commercial titled, "What a Day" set the creative mold for years of "slice-of-life" Hallmark advertisements to follow.

The spot follows a young career woman through a day in which everything seems to go wrong.

Throughout the spot, the viewer doesn't hear a word of dialogue, but the woman's expression tells everything they need to know.

Upon returning to her apartment at the end of the long day, she finds a Hallmark card among the bills.

Viewers never get to see the inside of the card.

But they see her open it. And, at last, they see her smile.

ABOVE: The Resting Place, *starring John Lithgow, aired in 1986.*

BELOW: *John Lithgow also appeared in Hallmark Hall of Fame productions of* The Country Girl *(1974) and* Redwood Curtain *(1995). But it was after his leading performance in* The Resting Place, *for which he was nominated for an Emmy Award, that he wrote to thank Don Hall for continuing to support him in a series of acclaimed roles.*

JOHN LITHGOW

Dear Mr. Hall —
Thank you for your kind note regarding my Emmy nomination for Resting Place! I was very proud to be in the show and very pleased at how it came out: a nomination was hardly necessary.
Thank you also for the support Hallmark gave the project. All of us felt it constantly — a continual assurance that we were working on something of great distinction.

Sincerely,
John Lithgow

In the short time that commercials have been eligible for Emmy Awards—since 1997—Hall of Fame spots have garnered three nominations and won the award once, in 2006.

"If we could put all of those commercials on one video disc, that collection would outsell every movie we've ever made," comments Moore. Moore's not worried about such a comment undermining his own program—he produces the commercials as well as the movies.

Consistent as it has been, there have been changes to the Hallmark Hall of Fame over the decades. At various times the program has appeared on NBC, CBS, ABC, and briefly, even PBS. The content of the programming has evolved as well. All the performances of the early years were live theatrical productions—the first taped show was an adaptation of the Broadway musical *Kiss Me Kate* in 1958. And while the show drew on the classics for much of its material throughout its first two decades, it increasingly incorporated more contemporary, and sometimes originally commissioned, work.

The evolution of Hallmark Hall of Fame programs had to do with public tastes and the reality of a more competitive television market. After all, when the series began there were a total of two networks—NBC and CBS. Today, the number of outlets for entertainment programming—on television and off—is virtually uncountable. Moore provides an early example of a programming change motivated by competition. "When PBS came along in the late '60s, early '70s, they started doing the classics—Shakespeare and loftier programming. So we moved toward more emotional programs."

Brad Moore took over the top spot at Hallmark Hall of Fame in 1982. Though the show still distinguished itself as quality television, he explains that there had been a drop off in the creative content over the preceding decade. The problem, as he sees it, was the programming model—still a holdover from the old days of "sponsorship" TV. "Our advertising agency at that time had kept a vestige of a programming department, but they were essentially buying programs off the shelf and selling them to Hallmark. They weren't baking them from scratch." He characterized the programs of the era as "very safe" and "very bland." "When you're Hallmark," says Moore, "that's just not good enough."

After a series of meetings with Don Hall, Moore and Parkinson developed a new plan. Remembering it today, Moore's voice still belies his excitement at the new beginning. "We stepped back in the middle '80s and said, 'Let's reinvent this thing. Let's start all over.' We said, 'We will develop the programs ourselves.' And not only did we start developing our own ideas, but a few years later we formed our own production company."

With Don Hall's strong encouragement, they determined to up the frequency of the franchise from two shows each year to three or four. To this day, Moore keeps a dog-eared memo from Don Hall with him at all times. It is dated June 10, 1985. He delights in reading an excerpt:

"The Hallmark Hall of Fame has been an absolutely unique image builder for this company. . . . It has broadly supported the aura of the whole enterprise in quality, taste, and even moral and ethical terms. ... I am not aware of any such tool, in or out of TV, available to any other company, with such a positive impact. With all the foregoing, I was delighted that we came to the strong conclusion to build our frequency back up to three, then four shows per year, in addition to giving it the high level attention it once had and surely deserves. The added investment of both time and resources are very worthwhile, in my opinion."

Moore and his team had a level of support—and creative freedom—that most movie developers and producers could only dream about. So they got busy.

The group's very first production following that reaffirming memo from Hall was one of its most groundbreaking—and one of the Hall family's favorites. *Love Is Never Silent*, a poignant story revolving around two deaf parents and their hearing daughter, thrust the Hallmark Hall of Fame back into the critical consciousness. The show won two Emmys and served notice that the Hallmark Hall of Fame still had plenty of stories to tell—and knew how to tell them in a way that could touch viewers deeply.

A year later, the Hallmark Hall of Fame managed to top that program—and in fact, top every program ever on television before or since—with a presentation called *Promise*. *Promise*, which first aired on December 14, 1986, told the story of two brothers, one afflicted with schizophrenia, in what the *Los Angeles Times* called a "sweet, tender, deeply affecting" way. Simply put, the film is the single most honored program in the history of television. Starring James Garner, James Woods, and Piper Laurie, *Promise* won five Emmys, a Christopher Award, a Humanitas Prize, a Peabody Award, and two Golden Globes, including best motion picture made for television. In every way, the show became one of the brightest jewels in the Hallmark crown.

Promise set the bar very high, but the Hallmark Hall of Fame has continued to reach for it without compromise. As in its early years of the series, a wave of critical praise seemed to follow each successive program.

As of this writing, the Hallmark Hall of Fame is the most decorated series in television history. It has earned 269 Emmy nominations and won the award 79 times—more than double any other series.

After nearly 60 years, the Hallmark Hall of Fame performances

James Woods

June 8, 1989

Mr. Donald Hall
Chairman of the Board
Hallmark Cards, Inc.
Kansas City, Missouri 64108

Dear Mr. Hall,

I was extremely pleased to receive your letter concerning **My Name Is Bill W.** Your kind words meant a great deal to me. We both know that this project was for all involved "above and beyond the call of duty." Your remarks do afford me the opportunity to share with you some thoughts I have expressed to others.

Because Hallmark is truly dedicated to excellence, not as some jingoistic "promotional gimmick," but from the heart, you may take your contribution to the arts almost for granted. I can tell you, however, that you and your organization are to those of us on the front lines the lifeblood of true artistry in the medium of television. This medium, the potential of which is virtually limitless, has been so exploited and reduced by so many others, while you remain a beacon in the wilderness. For those of us fortunate enough to rub shoulders with Hallmark and Donald Hall, the experience is an unforgettable one.

I wish you and your family all the best and look forward to years of fruitful collaboration with you, Sir, and Hallmark.

Yours truly,

James Woods

James Woods

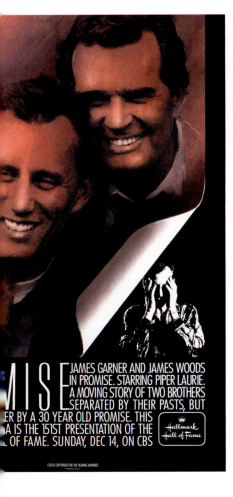

JAMES GARNER AND JAMES WOODS IN PROMISE. STARRING PIPER LAURIE. A MOVING STORY OF TWO BROTHERS SEPARATED BY THEIR PASTS, BUT ... BY A 30 YEAR OLD PROMISE. THIS ... IS THE 151ST PRESENTATION OF THE ... OF FAME. SUNDAY, DEC 14, ON CBS

ABOVE: *In 1982 the Academy of Television Arts & Sciences presented the Governors' Award to Hallmark for the Hallmark Hall of Fame's contribution to the television medium. Hallmark chairman Don Hall accepted the award.*

LEFT: Promise, *starring James Garner and James Woods, became the most decorated program in television history. It first aired in December of 1986.*

OPPOSITE PAGE BOTTOM: What the Deaf Man Heard, *starring Matthew Modine and James Earl Jones, first aired in 1997.*

BELOW : Sarah, Plain & Tall, *staring Glenn Close, won an Emmy in 1991.*

still have an almost preternatural knack for making deep connections with their audience. And even with unprecedented levels of competition, that audience is remarkably strong. Of the nearly 3,000 movies broadcast on television in the previous decade, the four highest rated were all Hall of Fame presentations.

The legendary quality of the productions has always attracted top-draw talent. The lineup of actors starring in Hallmark Hall of Fame movies includes some of the 20th century's (and 21st century's too) brightest lights. A full list would take too much space, but a sampling includes Helen Hays, Anthony Hopkins, Alec Guinness, Charlton Heston, Vanessa Redgrave, James Stewart, Elizabeth Taylor, Ben Kingsley, Anna Paquin, and Christopher Walken. All of these names bear something in common—they are all Oscar winners. In fact, a full one-quarter of all actors who have won Academy Awards have at some time appeared in a Hallmark Hall of Fame presentation.

In 2011, the Hallmark Hall of Fame will celebrate its 60th season on the air. Having spanned nearly the entire history of commercial television, the program stands alone as the longest running show on television. Its remarkable longevity would surely not have been possible had J.C. Hall's mantra—top entertainment but top quality, too—not been followed.

When Don Hall took over stewardship of the franchise in the late 1960s, he added a directive for more emotional programming—not to replace his father's guiding principals of quality and taste but to add to them. Don Hall Jr., the current CEO of Hallmark, has since defined the Hall of Fame's mission even more precisely. Moore well remembers a conversation with Don Jr. in the early 1990s. "He said, 'Why don't we agree that it's about quality, good taste, and enriching relationships?' So that's our statement to this day."

Like so many of the show's longtime fans, Don Hall Jr. fondly remembers watching the show with his family when he was a child. "It wasn't static entertainment," Hall says. "It was really about important life lessons that could be gained in a living room. There's something very magical about the shared experience of watching a show together that has great thought-provoking themes."

Through myriad changes in the television medium, and more recently in all the new media that has emerged to compete for viewers' attention, the Hallmark Hall of Fame still shines—a paragon of television broadcasting and a much-anticipated seasonal gift to its audience. The company's commitment has never flagged, even when economic conditions might have made a less committed sponsor give up on the admittedly expensive-to-produce endeavor.

"One of the big advantages we have over other television programmers and even over motion picture studios is that we know that the management is going to be here supporting Hallmark Hall of Fame next year and the year after that and the year after that," says Parkinson.

Brad Moore likes to tell a story of being approached by the head of media and advertising for a major U.S. automobile manufacturer. The executive was interested in replicating the success of the Hall of Fame for his own company.

"He called me up and said, 'Tell me the secret to the Hallmark Hall of Fame,'" recalls Moore with a mischievous smile. "I said, 'I'll tell you the secret. Take your company private. Take it private, and make sure that whoever owns it is a really good family." Moore pauses, then continues. "Then call me back, and I'll tell you the next step.'"

Just as his father reaffirmed the company's commitment to the Hallmark Hall of Fame franchise, giving it new vigor in the middle of the 1980s, Don Hall Jr. touts its continued relevance for the company today.

"The Hallmark Hall of Fame is still one of the most important ways we have to brand our business. We associate our brand with quality and good taste and—just as importantly—with stories that help celebrate the human spirit. By being associated with these stories, we connect with the brand in a very meaningful way. The Hallmark Hall of Fame enlarges the sense of the brand beyond particular product formats to be about caring and connection."

"Good television is good business," J.C. Hall once famously observed when questioned about his motives in sponsoring of the Hallmark Hall of Fame. Sixty years and two generations later, The Hallmark Hall of Fame is still good business—and very good television—but for the millions of viewers who have been moved, motivated, enlightened, charmed, educated, and uplifted by this extraordinary program, it is much, much more.

TOP: Love Is Never Silent, *first broadcast in 1985, was a landmark film for the Hallmark Hall of Fame for many reasons. Hallmark initially planned to air the movie on CBS, but network executives at the time resisted Hallmark's plan to cast deaf actors in the roles of two deaf characters. Hallmark stood its ground and made the movie with Phyllis Frelich and Ed Waterstreet in lead roles. The movie aired on NBC and went on to win Emmys for outstanding drama and best director.*

ABOVE: Front of the Class, *was broadcast December 7, 2008, as the 234th presentation of the Hallmark Hall of Fame. It was based on the true story of Brad Cohen, who overcame Tourette's Syndrome to become an award-winning teacher. Jimmy Wolk (center) starred as Cohen.*

LEFT: The Courageous Heart of Irena Sendler *was first broadcast April 19, 2009. Academy Award winner Anna Paquin played the title role in the true story of a brave Polish nurse who helped save the lives of 2,500 Jewish babies and children in the Warsaw Ghetto during World War II.*

The Hallmark Hall of Fame Programs

1951   1. Amahl and The Night Visitors †
1952   2. Amahl and The Night Visitors *
      3. Amahl and The Night Visitors *
1953   4. Hamlet †
      5. Amahl and The Night Visitors *
1954   6. King Richard II
      7. Macbeth †
      8. Amahl and The Night Visitors
1955   9. Alice In Wonderland
   10. The Devil's Disciple
   11. Dream Girl
1956 12. The Corn is Green
   13. The Good Fairy
   14. The Taming of the Shrew
   15. The Cradle Song †
   16. Born Yesterday
   17. Man and Superman
   18. The Little Foxes
1957 19. The Lark
   20. There Shall Be No Right
   21. Yeoman of the Guard
   22. Green Pastures
   23. On Borrowed Time
   24. Twelfth Night †
1958 25. Hans Brinker or the
       Silver Skates
   26. Little Moon of Alban †
   27. Dial M For Murder
   28. Johnny Belinda
   29. Kiss Me, Kate
   30. The Christmas Tree
1959 31. Berkeley Square
   32. Green Pastures (r)
   33. Ah, Wilderness!
   34. Winterset
   35. A Doll's House
   36. A Christmas Festival
1960 37. The Tempest
   38. The Cradle Song (r)
   39. Captain Brassbound's
       Conversion
   40. Shangri-La
   41. Macbeth †
   42. Golden Child
1961 43. Time Remembered
   44. Give Us Barabbas
   45. The Joke and the Valley
   46. Macbeth (r)
   47. Victoria Regina †
1962 48. Arsenic & Old Lace
   49. Give Us Barabbas (r)
   50. The Teahouse of the
       August Moon
   51. Cyrano de Bergerac
1963 52. Pygmalion
   53. The Invincible Mr. Disraeli †
   54. The Tempest (r)
   55. The Patriots
   56. A Cry of Angels
1964 57. Abe Lincoln in Illinois
   58. Little Moon of Alban *
   59. The Fantasticks
   60. Other World of Winston
       Churchill
   61. Amahl and The Night Visitors *
1965 62. The Magnificent Yankee

   63. The Holy Terror †
   64. Eagle in a Cage †
   65. Inherit the Wind †
   66. Amahl and The Night
       Visitors (r)
1966 67. The Magnificent Yankee (r)
   68. Lamp at Midnight
   69. Barefoot in Athens †
   70. Blithe Spirit
1967 71. Abe Lincoln in Illinois (r)
   72. Anastasia
   73. Soldier In Love
   74. A Bell for Adano
   75. Saint Joan
1968 76. Elizabeth the Queen †
   77. Give Us Barabbas (r)
   78. The Admirable Crichton
   79. A Punt, a Pass and a Prayer
   80. Pinocchio
1969 81. Teacher, Teacher †
   82. Give Us Barabbas (r)
   83. Victoria Regina (r)
   84. The File on Devlin
   85. The Littlest Angel
1970 86. A Storm in Summer †
   87. Neither Are We Enemies
   88. Teacher, Teacher (r)
   89. Hamlet
   90. The Littlest Angel (r)
1971 91. The Price †
   92. Gideon †
   93. A Storm in Summer (r)
   94. The Snow Goose †
   95. All the Way Home †
   96. The Littlest Angel (r)
1972 97. Love! Love! Love!
   98. Harvey
   99. The Price (r)
 100. The Hands of Corm Joyce
 101. The Man Who Came to
       Dinner
 102. The Snow Goose (r)
1973 103. You're a Good Man,
       Charlie Brown
 104. The Small Miracle
 105. Lisa, Bright and Dark
 106. The Borrowers †
1974 107. The Country Girl
 108. Crown Matrimonial
 109. Brief Encounter
 110. The Gathering Storm
 111. The Borrowers (r)
1975 112. All Creatures Great
       and Small
 113. The Small Miracle (r)
 114. Eric
 115. Valley Forge †
 116. The Rivalry †
1976 117. Caesar and Cleopatra
 118. Truman at Postdam
 119. The Disappearance of Aimee
 120. Beauty and the Beast
 121. Peter Pan †
1977 122. Emily, Emily
 123. All Creatures Great and
       Small (r)

 124. The Last Hurrah
 125. The Court Martial of
       George Armstrong Custer
 126. Have I Got a Christmas
       for You
1978 127. Taxi!!!
 128. Peter Pan (r)
 129. Return Engagement
 130. Fame
 131. Stubby Pringle's Christmas
1979 132. Beauty and the Beast
 133. All Quiet on the Western
       Front †
 134. Aunt Mary †
1980 135. Gideon's Trumpet †
 136. A Tale of Two Cities
1981 137. Mister Lincoln
 138. Dear Lair
 139. Casey Stengel
 140. The Marva Collins Story †
1982 141. The Hunchback of
       Notre Dame
 142. Witness for the
       Prosecution
1983 143. Thursday's Child
 144. The Winter of Our
       Discontent
1984 145. The Master of Ballantrae
 146. Camille
1985 147. The Corsican Brothers
 148. Love Is Never Silent †
1986 149. Resting Place
 150. Love Is Never Silent (r)
 151. Promise †
1987 152. The Room Upstairs
 153. Pack of Lies †
 154. The Secret Garden †
 155. Foxfire †
1988 156. Stones for Ibarra
 157. April Morning
 158. The Tenth Man †
 159. Promise (r)
1989 160. Home Fires Burning
 161. My Name Is Bill W. †
 162. The Shell Seekers †
 163. The Secret Garden (r)
1990 164. Face to Face
 165. Caroline? †
 166. Decoration Day †
 167. Foxfire (r)
1991 168. Sarah, Plain and Tall †
 169. Shadow of a Doubt
 170. One Against the Wind †
 171. Caroline? (r)
1992 172. O Pioneers! †
 173. Miss Rose White †
 174. An American Story
 175. Sarah, Plain and Tall (r)
1993 176. Skylark
 177. Blind Spot
 178. To Dance With the
       White Dog †
 179. O Pioneers! (r)
1994 180. Breathing Lessons †
 181. A Place for Annie †
 182. The Return of the Native

1995 183. The Piano Lesson †
 184. Redwood Curtain
 185. Journey
 186. Breathing Lessons (r)
1996 187. The Boys Next Door †
 188. Harvest of Fire †
 189. Calm at Sunset
 190. The Summer of Ben Tyler †
1997 191. Old Man †
 192. Rose Hill
 193. What the Deaf Man Heard †
 194. Ellen Foster
1998 195. The Love Letter †
 196. The Echo of Thunder
 197. What the Deaf Man
       Heard (r)
 198. Saint Maybe
 199. Grace & Glorie †
1999 200. Night Ride Home
 201. Durango
 202. Sarah, Plain & Tall:
       Winter's End
 203. A Season for Miracles
2000 204. Missing Pieces
 205. Cupid & Cate
 206. The Lost Child †
 207. The Runaway
2001 208. The Flamingo Rising
 209. Follow the Stars Home
 210. In Love and War
 211. The Seventh Stream
2002 212. My Sister's Keeper †
 213. Little John
 214. The Locket †
2003 215. Brush With Fate
 216. A Painted House †
 217. Fallen Angel †
2004 218. The Blackwater Lightship †
 219. Plainsong †
 220. A Painted House (r)
 221. Back When We Were
       Grownups
 222. Fallen Angel (r)
2005 223. The Magic of Ordinary
       Days †
 224. Riding the Bus with My
       Sister
 225. Silver Bells †
2006 226. The Water Is Wide †
 227. In From the Night
 228. Candles on Bay Street †
2007 229. The Valley of Light
 230. Crossroads: A Story of
       Forgiveness
 231. Pictures of Hollis Woods
2008 232. The Russell Girl
 233. Sweet Nothing In My Ear
 234. Front of the Class
2009 235. Loving Leah
 236. The Courageous Heart of
       Irena Sendler
 237. A Dog Named Christmas

    * Encore performance
    (r) Repeat
    † Award-winning program

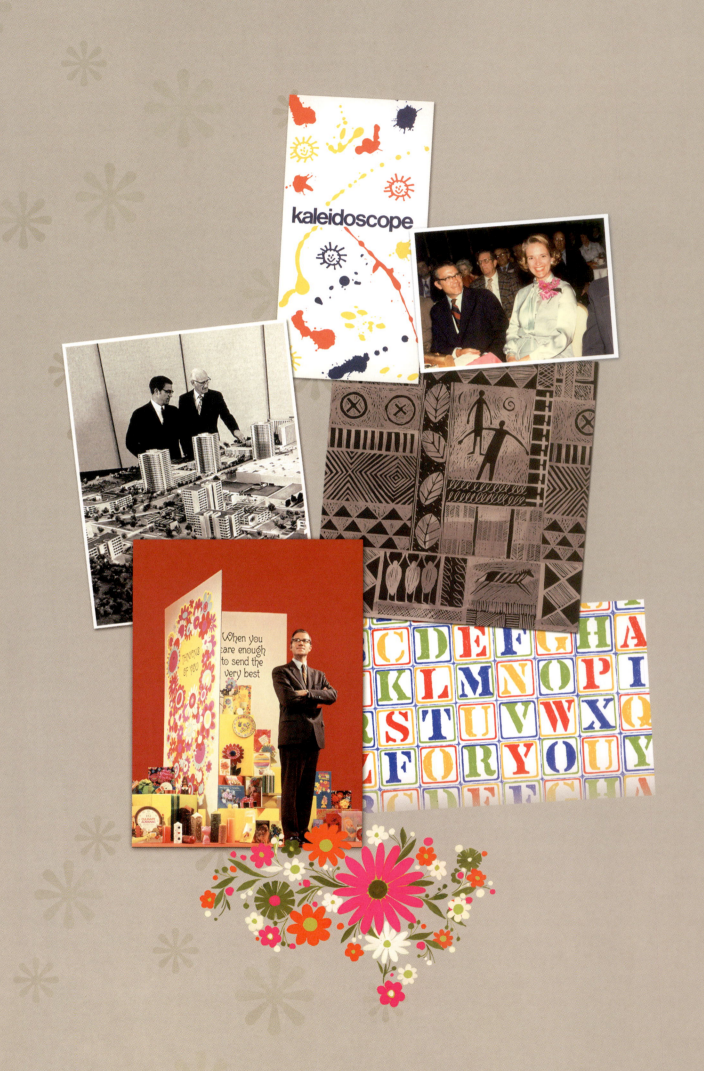

CHAPTER EIGHT

The Modernist

(1966–1980)

> # *"He can see 20 years into the future. That's what his real genius is... and he's got the guts to stick with his vision."*
>
> *— Charles Egan on Don Hall*

O N MARCH 16, 1966, DONALD J. HALL BECAME PRESIDENT AND CHIEF EXECUTIVE OFFICER OF HALLMARK CARDS. THE TRANSFER OF POWER WAS NOT UNEXPECTED. THE 37 YEAR-OLD HALL HAD BEEN BORN INTO THE COMPANY and groomed for leadership since childhood. Still, the enormity of the appointment is difficult to overstate. For 56 years, the ultimate direction of Hallmark Cards had been the purview of one man, its founder, Joyce C. Hall. The elder Hall would still lend his considerable presence to the company and continue to serve as chairman of the board. But on March 16, 1966, the seat of power shifted, and an agent of change assumed command.

Don Hall was ready. He'd been an observant student of his father's business all his life. He had heard the stories, absorbed the lessons, and become fluent in the often esoteric vocabulary of this unique business. For more than a dozen years, he had poured his heart and energy into his father's company, leading a push for modern management, updated technology, improved employee benefits, and a broader view of what the company could and should be. But Don Hall was just getting started.

The changes Hall would bring over the next two decades would be profound. But they wouldn't be flashy. Anyone who knew Don Hall then or knows him now will tell you that is not his style. With Hall, you get dramatic results but without the drama. According to David Hughes, the transition of leadership was essentially invisible to the ranks of Hallmark employees.

> *"Don had a very good rapport with the guys who reported to his dad. There was no palace revolt. But Don was looking for some different traits in the people he hired—for one, he wanted people who could think for themselves a bit more."*

Don Hall's twin priorities were product and people. His watchword for product was diversification. In the first 18 months of his presidency, the company would begin production of candles, puzzles, and gift books. And though such extensions of the Hallmark line were aggressive, they were always deliberate. The foremost thought in

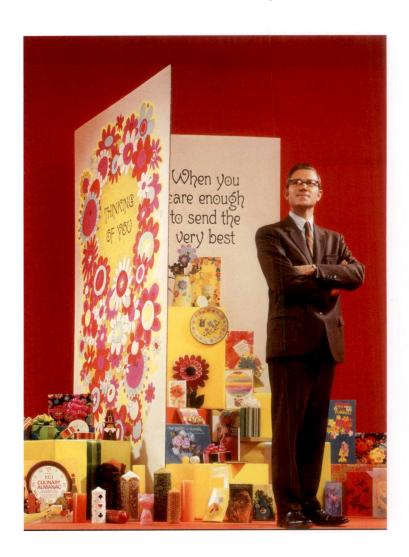

> "I TRY NOT TO STEER PEOPLE TOO MUCH. IF YOU HAVE FAITH TO MAKE THEM MANAGERS, THEY OUGHT TO HAVE THE FREEDOM TO PERFORM."
>
> *—Don Hall*

ABOVE: *When Don Hall took over as CEO of Hallmark Cards, one of his priorities was to take the company in new directions and expand its product offerings well beyond greeting cards.*

ABOVE: *Among puzzle aficio-nados, diemaker John Robrock was known for creating all of Hallmark's Springbok puzzle dies by hand. One of his challenges was giving each tiny puzzle piece a shape that was unique.*

BELOW: *The broad popularity of* Peanuts *made it the perfect licensed partner for experimenting with new Hallmark product categories—like playing cards, pencil erasers, and coin purses.*

diversifying its lines was always the needs of the independent card shop retailer.

It was with retailers in mind that Hallmark entered into the picture puzzle business in 1967. In the mid-1960s, puzzles were enjoying a renaissance of popularity in the United States. Much of the excitement was due to a new player in the field, a small company called Springbok Editions that created artful puzzles of excellent quality. In fact, Springbok's puzzles were so sought after that they retailed for as much as three times the average puzzle. In 1967 Hallmark acquired the company, greatly expanding its output and offerings. The popular puzzles were then made available exclusively in Hallmark shops. The move marked the first time Hallmark had used acquisition to diversify outside of its core greeting card business. The calculated gamble paid off. Within five years, sales of the Springbok line had increased sixfold.

By the dawn of the 1970s, Hallmark had diversified its lines even further, adding posters, children's books, and fine writing instruments worthy of the company's high-end stationery line. Each new product effort was held to the same standard set forth in the company's slogan—they had to be "the very best."

Making such significant additions to the product offering—while simultaneously expanding the traditional greeting card business—required incredible focus and plenty of talent. Having worked full-time at the company for a dozen years by 1966, Don Hall knew that there was no shortage of talent within the ranks, but he also saw opportunities to elevate the standing of some of his key lieutenants. In short order, he promoted Jeannette Lee to vice president and creative director, making her the first female corporate officer in the company's history. Lee, according to Hall, was "a star." "She could work with anybody, and she was, by nature, a person everybody liked.

She was an ideal person to be a role model for women in business, and we worked with her a great deal on elevating women in the company."

As part of the same restructuring that put Don Hall in the president's office, the decision was made to organize Hallmark's international business as a subsidiary corporation. To run the new business, Don Hall turned to another trusted veteran, his former mentor Ed Goodman. Members of Goodman's management team included Donald Gray (marketing) and Joe Kipp (director of international merchandising).

From the beginning, Don Hall exhibited a management philosophy in sharp contrast to that of his father. The younger Hall had long advocated what he calls "collegial decision making" and worked to create a more democratic workplace. Once at the helm of the company, he was able to usher in this new approach to business.

When talking about the changes and initiatives of the 1960s and '70s, Hall reflexively and invariably uses the pronoun "we," rather than "I." The "we" of Hall's inner circle included many familiar names and a growing number of new ones. There was Jeannette Lee, of course, and Harold Rice and Ken West were still setting the pace for technical innovations in lithography and production. Bill Harsh was an experienced and trusted counselor on personnel matters. New members of the executive committee included John Oakson (marketing) and Nathan Stark (operations). Hall also promoted bright, young managers David Hughes and Robert Stark to the vice-presidential level.

But Hall's democratic workplace extended well beyond the executive ranks. Interviewed in 1971, he explained, "I don't want us ever to decide we have all the answers. We need all the ideas we can get, and when our young people have ideas that can improve the company and the quality of our products, I want management to listen."

Despite their differences in management philosophy, Don Hall and J.C. Hall had many things in common, chief among them a steadfast belief in product quality and a commitment to supporting Hallmark's creative community. Jeannette Lee refers to the mid- to late-1960s as a period of creative explosion. "Everything changed," she explains. "Business changed. Product was different. The colors were so bold and exciting. We, the artists, all felt that it was just a wonderful time. The artists loved to travel, and we started sending them to Europe and Japan, and they'd come back and share the trends they saw."

If Don Hall's involvement in the creative ranks wasn't as hands-on as his father's, his support for their efforts was every bit as strong. In keeping with his approach to other branches

of the business, his strategy was to get the right people and give them genuine authority and freedom to do the job. A Hallmark executive of the era put it bluntly. "Don realized that the 'suits' needed to stay away from the creative groups." Hall explained his approach in a 1978 magazine interview:

"Restrictions and over-organization can impede creativity. It's important that our artists have the flexibility to stretch their wings."

"EVERYTHING CHANGED.
BUSINESS CHANGED,
PRODUCT WAS DIFFERENT.
THE COLORS WERE SO
BOLD AND EXCITING.
WE, THE ARTISTS, ALL
FELT THAT IT WAS JUST
A WONDERFUL TIME."

—*Jeannette Lee, on the creative
environment in the late 1960s*

THE WORLD IN THE 1960S

◆ In 1960, the U.S. Food and Drug Administration approves the use of the first effective oral contraceptive—the Pill, as it came to be known.

◆ Construction of the Berlin Wall is begun in the predawn hours of August 13, 1961.

◆ On April 12, 1961, Soviet Air Force Major Yuri Gagarin becomes the first man in space.

◆ Marilyn Monroe is found dead of an overdose on August 5, 1962.

◆ On October 14, 1962, an American spy plane detected a Soviet-supplied ballistic missle on the island of Cuba. For the next two weeks, the U.S.S.R. and the United States face the real prospect of nuclear war. In the end, the Russian government agrees to dismantle its weapons, as long as the United States agrees not to invade Cuba.

◆ AT&T launches the first communications satellite, "Telstar," in 1962.

◆ Martin Luther King Jr. delivers his transcendent "I Have a Dream" speech to 300,000 people gathered at the Washington Monument on August 28,1963.

◆ President Kennedy is assassinated in Dallas on November 23,1963.

◆ "Beatlemania" hits the U.S. as The Beatles stage their first American concert on February 11, 1964, in Washington, D.C. An appearance on *The Ed Sullivan Show* two days earlier was watched by 74 million viewers—about half the American population.

◆ Wilt Chamberlain, playing for the NBA's Philadelphia Warriors, scores 100 points in a single regulation-length game.

◆ The Gulf of Tonkin Resolution, which begins the war in Vietnam, and the Civil Rights Act are enacted in 1964.

◆ The first heart transplant is performed by Dr. Christiaan Barnard in 1967.

◆ The first Super Bowl is played between the Green Bay Packers and the Kansas City Chiefs in 1967. The Packers win 35–10.

◆ On July 21, 1969, American astronaut Neil Armstrong steps down from his *Apollo 11* landing craft onto the surface of the moon in "one giant leap for mankind."

◆ Four hundred thousand young people flock to a three-day music festival in August of 1969 on a farm in Woodstock, New York.

THE RESTLESS MIND OF HENRY DREYFUSS

"He has a great faculty and enthusiasm for finding and proposing ideas—and then backing away to let the ideas rise or fall on their own merit. Usually he has ideas faster than anyone around him can digest them. So if one idea doesn't work, the next one will."

—J.C. Hall on Henry Dreyfuss

For J.C. Hall, one of the great advantages of success was an ever-growing network of connections to the highest achievers in art, entertainment, science, and business. Often, he would seek out the acquaintance of someone he admired simply by asking a mutual friend to make an introduction. However, it was his longtime friend, advertising executive Fairfax Cone, who suggested—even insisted—that Hall meet the legendary industrial designer, Henry Dreyfuss. Cone told Hall, "He's the only man I know who is a professional shopper like you." Cone meant that both Dreyfuss and Hall "shopped for ideas, not purchases."

By the time Hall met Dreyfuss in the mid-1950s, the designer could already claim a record of achievement in his field that few, if any, had ever matched. From the 1930s on, Dreyfuss had invented, improved, or reimagined consumer products ranging from alarm clocks to locomotives. A partial list of his achievements includes the first combined handset telephone, the Hoover Model 150 vacuum cleaner, the Westclox Big Ben alarm clock, the streamlined Mercury train and locomotive, the Honeywell circular wall thermostat, safety razors, fountain pens, John Deere tractors, and the Polaroid Model 100 camera.

Throughout the 1930s, '40s, and '50s, Dreyfuss had consulted with dozens of the country's biggest and most innovative companies. But what could he do for Hallmark Cards? J.C. Hall wasn't at all sure, but from his very first meeting with the man, Hall knew that Dreyfuss brought an unmatchable intelligence and imagination to any conversation he joined. Hall recalled their first meeting in his book, *When You Care Enough*:

"I invited Dreyfuss to spend a day with us in Kansas City. After looking over our operation and meeting our crew of artists, he didn't see how he could be of much service. However, in getting to know him, I was convinced he could make a great contribution by bringing new ideas to us and improving old ones."

Dreyfuss took up that challenge, and from the early 1960s, until his death in 1972, he was a highly valued consultant to the company. His contributions covered the broad range one would expect from such an idea-rich iconoclast. They ranged from dashed-off suggestions regarding color palettes for greeting cards to in-depth consultations on the developments of the Crown Center complex, the Hallmark Gallery in New York City, and Halls Country Club Plaza department store.

Don Hall shared his father's admiration for Dreyfuss. He explains that though it may be hard for an outsider to identify Dreyfuss' contribution to the company, his influence was nonetheless ever-present. "No one," Don Hall has often said, "had the ability to stir us up creatively like Henry Dreyfuss did." When Dreyfuss died in 1972, Hall ruminated on his impact in the company's *Noon News* newsletter:

"Henry Dreyfuss' influence on Hallmark has been felt in many ways. Although there are few products or programs that are a direct result of his efforts, everything that we have done for many years has been influenced to some extent by his advice."

As for his thoughts on Hallmark, Dreyfuss, toward the end of his life, credited the company with starting him on a third career as a corporate consultant. (His first career, in the 1920s, was as a theatrical and set designer.)

In 1971, Hallmark staged a retrospective exhibit of Dreyfuss' work at the Halls Plaza store, which Dreyfuss had helped design. In an introduction to the exhibition, J.C. Hall wrote, "He had decided to retire from an active role in his industrial design firm but wanted to stay involved in creative work, and Hallmark seemed to point that way. Henry joined us as kind of a super dreamer. He liked this kind of dreaming so well he went on to serve as corporate consultant to John Deere, AT&T, and others."

"Our association has been so unusual," Hall continued. "We call him a consultant, but 'friend' might be a more appropriate word."

"He had the most creative mind I've ever known. It ran as smoothly and effectively as a Rolls Royce engine. His personality was equal to his ability. He was wonderful to be with—in spite of the fact that he left you mentally, though pleasantly, exhausted. He contributed taste, beauty, and quality to all our endeavors."

—J.C. Hall on Henry Dreyfuss

HENRY DREYFUSS

J,

"Pardon my language"

—but the attached has an (idea) in it — to make the message a bold part of the form. Does it deserve some explanation?

Henry

2.12.70

HENRY DREYFUSS

J. Would you consider some "animated" fruit for a series of cards? or a lot of it on one?

5.28.69

HENRY DREYFUSS

Jeanette,

Do you ever see N.M. mailings? This is a good one (missing are some ways to close (+open) envelopes which I've mailed to D. Hughes). I like the cover— front + back— Have you ever done a double-decker ice-cream cone card? Could the scoops of ice cream be round holes in the cover + in some

OVER →

magic Hallmark way let the recipient choose the flavors?

I prefer chocolate.

5.4.71

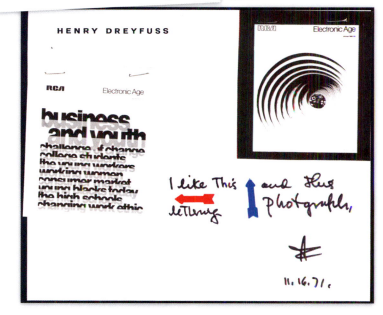

HENRY DREYFUSS

RCA   Electronic Age

business and youth

I like This ← lettering   and This ↑ Photographs,

11.16.71

HENRY DREYFUSS

Some fresh ideas for napkins.

I like the kids' drawings for Happy Birthday + wonder if REAL kid drawings wouldn't make a great + colorful party set.

ABOVE AND RIGHT: A few of the many idea cards and notes Henry Dreyfuss sent to Hallmark over the years.

Moving and Shaking

A quiet revolution was underway at Hallmark in the late 1960s. But outside its walls—all across America—a noisy, dissonant, and often violent upheaval was raging. Civil rights struggles, the escalation of the Vietnam War, assassinations, and political unrest all tore at the social fabric of the nation. Hallmark's hometown saw its share of tumult and turbulence. War protesters regularly filled Kansas City's Volker Park. And in the wake of Martin Luther King Jr.'s murder in the spring of 1968, several nights of looting and burning scarred the city's urban core. A series of construction strikes crippled the city, and downtown continued its decline as blight crept out from its increasingly abandoned edges. A 1966 article in *Fortune* magazine described downtown Kansas City as "a dead spot at the heart and crossroads of America."

Though the facts of downtown's decline were indisputable, that kind of assessment of his hometown was unacceptable to Don Hall. Those who know him are keenly aware that behind his low-key demeanor is an extremely high-energy worker—and a fighter. And Don Hall has always thought that his community was worth fighting for.

"I have strong feelings about this city," Hall explained in a 1974 interview with the *Kansas City Star*. "I think it's a super place to live and an extremely fine location to operate in the business world."

In his battle to keep Kansas City a viable place to live and work throughout the 1960s and '70s, Don Hall had two major

weapons: his formidable company and his seemingly unexpendable energy.

By the late 1960s, Hallmark had gained traction in many of the areas that had been priorities to Don Hall when he had taken over the company. Production and distribution facilities had been significantly upgraded or were in the process of being upgraded. Management was well coordinated, empowered, and poised for growth. And product diversification was making the card-shop-focused retail strategy an unqualified success. The net result of these actions was a company that was bigger, healthier, and better balanced than at any time in its history.

But to look out in nearly any direction from the top floor of Hallmark's headquarters was to see an urban environment that was not nearly so healthy. Over the next several years, in ways both small and audaciously large, Don Hall would lead a push to reinvigorate the city he loved.

He led by example. From the beginning of his career, Hall threw himself into Kansas City's civic and charitable communities. He typically slept only three to four hours a night throughout the 1960s and '70s. "Time is a flexible animal," Don Hall insists, and in those busy decades he stretched his waking and working hours to the breaking point.

His typical day started with a four-mile run in the dark. That was followed by a 7:00 a.m. breakfast meeting with other community and business leaders so that he could be at his desk by 8:15. A civic or business dinner often followed his workday, but he tried hard to be home with his three children in the evenings. When the kids went off to bed, he went back to work. All three of his children insist that they never saw him open his briefcase during the evening family time. (Adele Hall had a similar commitment to honoring time with family. One of her favorite sayings is, "Leave the dishes in the sink and play with your kids.")

LEFT: *Don Hall's tremendous civic contributions were formally recognized by the Greater Kansas City Chamber of Commerce when it named him "Mr. Kansas City" in 1972. His father won the award in 1961. Pictured (l. to r.) are Donald Hall Jr., Margi Hall, J.C. Hall, David Hall (front), Don Hall, and Adele Hall.*

"I'VE ALWAYS HAD TROUBLE GOING TO SLEEP. WHEN I WAS A LITTLE KID, I'D LIE IN BED AND STARE UP AT THE CEILING AND I COULD BE AWAKE ALL NIGHT. TO AVOID DOING THAT I LEARNED TO WAIT UNTIL I WAS TIRED ENOUGH BEFORE GOING TO BED. IN COLLEGE I'D START MY WORK WHEN EVERYBODY ELSE HAD GONE TO BED. AND IT'S STILL THE CASE. IF I KNOW I HAVE SOMETHING TO DO, I CAN START AT MIDNIGHT AND WORK AT IT PRETTY EFFECTIVELY UNTIL IT'S DONE. I LIKE TO FINISH THINGS, AND EARLY IN THE MORNING OR LATE AT NIGHT I FEEL SHARPEST."

—*Don Hall*

Don Hall's list of volunteer appointments during those years is prodigious. He served on the board of the Kansas City Chamber of Commerce, the Civic Council, the Full Employment Council, the Minority Supplier Development Council, the Harry S. Truman Library Institute, and a host of other organizations. At the same time, he was a director of the Federal Reserve Bank and a trustee of the Midwest Research Institute.

Often invited to sit on corporate boards, Hall was highly selective in accepting. Time spent on corporate boards, he knew, was time no longer available for the civic causes so important to him. "I said I'd never be on more than three (corporate) boards, and I counted ours as one," he said.

"I had a philosophy of not joining an outside commercial board unless I could learn something. I was asked to go on the board of Dayton Hudson at the same time I was asked to go on the board of Ford. Franklin Murphy (who had recommended Hall at Ford) couldn't understand my going on Dayton Hudson, but that was a retail operation and noted for great corporate governance. I thought I'd learn something there, and I did."

Hall knew the difference that even one dedicated person could make, and he encouraged his management team and all Hallmark employees to find ways to contribute to their community. "He wanted his officers to be on the boards of civic things and charity things," explained longtime friend and former president of Hallmark David Hughes, "not on corporate boards."

"BUSINESS IS NOW UNDERSTANDING THE OPPORTUNITY IT HAS TO HAVE IMPACT ON SOCIAL CHANGE, AND BUSINESS PEOPLE HAVE THE EXPERTISE TO AFFECT IT. THE PLACE TO START IS ONE-ON-ONE IN THE COMMUNITIES WHERE YOU DO BUSINESS."

—*Don Hall,* Madison Avenue Magazine, *1978*

"I HAVE TO OWN UP TO THIS—I DON'T HAVE PATIENCE. I NEVER WANTED TO CULTIVATE IT. ADELE HAS ETERNAL PATIENCE. I JUST DON'T."

—*Don Hall*

In his characteristically quiet way, Hall looked for ways to make his own company a better corporate citizen.

One byproduct of the 1960s civil-rights struggles was an emphasis on better job training for racial minorities and the economically disadvantaged. Both government-funded and private programs sprung up around the country. For private companies, altruism was not always the primary motivation. "A lot of companies started (job training programs) for PR purposes," explains Hall. "They made a show out of training but had no jobs for people when the training ended. We agreed that such programs were important to the community, but it just didn't seem appropriate to make it a public relations project. So we opened a training center in the most depressed area of the city, but one of the tenets of it was that we would keep it under our hats. We didn't let anyone know about it."

Even without a self-aggrandizing publicity campaign, the people who needed to find out about the training center—those in need of a hand up—did. Word spread through the inner city, and soon, in a nondescript one-story building at Eighth and Highland Street, without so much as a simple sign over the door, scores of so-called unemployables were learning not just job skills but also the fundamentals of arithmetic, literacy, and language. The only prerequisites were that they have dependents and an honest desire to work. Trainees became full-time Hallmark employees from their very first day.

"It was a marvelous thing," remembers Hall, "and very successful. After a period of time, when we felt they were ready, we'd move them into the regular workforce where they became indistinguishable from other employees as to pay, benefits, seniority, and future advancement."

It was a classic case of doing well by doing good. "Our longevity with those people was much better than those we hired through standard means," Hall points out. The program operated for a dozen years, and as far as Hall knows, it never garnered a word of positive press for the company. He didn't mind a lick. "It simply wasn't a motivation of ours. Our motivation was to get good people to work and to help people out."

Hallmark's distribution center in Liberty, Missouri (20 miles north of Kansas City), is a massive marvel of technology and efficiency. Opened in 1972 to fill and ship orders to retail customers in 32 states of the central, southern, and western United States, the center is one of the largest and most sophisticated warehouses in the country. In an average day, Liberty employees fill 9,000 orders, as 12 miles of electronically controlled conveyers move an average of 44,000 cartons through the distribution center's 37 acres of interior space. Even with this large volume, Liberty Hallmarkers maintain 99.8 percent accuracy in filing orders. About 60 percent of all Hallmark products are shipped out of the Liberty distribution center. Hallmark maintains a similar distribution center, which serves retailers of the eastern United States, in Enfield, Connecticut.

HAROLD RICE

On his Hallmark job application, Harold Rice wrote that he was "seeking the chance for advancement." He found it at Hallmark. Starting at the bottom as a lithography retouch artist in 1941, he retired 44 years later as a group vice president and member of the Hallmark board of directors. Dozens of breakthrough innovations occurred under his leadership. The center for technology and innovation, which he'd proposed, was under construction—and it was announced at his retirement dinner that this large addition to corporate headquarters would be named the Rice Innovation Center.

Harold Rice had three abilities prized at Hallmark: an artist's skill, an engineer's grasp of technology, and a gift for reconciling these often opposing disciplines in a language both could comprehend.

A Kansas City native, Rice graduated from Kansas City Junior College. His passion then was wildlife painting, and he never gave it up. He took the retouch job because there wasn't an opening for a wildlife painter. Then came an assignment that would get him noticed by J.C. Hall himself. Rice was asked to paint a set of 12 miniature wildlife paintings of upland game birds and waterfowl for the cover of a card featuring the work of Lynn Bogue Hunt, the dean of American wildlife art. Hunt had to approve the cover art, and he'd rejected four sets of paintings by the time Rice got the job.

Rice spent a weekend painting in his tiny apartment. His completed work was flown to New York City, where Hunt quickly okayed it. Rice was called to J.C. Hall's office where he got the news—and some rare words of praise. In a career with many high points, it's a moment that Rice always mentions first.

Harold Rice began his move up the corporate ladder inspired by a simple understanding. "We were selling art and color," he says. "If J.C. Hall approved artwork a certain way, he wanted the print that went out to the market to look as much like the original as possible." Over the years, no one did more to close the gap between original and reproduction than Harold Rice.

Rice was promoted to lithography supervisor in 1943 and head of the lithography department in 1946. In 1958, he was asked by J.C. Hall to lead a new Department of Creative Mechanics, in which all the toolmaking departments were brought together to get the best reproductions based on existing technology. "The idea was that the artist was always right," Rice says. "Always."

But the technology of the day had its limits, and soon Rice was leading the effort to push it forward. In 1965 he became director of advanced technical research. "Work was already moving from concept to reality on a variety of color reproduction improvements when I received my new assignment," remembers Rice. "It didn't start with me, but I was supportive of the work being done."

"Along with the new assignment came the realization that we could have a physics lab and not have anybody laugh at us if we hired the right people," Rice recalls. "We could have a chemistry lab, a laser lab, a computer center." With a team of researchers and engineers housed in a former garment building in downtown Kansas City, innovations came. There were new standardized inks, new ways of using cameras to make plates for printing those inks, ways to adapt litho color separation techniques to gravure printing, and a breakthrough method of etching gravure cylinders.

Some successes had no market application, while others were ahead of their time. For instance, a solar energy generator was conceived while researchers developed a successful three-dimensional printing process using plastic lenses to focus light. The generator was built, and it worked. But no company was interested in mass-producing it.

"We were doing fun things," Rice recalls. "But we were doing things that were important because we were learning to be really technical."

As Hallmark grew, Rice's responsibilities increased. He became director of manufacturing in 1967 and group vice president of operations in 1972. In 1975, he was elected to the board of directors. He even served as chairman of Crown Center Redevelopment Corporation for a year and a half in the early 1980s before returning to his position as head of operations.

Though Rice spent most of his Hallmark career as a top-level manager, his early passion for painting still inspired him as he shepherded many of Hallmark's advances in graphic arts and manufacturing.

"Harold's creative experience early in his career has given him an unusual insight to our company's goals," says Jeannette Lee, a longtime colleague.

Ken West, a lifelong friend as well as a Hallmark vice president, concurs: "Harold combines artistic ability with the ability to inspire and motivate people—a unique combination of talents."

"He believed strongly that when you take creative capability and combine it with technical expertise in a shared environment, you can spark new ideas and opportunities for us to grow through innovation."
—Patti Streeper, Vice President—Corporate Innovation

GAIL FLORES

In painting flowers for four decades—flowers in still lifes, flowers in garden landscapes, flowers in intricate patterns—it helps to like painting flowers. Fortunately, Gail Flores does.

"I lucked out," the artist says. "My passion was my profession."

Even her name is her profession—Flores in Spanish means flowers.

But when Flores was hired into Hallmark's illustration studio in 1961, she was not a floral specialist. She'd learned other skills while getting her bachelor's in illustration. But Hallmark used a lot of flower paintings, so she learned how. And it stuck.

"The training, the adventure, the experience of finding a job that matched my talents—that's what Hallmark was for me," she says.

Flores retired in 2000, but she still gets a kick from seeing her flowers on Hallmark cards. "Ten years later, I recognize them," she says. "Even when there have been changes to them on a computer, I can spot them. Fortunately, I'm a commercial artist and I like the business end. I like seeing my work on Hallmark products."

ALICE ANN BIGGERSTAFF

Alice Ann Biggerstaff discovered "wide-awake colors" on a trip to Mexico. In suitcases stuffed with shawls, bedspreads, and other handcrafts—in deep reds, lush oranges, and hot pinks—she brought these colors back to Hallmark.

She grew up in the Kansas City area and began in 1955 in Hallmark's Design Studio, where she became a leader with a paint brush, always working at the boards. Putting life and energy into shapes and textures, Alice Ann impressed Jeannette Lee and her longtime supporter, J.C. Hall. He knew she'd be a worthy match for the new color reproduction boom going on at Hallmark—that she'd push the technicians with her "wide-awake colors," which she did until retiring in 1987.

When Alice Ann died in late 2007, her friend, the award-winning children's book author Tomie dePaola, called her "one of life's true originals."

From Blighted to Beautiful: The Crown Center Story

As far back as 1936—the year his company moved into a new headquarters at Twenty-fifth and Grand Avenue—J.C. Hall had begun buying property adjacent to the plant. His motivation was simple. "We didn't want to wake up some morning with an undesirable operation in front of us."

The strategy was foresighted but not completely sufficient. By the time Hallmark had built its major addition in the mid-1950s, much of the surrounding neighborhood was an eyesore populated by dilapidated warehouses, vacant buildings, used car lots, and a smattering of substandard houses.

"The exodus to suburbia had a devastating effect on the city core. As more and more citizens moved out, the heart of the community weakened. Areas that had pulsed with life began to decay...tax bases dwindled, crime increased, and boarded-up windows became a more familiar sight.

If, as city planner Victor Gruen notes, the term 'decentralization' was on everybody's lips in the early '50s, it was soon coupled with 'urban renewal,' a federal government effort to shore up decaying downtowns."

—*Former Kansas City city manager and Crown Center president, Bob Kipp*

Perhaps worst of all was the prominent limestone outcropping standing a block to the west of Hallmark and just south of the city's stately Union Station. Home to a grand Bavarian-style beer garden and picnic ground called Tivoli Garden in the 1870s, nearly a century later the blocks-long bluff had long ago gone to seed. Its dubious contribution to the area's aesthetic now was the proliferation of garish billboards that covered its craggy sides. Signboard Hill, as the promontory was unofficially-but-universally known, was a Kansas City landmark but not a proud one.

"Someone who claims to have trekked up on top of Signboard Hill in recent times vows that he discovered rabbits and other species of wild game, a sort of graveyard of signboard skeletons, a few rusted tin cans, and some remnants of tarpaper shacks."
—*The* Kansas City Times, *Jan. 4, 1967*

When, in 1958, Signboard Hill came up for sale, J.C. Hall didn't hesitate. He purchased the property with the vague notion that it would be a fine place for a first-class hotel someday, something he believed Kansas City badly needed.

In the years that followed, even as the area continued its decline, Hallmark quietly acquired surrounding properties whenever they became available. "Before long, we were in the real estate business and wondered what to do about it," J.C. Hall wrote in his memoir.

Planning decisions weren't made hastily or without input—far from it. Don Hall recounted the process in a 1971 interview with *Nation's Business* magazine. "At first there was talk, mind-stretching brain sessions with old friend Walt Disney ('Get plenty of land, don't crowd yourself as we did in Anaheim'); with architect Ed Stone, who was designing the Hallmark Gallery in New York; and with our own executives such as Lynn Bauer (then president of Crown Center)."

Then came land-use studies by Victor Gruen, feasibility studies by economic consultant Larry Smith, development discussions with Jim Rouse, and the typical idea-packed input from industrial designer Henry Dreyfuss. In one memorable visit with I.M. Pei, Hall recalls the architect suggesting far-too-grand a plan to develop everything between Hallmark headquarters and downtown. As Don Hall remembers, "What was to become Crown Center grew, shrank, and changed in concept almost weekly." But with each iteration, one thing became increasingly clear, this endeavor afforded an almost unheard of opportunity to address myriad ills of an urban area in one great swoop.

On Wednesday, January 4, 1967, Don Hall led a group of Hallmark executives to City Hall where, amidst a buzz of TV cameras and reporters, he presented to Kansas City's mayor nearly 50 pounds

> "THERE HAD BEEN SOME HALFHEARTED ATTEMPTS AT DEVELOPMENT DOWNTOWN, BUT NOTHING SEEMED TO WORK. WE THOUGHT MAYBE THIS RATHER BOLD DEVELOPMENT RIGHT ON ITS SOUTHERN EDGE WOULD GIVE COURAGE TO DEVELOPERS DOWNTOWN."
>
> *—Don Hall*

ABOVE LEFT: *At 27th and Oak Street a row of abandoned storefronts wait to be demolished where the main Hallmark employee parking garage now stands.*

ABOVE RIGHT: *By late 1975 a new hotel, later to become the Westin Crown Center, stood at the foot of what had been known for decades as Signboard Hill.*

BELOW LEFT: *In May 1981 only a shell remained of the Brace Oldsmobile Building on the east side of Grand Street at 27th Street.*

BELOW RIGHT: *The first building of the Crown Center complex, now called the 2480 Building, went up across 25th Street from the main Hallmark headquarters building in the early 1970s.*

of maps, models, exhibits, affidavits, surveys, and photographs. Their proposal to the city was a whopper: complete redevelopment of 25 city blocks on the southern edge of the central business district.

"The intent of the visit to City Hall is to win an official blessing for a noble experiment. Let private industry take a crack at urban renewal. Let one firm replace 85 acres of blight with a model urban community."
—Don Hall, 1967

The plan, as presented, was for a true mixed-use development, including a million square feet of office space, a thousand hotel rooms, 2,500 apartments for 9,000 people, 7,000 concealed parking spots, and an innovative retail-cultural center—all surrounding a 10-acre park-like central square with fountains, museum-quality art installations, and a winter ice-skating rink. In essence, the plan proposed building a model city-within-a-city.

The reaction was immediate—and exuberant. Mayor Ilus Davis called the Crown Center plan a "majestic concept," and alluded to its potential to inspire even more development. "This is a milestone in Kansas City's growth," Davis said, "...a resounding vote of confidence by Crown Center in Kansas City's growth and international importance."

The media similarly endorsed the project. In its lead editorial the day after Hall's presentation, the *Kansas City Times* effused, "The concept is bold and so is the plan of execution." While noting that the development still hinged upon approval from the city planning commission and city hall, the endorsement went on to say, "We simply cannot conceive of anyone standing in the way of this tremendous opportunity."

"TODAY KANSAS CITY IS ON THE THRESHOLD OF A PROUD NEW ERA. THE OLD YEAR ENDED WITH THE TRIUMPHANT PASSAGE OF THE AIRPORT BONDS... THE NEW YEAR BEGINS WITH THE CROWN CENTER ANNOUNCEMENT. WITH SUCH MOMENTUM, OTHERS SHOULD BE ENCOURAGED TO DREAM BIG, TOO. WITHOUT A DOUBT, THE MID-1960S SHOULD BE LANDMARK YEARS IN THE HISTORY OF KANSAS CITY."

—Kansas City Times, January 5, 1967

ABOVE: *By June of 1977 the 26th Street Bridge spanning McGee Street awaited the wrecker's ball. In the background, to the right, the former Hall Brothers headquarters at 26th and Walnut housed Hallmark's candy factory.*

OPPOSITE TOP: *With the Crown Center complex in the background, excavation was underway on the Hyatt Regency Crown Center hotel by May of 1978.*

OPPOSITE BOTTOM: *Don Hall and J.C. Hall look over the master-plan model of Crown Center.*

"BECAUSE WE BELIEVE IN DOWNTOWNS, CROWN CENTER HAS BEEN DESIGNED TO COMPLEMENT THE CENTRAL BUSINESS DISTRICT RATHER THAN COMPETE WITH IT—ESPECIALLY IN RETAILING."

—Don Hall

An editorial in the city's other major daily paper took the praise even further, blithely suggesting that the city erect a statue of "a cigar as tall as the Liberty Memorial" in honor of the cigar salesman who persuaded a young Joyce Hall to move to town back in 1910.

Both J.C. and Don Hall were well aware of the plan's audacity—and its potential price tag—but Don Hall laid out the company's rationale in a 1971 interview. "First and last, we are businessmen. We believe in business and always seek a reasonable profit in our endeavors. Would Crown Center be good for Hallmark? Yes. Would it be good for Kansas City? Yes. Would it inspire private industry to get into the urban problem? Hopefully, yes."

City government embraced the plan without reservation. The

land was condemned and sold to the newly formed Crown Center Redevelopment Corporation at fair market value. Remarkably, only 19 residents were displaced by the land clearing. In the fall of 1968, the first ground was turned on what would be a decades-long construction project. The original vision for Crown Center had been his father's, but the execution of that dream was in the hands of Don Hall.

"Dad had a campus-type concept in mind," recalls Don Hall, "but this is the middle of a city and there's no way economically you can do that. We knew we'd have to build more densely to make it even remotely feasible." An early and important decision was the selection of Edward Larrabee Barnes as master planner for the development. He would coordinate the work of other architects and personally design the first office complex, the central square, and the retail center. His initial excitement about the project was reflected in a letter he later wrote to Don Hall:

"I'll never forget it. A great piece of empty land sloping away from the Hallmark headquarters with downtown Kansas City in the distance. And we were asked what to do with it—to shape a whole new section of the city. This was an architect's dream."
—Edward Larrabee Barnes, Crown Center master planner

Don Hall's personal interest in architecture is prodigious. "If I'm a frustrated anything," he has said, "I'm a frustrated architect." Together with Barnes and a handful of Hallmark executives, Hall started interviewing some of the nation's most prominent and progressive architects. The final list of contributors to the

Crown Center complex includes some of the country's best: Harry Weese, Warren Plattner, Norman Fletcher, Henry Cobb, and landscape architect Dan Kiley.

The bulk of Crown Center's construction was completed between 1970 and 1980, but the grand experiment in urban planning that began as a dream some 50 years ago is still evolving. And there is still room to grow—15 acres await further development (most likely residential) whenever demand dictates.

While the office and hotel properties have had consistent success over the years, the retail end has always proved a challenge due to the lack of a natural residential market. In the early 1980s, Crown Center management began placing more emphasis on entertainment, adding cinemas, a live theater, and more special events and exhibits. The Crown Center square, with its beautiful lawns, landscaping, and fountains, has also become a more consistent entertainment destination. In winter, the square offers outdoor ice-skating and is home to the mayor's Christmas tree and Christmas village. Summers are filled with free movies, concerts, and a diverse schedule of popular music and ethnic festivals.

Whether or not Crown Center had the effect he and his father had hoped—that it would spur nearby urban redevelopment—Don Hall will not hazard a guess. But a quick survey of the neighborhood would seem to support the notion. Since the time Crown Center was developed, the city's grand Union Station across the street has undergone a massive rehabilitation. It now serves as a multiuse entertainment destination linked to the Westin Crown Center Hotel by a glass and steel elevated walkway. Other nearby investments include a new Federal Reserve Bank building just south of Crown Center and the nearly $400 million IRS campus just to the west of Union Station on Pershing Road. That project included renovation of the city's historic Main Post Office. More recently, and farther north, construction of the new H&R Block headquarters, the Sprint Center Arena, and the Power & Light entertainment district have all brought new vitality to Kansas City's downtown. Perhaps even more encouraging—and closer to the hearts of Hallmark's own enormous artistic community—is the organic growth of the Crossroads arts district tucked in between Crown Center and downtown.

Whatever its role in inspiring the ongoing renewal of the city's core, Crown Center is no longer an oasis in a desert of decay but instead the cornerstone of an exciting urban revival.

RIGHT: *Panoramic view of Crown Center looking east from the Westin Hotel.*

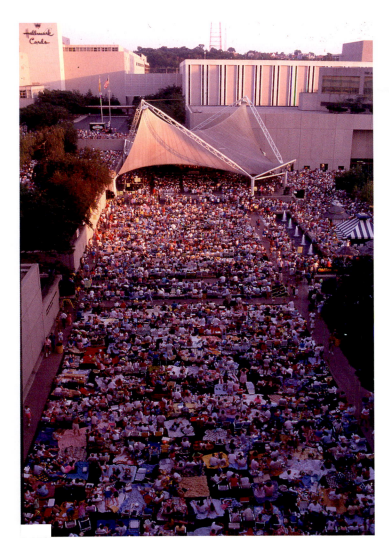

FAR LEFT: *Completed in 1973, the Westin Crown Center Hotel was designed by Chicago architect Harry Weese. Rather than leveling the building site, Weese incorporated Kansas City's prominent Signboard Hill into the building design. An indoor waterfall cascades 60 feet down what was once the hill's northeast face.*

LEFT: *Thousands gather on Crown Center Square for events ranging from outdoor movies to free concerts.*

ABOVE: *Hallmark's Crown Center Square opened its outdoor ice terrace in November 1973, with skating offered to the public from late fall to early spring.*

From the moment kids walk through the door of Hallmark's Kaleidoscope exhibit, the outside world recedes and they find themselves in a fanciful, imagination-fueled, new world where creativity is set free. At the end of a narrow, curving, rainbow-colored corridor, which serves as the coatroom, they pass by an outer-space room glowing with black lights. To the left is a whimsical cityscape where a gigantic bug serves as a work table. Just past that, kids encounter an under-the-sea room, a puzzle machine, a gizmo that lets you melt and paint with crayons, bins filled with ribbons, hearts, zigzags and stars, and plenty of markers, tape, and glue.

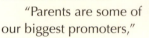

Kaleidoscope has been called an imagination machine. Everything there takes children on a failure-free journey of creativity. It's a place where kids can't possibly go wrong as long as they're making something and having fun.

Kaleidoscope began in the 1960s after Hallmark president Don Hall saw a hands-on art workshop for children at Kansas City's Nelson-Atkins Museum of Art. There was something magical about this event—it meshed perfectly with Hallmark's mission of helping people express themselves.

"It intrigued me," Hall remembers. "I thought it pertained to us a great deal." He liked it so much that he decided to expand the concept into a free public service, a place where the natural artist inside every child could come out to play.

First launched as a traveling exhibit in 1969, the Kaleidoscope art studio unfolded from two colorful semi trucks, and kids climbed aboard to create their own art. This traveling exhibit was retired in May 2004, but during its 35 year run it visited 12 cities across the country each year, inspiring

two-and-a-half million children. In 1975, Kaleidoscope became a permanent exhibit in the newly completed Crown Center complex where it's been ever since. Over 3 million youngsters have made art at Kaleidoscope's permanent home.

After nearly four decades, Kaleidoscope is more popular than ever. The 140,500 children going through the studio in 2008 represented an 18 percent increase over the 2007 attendance. Kaleidoscope administrator Regi Ahrens attributes part of the increase to Crown Center becoming a popular family destination. Kaleidoscope exhibit manager Linda Avery has another theory: Parents who enjoyed Kaleidoscope when they were kids are now making sure their own children get to experience that same fun.

"Parents are some of our biggest promoters," Avery says. "It's become a multigenerational tradition."

Besides media coverage and word-of-mouth promotion, Kaleidoscope sends invitations to organizations and schools each year. Independent sessions are targeted to school children aged five to twelve, while family sessions are open to children of all ages. Information on visiting the free exhibit can be found on the Web site www.hallmarkkaleidoscope.com.

In 2009, Kaleidoscope had seven full-time and thirteen part-time staff members. A full-time volunteer coordinator managed 125 regular volunteers. Kaleidoscope's smooth operation also depends on the 20,000 parent helpers who walk through its doors each year and volunteer their time.

Since Kaleidoscope's beginning, materials discarded in manufacturing Hallmark products have been recycled into art projects, with all Hallmark plants contributing their cast-offs. Kaleidoscope has also taken full advantage of the skills and ideas of Hallmark's creative staff, who enjoy the challenge of working on a scale considerably larger than the greeting card. Chris Duh, Kaleidoscope's designer, was a Hallmark artist himself before he led the 1995 effort to completely revamp Kaleidoscope's interior. He worked with a team of eight Hallmark artists to create a small-scale visual model of the new space, and when that was approved he set to work painting and molding the colorful fantasy environment that tells kids: "You're here to have fun."

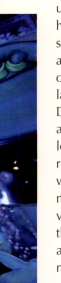

Inside Kaleidoscope, there are few right angles. The walls bend and bow, broken by mirrors, ship's portholes, and 3-D cartoon characters. Fanciful critters made of chicken wire and burlap cloth-mâché roam the premises. Duh even had students from Boone Elementary School in Kansas City help him design the big, bold, and blue contraption known as the "Thingamajine-Travel-Machine-Underwater-Submarine."

"One of my favorite things is to watch the kids running from one thing to another with these wide eyes," says Stacey Lamb, a *Hallmark master artist who worked on Kaleidoscope's design. "And when they get to something I might have helped design or paint, it totally fuels me."*

Duh strives to keep the Kaleidoscope experience tactile and interactive with a balance of low-tech and high-tech activities. He's worked with the Lifelong Kindergarten group at the Massachusetts Institute of Technology Media Lab in Boston to design art stations for Kaleidoscope. Kids visiting Kaleidoscope can now record musical pieces with their own voices using the Super-Duper Sound Looper developed at MIT.

In the years since Don Hall first conceived it, the Kaleidoscope philosophy hasn't changed much. It still focuses on nurturing kids' creativity and imagination in an environment of adventure where there's no such thing as failure or criticism.

"It's amazing that Don Hall would have this vision for Kaleidoscope 40 years ago," Ahrens says. "Because today, schools and industry value the type of creative, whole-brain thinking that Kaleidoscope has always stood for."

"It's not just about making pretty things," Avery adds. "We're not an art instruction center. We want kids to experiment and have a great time while exploring the creative process."

And when they leave through the winding, rainbow-colored coatroom back to the real world, kids take with them the extra creative confidence they've picked up at Kaleidoscope—along with a big bag stuffed with their artistic mementos.

To Hallmark artist Stacey Lamb, that's the whole point. "I love that there's no right or wrong way to do things there," says Lamb. "To me, every child who leaves Kaleidoscope with a bag of goodies is Monet."

PRIME TIME IN KANSAS CITY

January 12, 1970, was no ordinary Monday in Kansas City. Thousands of people flooded downtown streets in celebration. The day before, the city's professional football team, the Chiefs, had beaten the heavily favored Minnesota Vikings 23–7 in Super Bowl IV in New Orleans.

The social and political turmoil of the 1960s kept right on flowing into the 1970s, but in Kansas City—at this moment—there was much to celebrate and plenty of reasons for optimism. The city seemed to be on a roll. The state-of-the-art Kansas City International Airport would open in 1972, as would the Truman Sports Complex with side-by-side stadiums for the world champion Chiefs and the city's three-season-old Major League Baseball team, the Kansas City Royals. Tony shops and a new luxury hotel called the Alameda were opening for business in the Country Club Plaza shopping district, and down in the city's West Bottoms, work was underway on a new multiuse arena. Construction cranes dotted the city's skyline from north of the Missouri River to the ever-expanding southern suburbs.

The grandest construction project of all, of course, was happening in the backyard of Hallmark Cards. From 1968 to 1973, the landscape between Main Street and Gilliam Road from Pershing Road to Twenty-seventh Street was forever transformed as Crown Center took form. Though there was much construction still ahead, the complex celebrated its official opening in the spring of 1973.

"While (Donald Hall) doesn't 'run' Kansas City any more than Miller Nichols, any of the Kempers, or anyone else does, he definitely is working hard to improve it."
— *Kansas City Star, 1974*

In the thick of it all was Don Hall. Serving in leadership positions on seemingly every significant civic and business board or organization in town, he was rightly recognized as one of the city's most powerful nonelected leaders and biggest boosters. A profile of Hall that appeared in a national business magazine in the '70s said of him, "(He) wears a gentle cloak of privacy; a quiet man without a glimmer of grandeur or bravado...unless he's talking about Kansas City."

A desire to talk about Kansas City—and to lure new businesses here—is precisely what led Hall, in 1972, to begin an ambitious national campaign to promote the city and region. He enlisted a handful of other business and community leaders to help, chief among them the president of the Midwest Research Institute, Charles Kimball.

"Charlie Kimball and I were good friends and we talked a lot about the fact that Kansas City was having a boom. A ton of buildings were going up in 1971, '72, '73. There were billions being spent on big projects in Kansas City. Yet we weren't getting any attention and nobody was moving to town. We thought that the thing we needed to do was get some PR around the country, and we worked with (Hallmark PR Director) Bill Johnson and our public relations firm, Carl Byoir & Associates, to get articles in papers and magazines around the country. That was the beginning of Prime Time."

—*Don Hall*

To officially kick off the promotional effort, Hall and Prime Time's steering committee took their pitch to New York City. "We are here to report that Kansas City is in the midst of an unprecedented revitalization and is moving rapidly—and inevitably—toward a new national role," Hall told an audience of the national media at a press conference at the Pinnacle Club in the Saucony-Mobil skyscraper. He spoke of Kansas City's economic growth but also of its parks, fountains, boulevards, clean air, and quality of living, and he unveiled Prime Time's slogan: "One of the few livable cities left."

By any measure, Prime Time was a success. Media came first, and business followed. In the wake of the New York press conference, *National Geographic*, the *Saturday Evening Post*, the *New York Times*, and dozens of other publications featured stories on the city. The local Chamber of Commerce quickly adopted the plan and the city council backed it in a joint effort. By the fall of 1977, five years after its inception, the *Kansas City Times* reported that the Prime Time effort had resulted in 35 new companies moving their headquarters to Kansas City. At the time, Hall estimated the total addition to the community economy to be $60 million a year.

The Prime Time initiative, along with the city's subsequent boom in hotel and convention facilities, also gave a big boost to Kansas City's convention business, and in 1976 the long promotional effort paid off with a prize catch. When the Republican National Convention met in two-year-old Kemper Arena in 1976, Kansas City got the moment in the national spotlight for which Don Hall had so long worked.

The following year, Prime Time organizers cooperated with the Kansas City Chamber of Commerce to create a new, autonomous organization that would continue Prime Time's mission. The entity was named the Kansas City Area Development Council (KCADC). Don Hall and Charles Kimball were appointed KCADC's first co-chairs. As of this writing, nearly 30 years since its founding, the Prime Time/KCADC effort has attracted more than 500 new companies to the Kansas City region. "We wanted to put Kansas City on the map," Hall says with about as much satisfaction as his modest nature allows. "I think we succeeded."

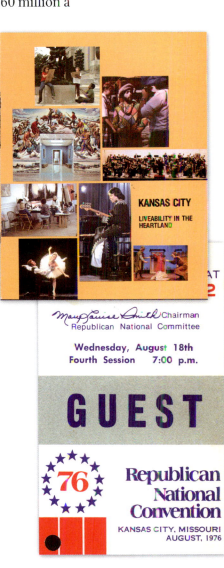

OPPOSITE PAGE: LIFE *magazine came to Kansas City in the early 1960s to do a feature story on Hallmark and the Hall family. In this outtake from the photo shoot, members of the family gather with J.C. and Elizabeth Hall to review cards. Don Hall is second from right. Barbara Hall Marshall's husband, Bob Marshall, who managed the Halls retail store in the 1950s, is pictured just left of him.*

GROWING IN EVERY DIRECTION

The mid- to late-1970s saw Hallmark return to its diversification and expansion strategy with gusto. In 1975, the firm made its biggest-yet venture away from its core business when it acquired a privately held and family-managed costume jewelry company called Trafari, Krussman & Fishel, Inc. Interviewed by *Business Week* at the time of the deal, Don Hall explained the logic of the acquisition. He pointed out that, like Hallmark, the company was design oriented with products that sold through department and specialty stores, and perhaps most importantly, were purchased largely by women.

That strategic acquisition and ones that would follow—like the purchase of a large picture frame company in 1979—were not only driven by a need to broaden the product lines in Hallmark's card and gift shops, but by an effort to even out the seasonal peaks and valleys that were symptomatic of the greeting card business.

Just as important were acquisitions that brought the company greater efficiencies and boosted the quality of its products. The purchase of the Litho-Krome Company in 1979 was such an inspired move. Located in Columbus, Georgia, Litho-Krome was widely recognized as one of the nation's most innovative, progressive, and high-quality lithography and printing companies. The company was well known to Hallmark—it had supplied color separations and proofs for the greeting card maker dating back to the mid-1950s. So interdependent were the companies, in fact, that at the time Litho-Krome became a subsidiary company—Hallmark work represented about half of the printing company's total revenue.

A third tactic of Hall's diversification and expansion strategy was to increase holdings in English-speaking overseas markets. In 1979, Hallmark International purchased The Specialty Press, an Australian card maker and its subsidiary company, the Dawson Printing Company of New Zealand. These companies became known as Hallmark Cards Australia, Ltd. and Hallmark Cards New Zealand, Ltd. In the early 1980s, it would acquire two significant greeting card makers in England and Scotland, greatly strengthening its presence in the strong card-buying U.K. market.

Commenting on the wave of acquisitions and joint ventures from the mid-1960s to the early 1980s, the *Journal of Buyouts and Acquisitions* had this to say: "The thrust of the acquisition strategy Donald J. Hall had implemented during this period was to build a larger house upon the basic foundation his father laid back in 1910. That mission he accomplished with distinction. To him belongs the real credit for taking the Kansas City-based company from the realm of an interesting, large greeting card company to a sprawling, diversified multinational business."

GOLD CROWN

"DONALD HALL OPERATES A FIRM MORE MASSIVE THAN HIS FATHER EVER DREAMED IT WOULD BE. THE COMPANY'S VOLUME TRIPLED IN THE 1960S AND ALREADY HAS DOUBLED THUS FAR IN THE 1970S, MAKING IT ONE OF THE LARGEST FAMILY—OWNED FIRMS IN THE COUNTRY. MUCH OF THIS GROWTH HAS COME AS A RESULT OF DIVERSIFICATION."

—*Kansas City Times*
August 26, 1978

INTERNATIONAL

"SO QUIETLY POWERFUL IS DON HALL THAT A REPORTER FROM A NATIONAL MAGAZINE WHO SPENT TWO DAYS HERE INTERVIEWING HIM RETURNED TO NEW YORK AND TOLD HIS EDITORS HALL WAS 'TOO DULL' TO WRITE ABOUT."

—*Kansas City Star*
December 16, 1974

Litho-Krome and Hallmark: Printing Pioneers and Perfect Partners

Looking back on Hallmark's long association with the Litho-Krome Company, it seems inevitable that two fast-growing, high-achieving companies—both leaders in their field—were bound to come together. Hallmark had long been seeking the holy grail of large-volume, accurate color reproduction, and in the mid-1950s the modest-sized commercial printing company, founded in 1932 in Columbus, Georgia, promised to provide it.

Much of Litho-Krome's success can be attributed to the determination and technical insights of one man, J. Tom Morgan, who'd been hired as an artist in 1933 and became the company's president 15 years later. Morgan had spearheaded the "Litho-Krome Process" using photographic masking to correct color, balance inks, and bring about standardized, repeatable methods to achieve stunning breakthroughs in four-color offset lithography.

Ken West

At the time, letterpress printing was the standard for commercial-color reproduction. But Morgan was to help change that. Industry expert Michael H. Bruno wrote of Morgan's achievements: "Tom Morgan has done more for the advancement of lithography as a process of choice than any other living lithoghrapher."

In 1949 Morgan proved to everyone what his methods were capable of when Litho-Krome reproduced a photograph called "Wine and Cheese" by famed commercial photographer Victor Keppler. This reproduction, which ran as a magazine insert, not only won first place in the New York Art Directors contest, but is now part of a permanent exhibit on lithography at the Smithsonian Institution. Bruno wrote that "Wine and Cheese" demonstrated "a level of quality for four-color lithography no other lithographer ever dreamed possible." And quality was what J.C. Hall was looking for.

Ken West, the retouch supervisor in Hallmark's lithography department at the time, was reading up on developments in the graphic-arts industry when he came across the news of Litho-Krome's success with "Wine and Cheese." Realizing that Litho-Krome had technical abilities that would be useful to Hallmark, West contacted Morgan.

The two men were kindred spirits, both determined and creative perfectionists, and they hit it off immediately. They openly shared their methods, with Hallmark adopting Litho-Krome's color charts and Litho-Krome using a dye-print preproofing method adapted from one perfected by West at Hallmark. They shared knowledge about photographic color separation until, as Morgan put it, "His (West's) methods and Litho-Krome's methods soon meshed."

"There were a number of improvements that Hallmark and Litho-Krome came up with independently—each a little different," West recalled. "We were able to share these, because they benefited both of us."

Tom Morgan

It was the relationship between West and Morgan that led Hallmark to hire Litho-Krome in 1955 to start making color separations. Litho-Krome bought a big 60-inch press—because 60-inch sheets were Hallmark's standard sizes—and began to print Hallmark cards in 1964. By then Litho-Krome was printing exclusively for Hallmark. "It was a decision we never regretted," Morgan would say years later.

Over the years Litho-Krome has made numerous improvements in the printing quality of Hallmark cards and introduced a wide range of processes, including embossing and foil stamping, with West overseeing the exchange of technical advances between the two companies. In 1979, when West was corporate vice president of graphic services, Morgan announced plans to retire, and Hallmark purchased Litho-Krome as a subsidiary. It was perhaps the ultimate demonstration of just how highly Tom Morgan's company and his breakthrough techniques were valued.

Wine and Cheese

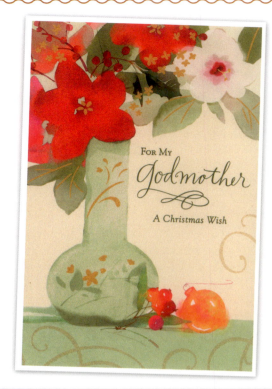

Comice
pears

Mission
Fig

Kiwifruit

Pomegranate

CRAIG LUECK

With Hallmark illustrator Craig Lueck it's easy to suspect that his "realistic" watercolor paintings have reality beat by a mile. But they're suposed to make you look...look hard...linger.

"The softer the edge, the longer the eye will linger," Lueck says. "To make something evocative it's important not to describe every detail."

Lueck's simple yet elegant watercolor landscapes reflect his love of nature. One high point of a Hallmark career beginning in 1983 was winning the Barbara Marshall Award in 2003. He spent his six-month sabbatical creating more than 100 landscape watercolors, traveling the United States and abroad, often visiting sites painted by artists who have influenced him.

He describes his own creative process as "instinctive, impulsive. . . I just shoot for honest, authentic responses in each piece."

Also, Lueck never stops painting—with an oil studio in the attic, a watercolor studio in the basement, and a palette and paint kit that fits in his Harley's saddlebags.

JEFF DALY

Humor writer Jeff Daly has been known to spend much of his working days playing with folded pieces of paper. Daly is one of Hallmark's masters of paper mechanics, the art of making cards that move by using cunningly designed pop-ups, slides, and flip folds. For Daly, being able to think visually, and often in three dimensions, is as crucial in creating his mechanical wonders as is his skill in writing a funny birthday message.

Though Daly got a university art degree and began his career as an editorial cartoonist, he was hired by Hallmark as a writer in 1975. At the time, Howard Lohnes and Bruce Baker were the deans of paper mechanics at Hallmark. But they tutored Daly in the artform, and he discovered he had a knack for it.

"It really helps to think like an animator, visually and verbally," he says. "It's the card's action that gives a big part of the payoff."

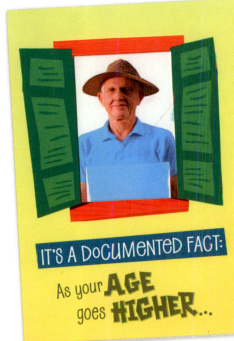

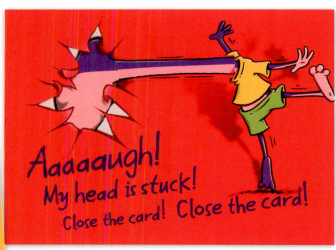

189

HALLMARK KEEPSAKE ORNAMENTS: FROM SIDELINE TO SENSATION

"Do you think you could sell these?" That was the question asked in 1972 when Hallmark shipped boxes, each containing four Christmas ornaments, to selected retailers across the country. The answer would be important. Not only were these ball ornaments decorated with original designs, unlike anything seen before, but they were samples of what the company hoped would become a new product line.

A painting called *Elves* by Hallmark artist Sue Tague was reproduced on one of those first four ornaments. Tague still remembers the uncertainty surrounding the new venture. "At the time I hadn't seen Christmas ornaments with original artwork on them," Tague recalls. "I remember asking myself if anyone would like them. I guess they did."

After previewing the ornaments with their customers, retailers responded with an enthusiastic "yes!" Hallmark's Christmas ornament line was launched the following year with 18 ornaments, including four from that first sample box.

These days, Keepsake introduces roughly 300 new Christmas ornaments each year—everything from miniatures to ornaments with motion, light and sound, from Tinker Bell to classic American cars, and from sports stars to *Star Wars*.

The Keepsake Ornaments line earned its reputation on the strength of intricately sculpted characters and detailed scenes. They typically begin as rough sketches, then as sculptures carved in clay, wax, or wood. After each sculpture is hand painted, a technical artist creates a prototype of the ornament to be used in actual production. A growing number of Keepsake artists also consider the computer another vital tool in their work. Software programs allow them to sculpt digitally—turning and viewing the image in three dimensions—and then to send these digital files to a rapid prototyping machine that creates the production model.

Over the past four decades, Keepsakes has discovered that ornament series are especially popular with collectors. Artist Betsey Clark's signature ragamuffins and waifs appeared in the first series, which began in 1973 and lasted 13 years. The rocking horse series, one of Keepsake's most popular, began in 1981—though it wasn't intended to be a series. Hallmark artist Linda Sickman had simply painted a bunch of rocking horses, then couldn't decide which one she liked best. Her art director liked them all too, so it was decided to run them as a series. Frosty Friends, begun in 1980 by sculptor Ed Seale, has been the longest-running series. Other successful, longtime series include Mary's Angels, based on the work of Mary Hamilton, and Nostalgic Houses and Shops.

Over the years, Keepsake creations have reflected not only the fun and nostalgia of the Christmas spirit, but also the ever-changing face of popular culture. The art of Norman Rockwell and Currier & Ives appeared in 1974. In 1977, the *PEANUTS* gang and Disney characters were introduced. Barbie and *The Wizard of Oz* characters followed. The year 1991 saw two milestones. Not only did the first *STAR TREK*™ ornament—the Starship Enterprise—come out as a Keepsake, but ornaments intended for men were introduced when Don Palmiter sculpted a 1957 Corvette for the first in the Classic American Cars series. The Beatles even joined the line in 1994 when Keepsake celebrated the 30th anniversary of the Fab Four's first appearance on *The Ed Sullivan Show*. The Beatles gift set by artist Anita Rogers took a month to sculpt and marked another milestone— the first time a Keepsake sculptor had attempted likenesses of real people.

Keepsake's yearly offering of "Magic" ornaments began in 1984 with 10 designs of illuminated Christmas scenes. Today, Keepsake's Magic ornaments are elaborate creations that play music, put scenes into motion, record messages, and promise to do even more as technology improves. Staging such big productions on such a tiny scale requires imagination and collaboration between artists and technical engineers. Though many of Keepsake's sculptors create Magic ornaments, Ken Crow is most closely associated with the genre. With his immensely popular "I'm Melting! Melting!" ornament—which recreates the famous scene from *The Wizard of Oz*—Crow figured out how to have the Wicked Witch appear to melt into the castle floor.

By the mid-1980s, dozens of local ornament clubs had sprung up across the country, made up of devoted Keepsake Ornament collectors who met regularly to share stories and tips for decorating with ornaments. Making official what had begun as a purely grassroots phenomenon, Hallmark formed a national Keepsake Ornament Club in 1987. With its own staff within Hallmark, the club provides about 100,000 national members with information—through a newsletter and Web updates—on Keepsake artists, new series, club-exclusive ornaments, and other member perks. It organizes artist-signing events across the country and stages big annual conventions where enthusiastic collectors buy and swap ornaments, dress up as their favorite ornament characters, and treat the overwhelmed artists like rock stars.

Hallmark Keepsake Ornaments today are a far cry from the humble offering of four ball ornaments in a box back in 1972. But the inspiration for the venture hasn't changed over the years. There's the same commitment to creativity and craftsmanship, but there's also the connection between Keepsake and Hallmark's fundamental mission, which makes ornaments a perfect product fit. There's no better testament to Keepsake's importance to Hallmark than the fact that Hallmark CEO Don Hall Jr., during his rise up the corporate ladder, served as Keepsake's general manager from 1993–95. "Some might say we are a greeting card company that makes Christmas ornaments," Hall Jr. says. "But making ornaments has been a natural progression of what we do. Keepsake ornaments are more than decorations. Like greeting cards, they speak to what's universal in the human heart by helping people preserve memories, commemorate milestones, and nurture relationships."

BELOW: *A Hallmark Keepsakes ornament goes through several phases between initial concept and final product. From left to right, a Wizard of Oz ornament progresses from concept sketch, to rough prototype, to computer-generated art, to hand-crafted wax model, and finally to painted prototype.*

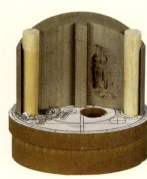

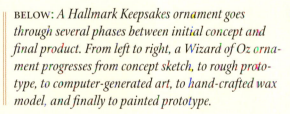

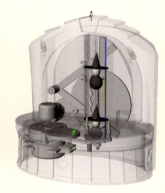

CHAPTER NINE

Traditions, Transitions, Expansion & Explorations

(1981–2002)

"I cannot conceive of a community-wide enterprise in this city succeeding without the support of Hallmark; indeed, it might be said that Hallmark's brand on charitable and community activities carries the same power as it does on greeting cards."

— Morton Sosland, chairman, Sosland Companies, Inc.

IN 1980, HALLMARK ACHIEVED SOMETHING THAT MADE ITS CHAIRMAN, DON HALL, EXTREMELY PROUD. DURING ITS ANNUAL UNITED WAY CONTRIBUTION DRIVE, THE COMPANY— and its employees—pledged the largest amount ever contributed by a single firm in Kansas City history.

There are many fine companies headquartered in Kansas City. There are local companies that employ more people than Hallmark. But this singular achievement offers up a telling insight—there's no company quite like Hallmark—and no employees quite like Hallmarkers.

Former city manager and Crown Center president Bob Kipp recalls encountering that insider-coined appellation, "Hallmarker," in his early days with the company in the 1980s. He remembers puzzling over its use by his new associates as they discussed the relative merits of job applicants. "The question was always, 'Is she or he Hallmark?' or 'Is this a Hallmarker?'" says Kipp of the esoteric verbal shorthand. "I didn't get it. Only after awhile did it soak in that it has to do with that value system. They meant, 'Is his or her behavior consistent with the Hallmark value system.'"

Boiled down to its essence, the value system internalized by true Hallmarkers touches upon three major points—the quality of the product the company produces and sells, a sincere respect for the people who work at the company, and a commitment to the communities where the company operates.

The values had been unstated, but understood, for decades. They're what inspired J.C. Hall's mantra, "I'm hell-bent on quality." They're what compelled Bill Harsh to show up at the hospital when an employee was laid-up—often with a check to cover unforeseen expenses. They're what motivated Don Hall to form the "25-year club" and recognize those employees each and every year with a grand dinner—a dinner for which the guest list in recent years has included roughly 7,500 names.

Throughout much of Hallmark's history, the tenets of its philosophy were taught by example. Passing along these values was easy when the company was small enough that few fellow

ABOVE: *In a family tradition that dates back for decades, Don Hall and members of the Hall family ring bells for the Salvation Army outside of the Halls Country Club Plaza store each year before Christmas.*

RIGHT: *Hallmark volunteers Shannon Kinney-Duh and Chris Duh put final touches on the "Wall of Hearts" that recognizes charitable donors to the Ronald McDonald House. Chris Duh was art director for the year-long mosaics project, which was completed in the fall of 2006.*

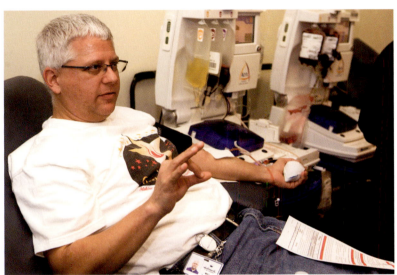

TOP LEFT: *Each spring hundreds of Kansas City-area Hallmarkers, family members, and friends volunteer their labor planting, painting, building fences, and mulching at the Hallmark-sponsored Wild Saturday at the Zoo, which began in 1999. Hallmark's Topeka plant sponsors a similar day of service at the Topeka Zoo each year. At the May 2009 event in Kansas City, Ben Stallbaumer, brother of Hallmarker Kate Stallbaumer, and Larry Gessner teamed up to clear brush.*

ABOVE LEFT: *Hallmarker Mike Schwabauer leads the twice-annual blood drives that in 2008 collected over 700 pints of blood for Kansas City's Community Blood Center. "Giving blood," Schwabauer says, "is one of the few things that people can do that actually can save a life."*

TOP RIGHT: *Hallmark volunteers Debbie Neff and Eric Muetz fill a wheelbarrow with mulch for new spring plantings during Wild Saturday at the Zoo in Kansas City in 2009.*

ABOVE RIGHT: *Hallmark volunteers donated their labor, lunch hours, and creativity in the Kaleidoscope workshop at Crown Center to create the mosaics that now decorate the Ronald McDonald House for children and families just across the street from Hallmark headquarters and Children's Mercy Hospital in Kansas City.*

workers were strangers. It became more difficult as the company grew larger and more geographically extended.

In 1989, Don Hall decided it was time to put these ideas down in writing. That year, the company adopted a formal expression of its guiding principles called the Beliefs and Values statement.

Admittedly, corporate "mission statements" were much in vogue in the 1980s, but a closer reading of this particular statement—and a direct interpretation of it provided by Don Hall—supports the notion that Hallmark's Beliefs and Values were anything but run-of-the-mill.

Shortly after the Beliefs and Values statement was introduced, Don Hall made it the keynote of his regular speech to new employees. In it, Hall explained and expanded upon the thinking behind the statement's principles. Two of his points, in particular, provide important insight into Hallmark culture.

"Distinguished financial performance is an absolute must," Hall told employees, "but the dollar is not almighty, in spite of what some business schools teach. If we behave as if it is, we cheat ourselves of some of life's greatest opportunities."

A bit later in the speech, Hall touched on another of his long-held convictions:

"We are responsible to our city and to our communities not merely because thriving cities and communities indirectly—or even directly—benefit our company economically. Rather, it is a responsibility born out of the kind of natural, loving, and moral commitment that binds each of us to our own individual families."

These two notions—that profit should not come at the expense of principles, and that a corporation bears a real responsibility to its community—should certainly not have been radical ideas. However, when espoused at the height of the go-go, "greed is good" era that was the late 1980s, they bear noting.

Long before Hallmark's Beliefs and Values statement was first drafted, Don Hall was already advocating for more community partnership and commitment from corporations. In the late 1970s, he delivered a speech to his alma mater, Dartmouth College, in which he coined a phrase that summed up this philosophy: *social responsibility plus*.

In the speech, Hall argued that the term "corporate social responsibility" had been overworked, stretched, and misused to the point that it was almost a cliché.

"In my view," Hall told the audience, "we aren't socially responsible just because we obey the law, comply with regulations, or provide service to our customers. These are expected and required of businesses and merely represent good practices."

> "DISTINGUISHED FINANCIAL PERFORMANCE IS AN ABSOLUTE MUST, BUT THE DOLLAR IS NOT ALMIGHTY, IN SPITE OF WHAT SOME BUSINESS SCHOOLS TEACH. IF WE BEHAVE AS IF IT IS, WE CHEAT OURSELVES OF SOME OF LIFE'S GREATEST OPPORTUNITIES."
>
> —*Don Hall*

THIS IS HALLMARK

WE BELIEVE:

That our PRODUCTS and SERVICES must enrich people's lives.

That CREATIVITY and QUALITY—in our products, services, and all that we do—are essential to our success.

That INNOVATION in all areas of our business is essential to attaining and sustaining leadership.

That the PEOPLE of Hallmark are our company's most valuable resource.

That distinguished FINANCIAL PERFORMANCE is imperative to accomplish our broader purpose.

That our PRIVATE OWNERSHIP must be preserved.

WE VALUE AND ARE COMMITTED TO:

EXCELLENCE in all we do.

High standards of ETHICS and INTEGRITY.

CARING and RESPONSIBLE CORPORATE CITIZENSHIP for Kansas City and for each community in which we operate.

These beliefs and values guide our business strategies, our corporate behavior, and our relationships with business partners, suppliers, customers, communities and each other.

> "HE WENT ON THE DAYTON HUDSON BOARD FOR TWO REASONS. ONE, IT WAS A FAMILY BUSINESS; BUT TWO, HE THOUGHT THEY WERE THE BEST AT SOCIAL RESPONSIBILITY IN THE COUNTRY. HE ADMIRED THE DAYTONS BECAUSE THEY WERE VERY COMMITTED TO THE COMMUNITIES IN WHICH THEY OPERATED."
>
> —*Bill Hall discussing Don Hall*

ABOVE: *Every two years Hallmark creates a new "For America's Babies" greeting card to remind parents of newborns to have their children immunized. The philanthropic program, a partnership with state governors, began in 1998. The 2009—2010 card was designed by Hallmark artist Karla Taylor. An immunization record is printed on the back of the card.*

OPPOSITE PAGE: *Since 1989 all new Hallmark employees receive a copy of the Beliefs and Values statement, which contains the essence of the company's philosophy of commitment to quality and community service.*

"EVERYONE IN HALL-MARK'S VOLUNTEER OFFICE IS VERY OPEN TO ALL THE WAYS THAT PEOPLE WANT TO HELP, WHETHER IT'S THROUGH FINANCIAL DONATIONS, GIVING TIME AND LABOR, OR USING YOUR SPECIALIZED SKILLS TO CONTRIBUTE."

—Mike Schwabauer,
a 20-year Hallmarker who leads in-house corporate blood drives for the Kansas City Community Blood Center

"We should be thinking in terms of a higher standard, a standard I call social responsibility plus. This means doing those things that go beyond what is expected. It is using a portion of our corporate resources to benefit society. We have the opportunity to apply our corporate and personal talents to make a significant difference in our communities. Social responsibility plus is really social opportunity—the opportunity to bring the skills of business and people in business to bear on public problems."

Reaction to the speech was strong—strong enough that Hall was called upon to reprise it several times over the following months and years.

At Hallmark, Hall challenged his employees to live by these principles—and Hallmarkers responded—not just through their support of the United Way but in hundreds of other ways. Not only with financial contributions but with personal, physical involvement in not-for-profits and charitable organizations throughout the Kansas City community.

Below are a few, but only a few, of the ways that Hallmark—and Hallmarkers—make a difference:

• Kaleidoscope: Hallmark created this "imagination workshop" in the 1960s as a gift to children for their creative self-expression, enrichment, and pleasure. *(See sidebar feature on pages 182 and 183)*

• Through its Community Assistance Program (CAP), Hallmark employees who are experiencing low work levels (due to the seasonal nature of the social expression business) are deployed to help with small, light construction projects in the community.

• Hallmark volunteers: Hallmark employs a full-time volunteer manager to match Hallmarkers to volunteer opportunities in the community.

• Immunization cards: These cards, created and printed by Hallmark, are supplied at no cost to the nation's governors to send to every new parent in their state to encourage them to stay current with their child's recommended immunizations.

• Harvesters Community Food Network: Hallmark is a lead volunteer in the food bank's "BackSnack" program, which provides roughly 8,000 low-income children in Kansas City with a small backpack of nutritious food to eat over the weekend—when subsidized school meals aren't available. Hundreds of employees volunteer to fill the backpacks each week at Hallmark headquarters.

This list could go on for pages, but the point made would be the same: Hallmark believes that members of a community—especially those with the resources and means—bear a responsibility to make a positive impact on that community. And Hallmarkers have long held a reputation for doing just that.

REIMAGINING THE NELSON-ATKINS MUSEUM

"Without Don's fierce determination in support of the museum, the Nelson-Atkins would be a pale shadow of its present eminence as one of the nation's finest art museums. He deserves credit for leading the museum to the wonder it is today."

—Morton Sosland, Chairman,
Sosland Companies, Inc.

In 1981, Don Hall was asked to become one of three trustees of Kansas City's Nelson-Atkins Museum of Art. He was eager to accept but with a few conditions—well, to be precise, 36 conditions. Hall had long thought that the venerable museum needed to make some changes—most of them to do with making it more welcoming to visitors and more vital to the community—so he presented a list to the other trustees. "I don't know why I had the guts to do that," Hall recalls today, "but I did."

Despite the list of demands—or perhaps because they represented some fresh and long-overdue thinking about the institution—the trustees welcomed Hall to the board. It would take many years, but over time he was able to check off all the items on his agenda for the museum.

One of the main components of Hall's plan for the Nelson was to increase the size of its governing body. Under his guidance, the board increased from a group of three—the University trustee trio which had been established by founder William Rockhill Nelson—to 21. To Hall's mind, more people meant more energy, more opinions, and more ideas.

The museum was also short on space. Largely unchanged since its construction in 1933, the classical Beaux-Arts style building housed one of the country's finest collections of art but could only display a small percentage at any given time. By the early 1990s, Hall had become chairman of the museum's board. He kicked off a capital campaign to fund additional display space, and within a few years the group had built a fund of more than $50 million.

Now the fun part started—choosing an architect and a plan. Hall formed a search committee that traveled the world reviewing the work of architects. An initial list of about 30 was whittled down to five or six. Somewhat remarkably, the group was unanimous on their top choice: American architect Steven Holl was chosen to design the new addition in 1999.

While still on the drawing board, Holl's design began attracting attention—not all of it kind. The addition, called the Bloch Building after Henry Bloch, H&R Block co-founder and one of the museum's longtime trustees, was assailed as looking boxy, industrial, and incongruous with the museum grounds.

Don Hall formed his own opinion. "I liked Steven Holl's design as soon as I saw it," he remembers. "It was a unique plan. Its creativity was terrific because the big challenge was to avoid covering, changing, or overwhelming the old building. It's an icon, and people would be disappointed if you messed it up. Yet some substantial square footage was needed, and to achieve that without obstructing or damaging the architecture of the old building required a unique and bold plan."

However, Hall's was a minority position. Local grumbling only increased as the building took shape, and ultimately the architect was compelled to hold a "town meeting" to address the negative talk. In it, he asked the public for one thing, "patience." He promised that the building would begin to make more sense when it was closer to completion.

When the addition opened in the summer of 2007, Holl—and Hall's committee—were vindicated. The architect's design, which incorporated five irregularly shaped, glass-clad structures (called "lenses" by Holl) that march down the perimeter of the museum grounds east of the old Nelson-Atkins, was met with almost universal raves—locally, nationally, and internationally. Though most of the exhibits in the addition are underground, natural light from the lenses illuminates the artwork. Among the critical praise was a lengthy review in the *New Yorker* magazine. *TIME* magazine ranked the building at the top of its "10 Best Architectural Marvels" list in 2007.

"As it turns out, the building… is not just Holl's finest by far but also one of the best museums of the last generation. Holl's five glass structures, punctuating the hill, don't mock the old building as you might expect; they dance before it and engage it."

"Almost everything the Nelson-Atkins has put into the building—for example, its excellent collection of abstract expressionist and contemporary art—looks better than it did before."

—Paul Goldberger, the New Yorker

RIGHT: *In 2006, the Nelson-Atkins Museum of Art acquired the Hallmark Photographic Collection through a combination gift and purchase. Primarily American in the scope of its holdings, the collection spans the entire history of photography, from the birth of the medium in 1839 to the present. Considered one of the finest private collections of American photography ever assembled, at the time of its acquisition by the museum it included more than 6,500 works by 900 artists.*

TOP: *The new Bloch building, designed by Steven Holl, sits to the east of the original Nelson-Atkins Museum.*

ABOVE: *The Hall Family Foundation collaborated with The Nelson-Atkins Museum to create a 17-acre sculpture garden featuring the work of English artist Henry Moore and other noted 20th century artists. After two years of work, the artistic green space that the* New York Times *called, "a garden of precisely the right sort," opened to the public in 1989. Some 60 Henry Moore sculptures were given by the Hall Family Foundation to the Nelson-Atkins.*

THE HALL FAMILY FOUNDATION

The Halls, Hallmark, and Kansas City. The connection between family, firm, and city goes back for a century, but to define the relationship by number of years alone doesn't begin to tell the story. There is depth to this partnership, not just length. And there is untold breadth to the benefit it brings to all three entities. After 100 years, the connection between firm, family, and hometown is deep rooted, symbiotic, and strong.

Since founding the company that would become Hallmark in 1910, Joyce C. Hall always contributed at least 5 percent of annual profits to charity. The net amount wasn't much in those early years, of course. The money was distributed to a range of worthy causes—with one thing in common—they were local. The contribution was Hall's way of giving back to the city that he felt had given him so much.

In 1943, J.C. and Elizabeth Hall established the Hallmark Educational Foundation (which would change its name to the Hall Family Foundation in 1993) to formalize the family's philanthropic effort. The foundation's first three contributions were to a Kansas City-area Boy Scout camp, the Pembroke Country Day School, and toward a fund to establish an independent, not-for-profit research facility that would become Midwest Research Institute. Another early beneficiary was Children's Mercy Hospital, which in 1970 would relocate from Independence and Woodland Avenues to Kansas City's Hospital Hill—just across the street from Hallmark headquarters. With J.C. Hall, generosity began at home—and benefitted those close to it.

As Hallmark has grown, the foundation has too. For the past three decades, guiding that growth and overseeing the daily operation of the foundation has been the responsibility of William (Bill) Hall.

Though Bill Hall has no direct lineage to the J.C. Hall family, it seems not entirely accurate to say that he is not a member of the

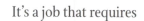

Elizabeth and J.C. Hall

Hall family. After more than 30 years of service in dual roles as head of the foundation and as Don Hall's assistant for non-Hallmark activities, Bill Hall is about as close as one can get to family without actually being related.

Bill Hall was hired by Hallmark in 1968 and assigned to a career development program intended to move him around to a variety of departments. While he was working in the company's finance department in the late 1960s, Don Hall put him in charge of a real-estate project in Lawrence, Kansas. Hallmark's CEO was impressed with the young man's financial acumen and shortly thereafter asked him to manage the family foundation's stock and bond portfolio. At the time, the portfolio totaled about $6 million. It grew considerably larger when Elizabeth, and then J.C. Hall, passed away. Today, Hall oversees about $700 million in foundation capital. Five years after he began management of the foundation's assets, Hall took on the additional responsibility of overseeing the foundation's grant making. He became president of the Hall Family Foundation in 1982.

It's a job that requires tremendous insight into Don Hall's and the board's priorities and values. "I'm trying to carry out their vision," says Bill Hall. "Because of all the years we've worked together, I have a good sense of that vision."

There are many substantial and active foundations operating in Kansas City today, but according to Bill Hall, that wasn't always the case. "The Hall Family Foundation was, for a long time, the philanthropic gorilla because there weren't any other large foundations in Kansas City," explains Hall. The late 1980s brought a change to that scenario when private estates were used to establish the William T. Kemper Foundation, the Kauffman Foundation, and the Stowers Foundation, among others. At around the same time, Don and Adele Hall helped establish the Greater Kansas City Community Foundation.

Each of these foundations has its own area of emphasis, and all of them have helped put Kansas City on the philanthropic map. "At one time, Kansas City had low philanthropic capital per capita," says Bill Hall. "Today that number is very high."

Bill Hall emphasizes that the foundation he runs is not part of Hallmark but is an entirely family-funded charitable organization. Still, he concedes that it is the company's history of doing well that has allowed the family foundation to do so much good. And while the level of the foundation's philanthropic giving has increased markedly over the decades, its focus is very much the same.

"First and foremost, it's greater Kansas City," says Hall. "That's our geographic limitation. Our work falls into four main areas of emphasis: children, youth, and families; the arts; education; and community development." In the last 10 years alone, the Hall Family Foundation has contributed more than $340 million to its grantees in the Kansas City community.

Although he clearly loves his job, Bill Hall will tell you that "giving away money" isn't nearly as easy as some would think. By law, the foundation—every foundation—must give away 5 percent of its value every year. "We develop a plan—with people both internally and outside—for each of our four areas of emphasis," says Hall. "We are strictly grant makers. We don't run any of our own programs but work with people in the community who have parallel interests to the foundation. Children's Mercy would be one of those, as would the University of Kansas , the Nelson-Atkins Museum of Art, and many, many small organizations—like Southwest Boulevard Family Health Care. We partner with these organizations to carry out the strategies of the foundation."

To do the job correctly—that is, to make sure that each dollar gifted does the most possible good— requires an ultimate

insider's knowledge of the Kansas City community. Bill Hall cites the collective knowledge and connectedness of the foundation's board of directors—which includes Bob Kipp, Margi Pence, Sandra Lawrence, Richard Green, Morton Sosland, former University of Kansas Chancellor Robert Hemenway, Don Hall, and executive director of the Mid-America Regional Council, David Warm, among others. "We have a very engaged board," Hall says. "Nobody knows more about this community—what has gone on, what is going on, and what will go on—than the members of our board. They are a tremendous resource."

Though he's quick to cite the qualifications of others, when it comes to knowing the pulse of the Kansas City community, Bill Hall himself is surely anyone's equal. In 2007, Hall was awarded the Kansas Citian of the Year Award by the Greater Kansas City Chamber of Commerce, a designation given annually "to those whose civic contributions and achievements reflect the insight, creativity, and consciousness necessary to build and maintain a quality urban community." Past recipients of the award include J.C., Don, and Adele Hall. Bill Hall cites the latter two as the greatest possible examples and inspiration for anyone interested in community involvement.

"The vitality of the Hall Family Foundation is a direct reflection of Don's and the foundation board's engagement in the community," he says.

"Don would tell you," Hall continues, "it isn't just the money. The money's important, but you've got to be in the community and engaged. We don't like 'ivory tower' philanthropy. You have to volunteer. You have to get involved in the charitable process. You have to be a part of the community."

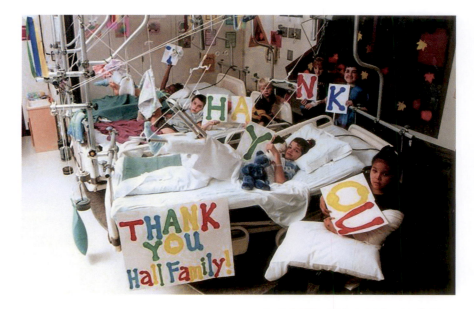

LEFT: *A Teach For America "corps member" interacts with students at Wendell Phillips Elementary School in the Kansas City, Missouri, School District. This nationally acclaimed program recruits outstanding college graduates to teach for two years in low-income schools. With support from the Hall Family Foundation, the program began operating in Kansas City in the 2008–2009 school year.*

FAR LEFT: *A "Big Brother" and "Little Brother" from the Kansas City area share a pizza during an outing sponsored by Big Brothers, Big Sisters of Greater Kansas City. Over the years, the Hall Family Foundation has supported the organization's efforts to expand the mentoring program within the greater Kansas City area.*

BLUE SKIES AND BOLD AMBITIONS

As the 1980s began, the outlook for Hallmark could scarcely have been more bright. The company enjoyed a strong position in its core business of greeting card publishing, accounting for roughly 30 percent of the U.S. market. Activity overseas was also strong as Hallmark made several moves that expanded its presence in the U.K., Australia, and New Zealand. In 1980, the firm further committed to its successful retail strategy by acquiring the 160-store chain of Evenson Card Shops.

Meanwhile, the Crown Center complex continued to grow. Just south of the Crown Center shops, side-by-side condomini-um and apartment buildings, the 30-story San Francisco Tower and seven-story Sante Fe Place, opened up the late 1970s, adding a vital residential element to the development. In 1977, plans were announced to build a second luxury hotel—to be run by the Hyatt corporation—at the northeastern edge of the complex.

The Hyatt Regency Hotel hadn't been part of the original master plan, but when the Hyatt corporation had trouble getting a facility built in downtown Kansas City, it turned to Crown Center instead. The success of the Westin was all the encouragement Hall needed to move ahead with the deal.

Charles Egan recalls the deliberation that went into the decision. "Don had always been supportive of renewal down-town," says Egan. "One of the things that was going to be a major factor in capitalizing a renewal was a hotel downtown, but for various reasons the civic effort to get that done had aborted, and that's why he went into the Hyatt."

As Missouri's new tallest building, the Hyatt Regency Crown Center hotel drew attention and admiration from the day it opened in July of 1980. The 40-story hotel, boasting more than 700 guest rooms, a soaring 60-foot-high lobby, and a revolving rooftop restaurant, was every bit as impressive as the Westin Crown Center hotel opened seven years earlier just a block away.

A sense of contentment reigned at Hallmark as business thrived and new challenges were met with a sense of relish and can-do spirit. But despite the rosy outlook, the early years of the 1980s would hold some wholly different kinds of challenges for Hallmark—and for the Hall family—both personal and painfully public.

LEFT: *The exterior of the Hyatt Regency Crown Center photographed in 2009.*

The Sky Falls

In the summer of 1981, Kansas City residents had found a new way to beat the heat and enjoy a pleasant evening's diversion. On Friday evenings, couples of all ages flocked to the city's recently opened Hyatt Regency at Crown Center to participate in tea dances in the hotel's breathtaking multi-story atrium lobby.

On the evening of July 17, a crowd of around 2,000 people had gathered in the hotel's atrium for the weekly dance. Hundreds more watched the dancers from surrounding balconies and two elevated walkways, or skywalks, that spanned the hotel's lobby. Just a few minutes after seven o'clock, as the evening sun streamed through the lobby's west-facing glass wall and the band played Duke Ellington's "Satin Doll," the unthinkable happened.

The fourth-story skywalk tore loose from its suspension rods and came crashing down on the second-story bridge directly below it. The combined force brought the entire mass of concrete and steel down on the lobby floor. Scores of people were killed instantly. Many more were injured severely and trapped under the twin concrete slabs. No one in the vast room would ever forget the horror of the moment.

A few hours before the collapse, Don and Adele Hall had left the city for a weekend at the Lake of the Ozarks. Arriving after the two-and-a-half hour drive, they were immediately informed of a catastrophe at the hotel. Don Hall reached the manager of Crown Center on the phone, but details were still sketchy.

"THE PAST 18 HOURS HAVE BEEN THE DARKEST OF MY LIFE AS WELL AS ONE OF THE WORST NIGHTS IN THE HISTORY OF KANSAS CITY."

—*the first line of a statement issued by Don Hall on Saturday, July 18, 1981.*

ABOVE: *The atrium and lower skywalk at the Hyatt in 1981. The walkway above this one (not shown) is the one that failed first.*

BELOW RIGHT: *Diagram from a report commisioned by the Kansas City Star explaining how the failure occurred. The report stated:*
"A change had been made in the design of the vertical rods that supported the walkways, which doubled the stress on the top walkway. Instead of running continuous rods from the second-floor walkway on to the ceiling, as the original plans dictated, builders installed staggered sets of rods. One set attached the lower walkway to the floor of the upper walkway; another set ran from the upper walkway to the ceiling. The top walkway was being pulled from above and below."
The National Bureau of Standards report released in February 1982 stated "the walkways...had only minimal capacity to resist their own weight and virtually no capacity to resist additional loads imposed by people."

204

> *"History, despite its wrenching pain, cannot be unlived but if faced with courage, need not be lived again."*
>
> —*Maya Angelou.*

"We got back in the car and started driving back to Kansas City," Don Hall recalls. "We were listening to news reports on the radio and it got worse and worse and worse. We went directly do the Hyatt." Nearly 30 years later, he still finds it hard to describe what he saw. "They were carrying body bags out. It was awful."

By then, the rescue effort was well underway. A thousand workers—fire fighters, paramedics, and volunteers—worked through the night, using jackhammers, blowtorches, and construction cranes to unsnarl the wreckage and lift it off the trapped victims.

Ultimately, the death toll reached 114 people. Nearly a hundred more sustained injuries requiring hospitalization. The loss of life would give the disaster the grim distinction of being the deadliest structural collapse in U.S. history.

How could this have happened? At the time, the question wasn't just a rhetorical entreaty but voiced an urgent search for a physical cause. A wide range of possibilities were advanced in the chaotic days immediately following the skywalk collapse. Angry finger pointing accompanied nearly every theory.

"It was obvious that this would turn into a legal nightmare, but we didn't know the dimension of it at that time," recalls Hall. "And of course nobody knew the real cause for a long while."

The true cause, determined after an investigation that stretched on for many months, was a simple but critical change in the way the walkways were supported. A modification of the engineer's original plans was made by the steel fabricator—a shop change—and later approved by the engineering firm, GCE International.

"One of the ironies of the Hyatt is that the cause of this extraordinary catastrophe was so simple," says Charles Egan, who served as Hallmark's general counsel at the time of the disaster. "Everyone was expecting that there was going to be a scandal out of this, and the newspaper was playing to that point of view. That wasn't the case, but it took the better part of a year to disabuse people of that."

In 1985, a Missouri administrative law judge ruled that two engineers of GCE International exhibited "a cavalier attitude" in designing the walkways and revoked their engineering certificates in Missouri and Kansas. The judgment had, in essence, answered the question of who was at fault.

HEALING A CITY

Pinpointing the physical reason for the structural collapse was simply a matter of examining evidence. Don Hall was confident that the independent investigation would settle that matter—and that Hallmark would ultimately be found inculpable. For his part, Hall worried less about who was to blame for what went wrong than about what could be done to make things right for the people whose lives were devastated by the catastrophe.

From the beginning, Hall had no illusions but that his company would bear the financial brunt of the disaster. Charles Egan explains the situation in plain terms: "The reality of something like the Hyatt disaster is not who's responsible, but who can pay."

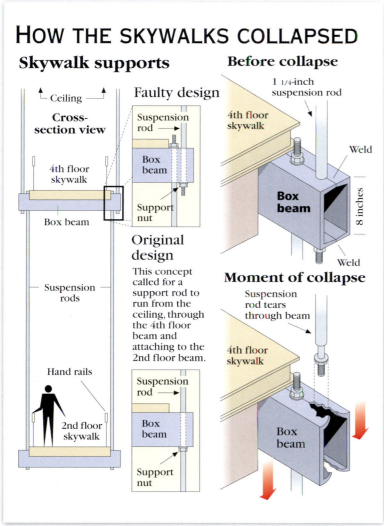

HOW THE SKYWALKS COLLAPSED

Skywalk supports

Kansas City Star

205

Nearly 2,000 separate damage claims were filed in court. "The plaintiffs got busy pretty fast," remembers Hall. "The problem was the people at fault had a million or 2 million dollars insurance—not enough to settle even one of these claims. Only the Hyatt and ourselves had deep pockets, so it turned out that we soon had something like $3.5 billion in suits against us." At the time, Hall points out, the company wasn't even worth $1 billion dollars. Culpable or not, the firm was in legitimate danger. "Yes, we worried that it could take the company down," Hall recalls. "We could have been defunct."

Soon after the tragedy, it became apparent that the liability insurance carried by the Hyatt wasn't nearly sufficient. With the looming prospect of drawn-out court battles over who would take responsibility for the financial burden, Hall believed that Hallmark should take action on its own. Charles Egan recounts how the matter was resolved:

"Don wanted to heal the city. He wanted the victims and their families fairly compensated, so that they could get on with life to the extent possible with these injuries. Don knew that Hallmark was going to take the hit in the financial sense, so he supported the idea of putting together a comprehensive settlement, so that we weren't fighting this thing for years and years and years."

After several months of meetings with legal teams representing the lead contractors and architects and even more protracted meetings with the leaders of the plaintiffs' group of lawyers, Hallmark agreed to admit liability and fund all of the settlements. Damages would be negotiated on an individual basis. Payouts ultimately exceeded $100 million.

"We were able to get a comprehensive settlement structure in place in about 18 months," Egan continues. "That's unprecedented. It couldn't have happened if Don hadn't supported it."

Like thousands of other Kansas Citians, Don and Adele Hall will forever carry the weight of July 17, 1981, in their hearts. The tragedy, according to friends, devastated them both. For Don Hall, the aftermath was little better. After a year and a half of battles with recalcitrant insurers and wrenchingly emotional negotiations with plaintiffs, he found himself in unfamiliar territory. "I was tired," he remembers. "It was demolishing."

It is often said in Kansas City that the loss surrounding the Hyatt disaster was great enough, and the city small enough, that everyone knew someone who was personally touched by the tragedy. The Hall family was no exception and neither was the Hallmark family.

On Monday, July 20, a letter written by Don Hall was distributed to all Hallmark employees. In it, Hall commended the bravery and energies of the people who worked through the night and asked for prayers for the families of the victims. At the end of the statement were the names of two Hallmarkers who had lost their lives at the Hyatt over the weekend.

In the wake of the Hyatt disaster, the Crown Center Redevelopment Corporation commissioned a complete review by independent mechanical and electrical engineers of every structure in the Crown Center complex. And after extensive repairs and thorough inspection by two leading engineering firms, the Hyatt Regency hotel reopened on October 1, 1981.

TheNoonNews

Monday
July 20, 1981
Hallmark Cards Inc.

A Statement by Donald J. Hall, president, Hallmark Cards, Inc., concerning The Hyatt Regency tragedy (Issued at 2 p.m., Saturday, July 18, 1981)

The past 18 hours have been the darkest of my life as well as one of the worst nights in the history of Kansas City. I find it difficult even to talk about the events of last night, as I know many of you do.

The catastrophe and the suffering of the injured bring forth a personal and community grief that requires all of our prayers.

While it is difficult to concentrate on anything other than compassion for those who have lost loved ones and the many who suffered injuries, I would be remiss if I did not commend the bravery and energies of the people who worked throughout the night to relieve the suffering of the victims.

Our police and fire departments, assisted by Belger Cartage, were superb. All those involved in essential emergency services were tireless and expert. Blood donors sensed the crisis and responded early in the evening, in large numbers. The Red Cross and the Salvation Army were promptly on the scene and were as devoted and effective as always.

The staff at the hotel was excellent, even in sorrow, as was the executive staff who manages the facility so beautifully. Numerous reports during the night mentioned their courage and concern. Without exception the people called to the scene proved to be this community's finest, even though the hour was our darkest.

It is impossible at this time even to speculate on what might have caused the events of last evening. Our thoughts have been preoccupied with the human suffering.

Investigations are beginning by all concerned parties. We too have launched an extensive investigation of our own into the causes of the accident and we will engage independent experts.

In the days and weeks and months ahead, much work must be done. Now it is a time for prayer and compassion and grief.

The following Hallmarkers have been identified as victims of the tragedy:

Deceased:

Julia Ann (Julie) Lamar, 33, senior Tel-Sales account representative — Hallmark Tel-Sales.

William V. (Bill) Longmoor, 56, account executive — Multimedia Forum.

Injured:

Pauline V. Kresin, personnel records clerk — Personnel Administration Services.

The Noon News, along with all Hallmarkers, extends sympathy and condolences to the injured and to the families and friends of the deceased.

"EVERYBODY IN THE INVESTMENT WORLD KNOWS WE'RE PRIVATELY HELD, AND I THINK TO A MAN THEY'D LIKE TO BE A PARTY TO CHANGING THAT. BUT THERE ARE NO ADVANTAGES I CAN VISUALIZE TO GOING PUBLIC."

— Don Hall

"UNDER OUR PROFIT-SHARING PLAN, EMPLOYEES OWN ABOUT ONE-THIRD OF THE COMPANY. IF WE HAD BEEN PUBLIC, THAT WOULD HAVE BEEN A PRETTY HARD THING TO ARRANGE."

— Don Hall (1977)

FAMILY MATTERS

It's impossible not to take away important insights from an experience like the Hyatt tragedy. For Don Hall, the incident re-affirmed his conviction to preserve Hallmark's status as a privately held company. To his thinking, the relatively quick legal and financial settlements surrounding the episode would have been virtually impossible if Hallmark had been a publicly traded company.

The resolution to maintain family ownership of Hallmark began, of course, with J.C. Hall. The senior Hall had a history of attempting (and usually succeeding at) endeavors that would almost certainly have been impossible had there been Wall Street bankers to keep happy. Advertising and promotional campaigns, the Hallmark Hall of Fame, the employee profit-sharing plan, and the Crown Center development itself are just a few of the company institutions that would likely never have seen the light of day in absence of committed family leadership—and ownership. J.C. Hall received, and declined, the first offer to buy his company way back in 1925. The offers continued unabated over the years, but the answer was always "no"—and a quick "no" at that.

The more dominant Hallmark became in its industry, the more prized it became to investors. But, like his father, Don Hall never wavered on the point of private ownership. Interviewed by the *Chicago Sun-Times* in the late 1970s, Hall left little question about his position on the matter. "Everybody in the investment world knows we're privately held, and I think to a man they'd like to be a party to changing that. But there are no advantages I can visualize to going public."

More than 30 years after that interview, he's more adamant

"WHEN YOU'RE PUBLIC, YOU'RE LISTED ON THE STOCK EXCHANGE AND YOU'RE JUDGED BY PERFORMANCE. BUT SOMEWHERE ALONG THE WAY, INSTEAD OF ANNUAL PERFORMANCE IT BECOMES QUARTERLY AND EVENTUALLY MONTHLY PERFORMANCE, AND THAT'S NOT THE WAY TO RUN A BUSINESS. YOU STAY A COURSE AND SEE IT THROUGH. ... WE HAVE SPECIAL FEELINGS ABOUT PEOPLE—EMPLOYEES AND THE COMMUNITY—AND WE REALLY COULDN'T CARRY OUT CERTAIN THINGS TO THE DEGREE WE WANTED TO IF WE WERE PUBLIC."

—Don Hall

than ever. Don Hall has always been a man to take the long view. Public companies, he points out, rarely have that luxury.

"When you're public, you're listed on the stock exchange and you're judged by performance," Hall explains. "But somewhere along the way, instead of annual performance it becomes quarterly and eventually monthly performance, and that's not the way to run a business. You stay a course and see it through." Furthermore, some decisions, Hall intimates, just don't come down to the bottom line. "We have special feelings about people—employees and the community—and we really couldn't carry out certain things to the degree we wanted to if we were public."

When he joined the company full time in the 1950s, Don Hall took advantage of its private ownership status to push through a virtually unprecedented line-up of benefits including the employee profit-sharing plan and career rewards program. Ticking off the myriad benefits championed and instituted by Don Hall, Charles Egan reminds, "these were all new ideas at the time—not just new to Hallmark—new to the world."

The company's commitment to providing a generous benefit package for its employees has become part of its operating philosophy over the years. And it hasn't gone unnoticed. In 1982, Hallmark was listed among the top ten in *Fortune* magazine's 100 Best Companies to Work for in America. Similar honors have followed ever since.

Simply put, Don Hall, like his father before him and his sons who have followed him into the business, believes that private ownership allows Hallmark management to make the best long-term decisions for the company and its employees. They are serious enough about their commitment to private ownership that when a company Beliefs and Values statement was created in 1989, the preservation of private ownership was included as a key tenet.

Of course, Hallmark is more than just a privately owned company. It is a family-owned company—status that adds further layers of complexity and requires patience, coordination, and communication throughout the branches of an ever-broadening family tree. For decades, the extended family of J.C. Hall has met quarterly at the Hall family farm—J.C. Hall and Elizabeth Hall's former home—to be kept up to date on company matters but also to encourage input from all members of the family.

From the beginning, Hallmark's corporate values were a direct reflection of J.C. Hall's personal values. As remarkable as it sounds, unity among his descendents—not over every minor detail but on the things that matter most—has made it possible for the company's values to reflect those of the Hall family to this day.

HALLMARK'S FAMILY CONNECTIONS

Hallmark is widely known as a family business—owned and operated. But it's not just the Hall family that has lent generations of talent to company. Over the decades, Hallmark has attracted multiple members of many families.

So, what's it like to know Hallmark not only as a supportive, family-centered company, but as a place where a relative (or two. . . or five) also works?

"It's all about love...and I love that I work near my dad and at Hallmark," says Monica Delaorra, a senior editor. Monica knew she wanted to be a Hallmarker when her father brought her in on a "Take Your Daughter to Work Day" when she was 12. "It's such good fortune to be working for a company built by family and based on connecting," she says.

Others talk about being destined for a career at Hallmark. "If you asked me about my parents, two of the first things I'd tell you is that they're both artists, and they've both worked for Hallmark," says editor Lauren Benson. "Whether it was fate, luck, or being raised with the peculiar habit of leaving notes on 3x5s, the longer I'm here, the more grateful I am that I came."

Lisa Chepren, a Hallmark designer, had both parents and a younger sister in the creative division. She was won over to Hallmark as a child. "As a kid, Hallmark seemed like a magical place, with colored pencils and endless supplies of markers and paper. Even back then, it felt like my destiny."

Chanda Fanolio, a creative account manager in the licensing studio, agrees: "Hallmark has always been a presence in my life. My mother and father both had their careers here, and I always knew that someday I would too."

Among the many employees, current and retired, who share blood ties at Hallmark headquarters, these families were featured in a 2009 photo exhibition by Hallmark photographers Steve Wilson and Donald Lesko. ABOVE: Lauren Benson and parents Jack and Lynn Benson. TOP LEFT: (clockwise) MyDung Cong and her sister Hanh Crow; Jill and Richard Fanolio and their daughter Chanda Fanolio; (center left) Elizabeth Baddeley, her mother Gayle Baddeley, and Gayle's niece Colleen Belton; Tyler Richmond and mother Becky Richmond; Marilyn Nixon and sister Shirley Cooper; (bottom) Marco and Carlo Pascolini, parents Barbara and Asterio Pascolini and sister Lisa Pascolini DeRousse; Shara Eaton and nephews Jeff Jones and Brad Dunlevy.

Barbara Hall Marshalll: An Eye for Detail

For as long as she can remember, greeting cards have held a strong appeal for Barbara Hall Marshall. As the middle child of J.C. and Elizabeth Hall, she certainly had plenty of exposure to these small works of artistic expression. In fact, it was Barbara, far more than her siblings Jimmie and Don, who most enjoyed reviewing the day's production of designs with her father at home every evening. Even then, she showed a natural talent for knowing which designs would strike an emotional chord with consumers.

Looking back now, she realizes that it wasn't just the art and illustration that appealed to her—but the diminutive size of the works. "As a child I always saved little pictures of things. I love little pictures—maybe that's part of the allure of greeting cards."

Those two interests—art and small things—would grow into abiding passions as Barbara Hall grew up. And her life, in many ways, would grow to revolve around them.

Barbara has served as an official advisor on Hallmark greeting card designs for more than 60 years. From the 1950s through the 1980s, she was a fixture on the "Okay Committee" that reviewed every card or specialty product produced by the company. Her father (and later her brother, Don) learned to trust her judgment as she stood in as a "consumer's advocate," offering comments on color, processes, design, and overall taste. It was a natural extension of those childhood evenings spent looking over her father's shoulder, and it was a role she cherished.

It wasn't always easy. "It taught me to give criticism," she says. "That can be very hard when the artist who created the work is in the room with you, but you still have the responsibility to say what you think."

Barbara's standing among the artists whose work she reviewed didn't suffer for her honesty. In fact, among the artistic community at Hallmark, she is respected and revered. She has always been an advocate, something that is not lost on Hallmark artists.

"She always seemed to be so right in her judgments about the artwork. She really knew the card lines and our consumers. And she was always very kind in her comments, even if it meant you had to redo something. All the artists admired her so much."
—*Mary Hamilton, Master Artist*

Barbara brought a consumer's insight to the review of greeting cards, not just because she happened to fit the profile of a "typical" greeting card buyer but because she worked for many years in the Halls' downtown retail store. "I worked in the card department," she explains, "so I got to hear what people said about cards." From 1943 until she was married in 1949, Barbara would work at the Halls' store until late afternoon and then head straight to company headquarters for the daily creative review. That inside/outside arrangement gave her a perspective on greeting cards that few others shared.

In 1998, in recognition of her 50th anniversary of service to the company, Hallmark established the Barbara Hall Marshall Award. The award recognizes top talent within the creative division and gives recipients a sabbatical opportunity to explore various creative disciplines. At the end of the sabbatical, award recipients share their work with peers and colleagues to provide inspiration and education across Hallmark's creative community.

The six-month sabbatical speaks volumes about the company's commitment to nurturing creative people. "It recognizes the spirit of creativity that Hallmark was founded on," says Don Hall, Jr., current president and CEO. "It allows time for innovation and creative exploration. In doing so, the award and its recipients inspire our entire creative community."

As great an impact as she has had at Hallmark, and around Kansas City, Barbara Hall Marshall is perhaps better known for her work outside the company. In 1982, she and a longtime friend, Mary Harris Francis, founded the city's charming Toy and Miniature Museum. An avid collector of mostly diminutive items since childhood, Barbara well remembers the spark that set her on a long path toward establishing the museum.

"I was in New York with my husband in the early 1950s, and I saw a display of this little furniture in a store window," she says "I was so charmed by these pieces that I bought a little chair—one little chair. After that, each time we would visit the city, I would treat myself to another little piece."

It took years for her to compile this small collection—and she might have been content with it. But around the same time, she learned that her best friend's sister, Mary Harris Francis, collected antique toys. The two shared their passions with each other and soon, "Well, now you've got someone egging you on," explains Barbara with a little laugh. "Pretty soon, we both had our treasures all over our houses. Finally, Mary Harris' mother said, 'If you girls get one more thing, you're going to have to start a museum.' We looked at each other and thought, 'That's what we should do!'"

After a long search, the two women found the perfect site and in 1982 opened the Kansas City Toy and Miniature Museum in a century-old mansion on the campus of the University of Missouri-Kansas City. The museum, with its world-class collections of fine-scale miniatures and vintage toys, thrills thousands of visitors each year and has been acclaimed as one of the finest of its kind in the world.

Though she has always had a keen eye for the small, Barbara Hall Marshall's impact on the Kansas City community has been anything but. She is a longtime trustee of both the Kansas City Art Institute and the University of Missouri-Kansas City and an ardent supporter of the local arts community.

More than 60 years after she started working for the family company, Barbara still enjoys sharing her ideas and thoughts with members of the Hallmark creative staff.

"I love art," she says. "But I love even more the people who make art."

Edythe Kegrize

Gary Head

Ken Crow

When he completed his military service in 1953, Don Hall returned to Kansas City ready to work. His job was at Hallmark, but his work would extend far beyond its walls. Don Hall came back determined to make the city he loved an even better place to live.

Hall brought to his hometown a keen desire to get involved—but he also brought something every bit as powerful and energetic—his new wife, Adele. And, as Don Hall and the Kansas City civic community would soon find out, in Adele Hall, Don had met his match in more ways than one.

"She certainly has been his partner in all the civic activities—in fact, Don would say, she's been his senior partner."
—Bill Hall

The young couple wasted no time in getting involved in their community—sometimes together, but often independently—after all, they could cover more ground that way.

Through his involvement with the city's Civic Council, Don Hall sought out other area business leaders who shared his passion for making Kansas City a better, more effective, and more liveable city. With each point of contact he invariably took on another responsibility. He found a mentor and kindred spirit in Charlie Kimball, director of Midwest Research Institute, and in so doing became involved with a group called the Science Pioneers, which promoted the study of science among school children. He admired Dr. Franklin Murphy, chancellor of the University of Kansas and an early member of the Hallmark board of directors. Through Murphy, Hall developed strong ties to the nearby university and deepened his commitment to supporting higher education in the Kansas City area.

In the mid-1960s, while serving as chairman of the Civic Council, Hall initiated two new programs: an organizing association for Kansas City neighborhoods and the Minority Supplier Development Council—both were firsts for the city. Asked why he had such an abiding interest in the diverse causes and committees he volunteered for, Hall gives a typically matter-of-fact response. "There were just things to do," he says.

Don Hall's line-up of civic involvements and charitable board appointments continued to grow. So ubiquitous was his presence on the civic scene that a magazine article from the

1970s referred to him as "city Hall." But Hall didn't say yes to every entreaty for help or directorship proffered. He had his own acid test. "I chose to do things on the basis of whether or not I could really accomplish anything," he explains. Hall avoided "figurehead" positions. "Personal involvement," Hall says, "is the key."

Don Hall's commitment to the community did not go unnoticed. In 1972, he was honored as "Mr. Kansas City" by the Greater Kansas City Chamber of Commerce—an honor that had been bestowed upon his father 11 years earlier. (Adele Hall would become the first woman to be honored with the award in 1990, necessitating that the name be changed to "Kansas Citian of the Year.")

Even as the mother of three young children in the 1950s and '60s, Adele Hall began building her own reputation as a key contributor to charitable and civic efforts in her new hometown of Kansas City. "I remember going door to door with the kids collecting for United Way," she says. "They would stuff envelopes and go to meetings with me when I couldn't find a babysitter—it was just a way of life."

"Don married this marvelous woman who can't say, 'no.'
I used to tell her that I was going to make her a little sign
to put by her phone that read, 'Hello. No.'"
—David Hughes, discussing Adele Hall's
prodigious list of civic involvements

Though energized and encouraged by her husband, Adele Hall credits her own commitment to service to her civic-minded parents—her father, particularly. "He had a commitment to his community practically above all else," she says. "I grew up with this idea that you just did your duty."

Still, she points out, "getting hooked up with the Hall family caused me to realize that what I was doing was worthwhile

because Don thought it was worthwhile too. It just underscored the importance of making a contribution."

She has been called the most powerful woman in Kansas City—a characterization that would surely make this modest woman cringe. But everyone who knows Adele Hall (and that includes a lot of people), and everyone familiar with her work in the community, realizes that in this case "powerful" means "the power to do good".

Mrs. Hall is perhaps best known for her work with the United Way. In 1977, after 24 years of service to the organization, she became the first woman to be named president of the Heart of America United Way. She would also rise to play a prominent role in the charity's national organization, eventually serving as vice-chairman of the board and chairman of the executive committee.

Adele Hall is one of the few members of the Kansas City community whose list of civic and charitable involvements rivals her husband's. The United Way is one prominent organization among many that benefit from her active assistance and seemingly bottomless energy. But the organization that is perhaps closest to her heart is Kansas City's Children's Mercy Hospital.

Hall's association with the children's hospital dates back to her first year in Kansas City, 1954, when she began regularly volunteering there and at the Crippled Children's Nursery School in midtown Kansas City (which would later become part of the hospital). Her first contributions were literally hands-on. She sat with ill or injured children, working puzzles, reading books, teaching numbers, and soothing fears. Her bedside and waiting room volunteering has continued for decades—but Hall also gradually took on more organizational responsibilities and was asked to join the hospital's board of directors in the mid-1970s. In that capacity, she helped steer the hospital through years of tremendous growth.

"I was struck with their mission, which was to take care of any child, regardless of their ability to pay, with the same standard of care. I knew I wanted to help those little kids in any way I could."
—Adele Hall, discussing Children's Mercy Hospital

When Hall began volunteering in the 1950s, the hospital didn't even have any full-time physicians. Today, Hall is an emeritus member of the hospital's board and still sits on the Children's Mercy Foundation Board. Her daughter, Margi Hall Pence, shares her mother's commitment to the hospital, having served as a long-time board member and as chairwoman in 2001 and 2002.

In late 2007, Children's Mercy announced a planned 15-year, $800 million expansion. Within a few months, the Hall family—through the Hall Family Foundation and its donor-advised funds at the Greater Kansas City Community Foundation, gave the single largest gift in the hospital's 110-year history.

Over the years, Don Hall had come to see the tremendous good that a dedicated foundation could have when locally focused and well managed. By the late 1970s, Hall—along with a small group of like-minded philanthropists—was convinced that more members of the Kansas City community could afford to, and would benefit from, being involved in philanthropic efforts.

The Halls met George H.W. Bush in the 1970's while attending a picnic for the Campfire Girls, and his wife, Barbara, soon after. The couples stayed in touch over the ensuing years and by the time Mr. Bush became Vice President in 1981, they had become close personal friends. Shortly after Mr. Bush became President in 1989, he appointed Don Hall chairman of the President's Committee on the Arts and the Humanities. Adele Hall would serve on the same committee under Bush's son, George W. Bush. In 1997, the senior Mr. Bush, asked Adele Hall to join the board of the Points of Light Foundation, a national organization he founded to promote volunteerism. She served on the foundation's board from 1997 to 2007. Pictured above are Don and Adele Hall with Mr. Bush on his boat in Kennebunkport, Maine.

The story of the founding of the Greater Kansas City Community Foundation has taken on the patina of legend. Though the exact amount of seed money is playfully disputed, Adele Hall remembers the genesis of the foundation well. "Charlie Kimball passed a hat—something like $237 was collected from the seven friends present and that was the beginning of the Community Foundation."

The idea behind the foundation was simple: charitable giving should be the responsibility of many, not just a select few. By partnering with a community foundation, donors could benefit from the simplicity and tax advantages of a public charity combined with the personal involvement and flexibility of a private foundation.

"The idea was that philanthropists could do more together than individually, and if they were to come together, they could attract other philanthropists with similar vision and passion to join with them. Together you can do more."
—Adele Hall, on the Kansas City Community Foundation

The Community Foundation has succeeded beyond all expectation. Three decades after its creation, it has grown to become one of the largest and most entrepreneurial public charities of its kind. Today, the Community Foundation manages more than $1 billion in assets and oversees more than 2,200 charitable funds established by individuals, families, and businesses. In total, the foundation has provided more than $1.25 billion in grants since its inception and impacted more than 3,100 nonprofits in greater Kansas City.

MOURNING A GIANT

Never was generational continuity more on the minds of the Hall family—and the Hallmark family—than on October 29, 1982. Joyce C. Hall, the founder of Hallmark and the man who, more than anyone before or since, helped define and develop the greeting card industry, passed away in his sleep at the age of 91.

Hall was still chairman of the board at Hallmark and until a few years before had maintained a semi-regular presence at the office. His death was mourned far beyond the complex of buildings surrounding 25th and Grand Avenue. The mayor of Kansas City asked that flags at city buildings be lowered to half mast and suggested that Kansas Citians do the same, "in memory of one of our greatest citizens and one of the nation's greatest citizens." Similar testimonials poured forth from other local business and community leaders.

Joyce Hall's death spurred news stories and tributes from the nation's leading newspapers. Like scores of other news outlets, the *New York Times* and the *Washington Post* recounted his rags-to-riches story while reporting that the company he founded 72 years earlier now boasted annual sales of $750 million. The *Los Angeles Times* focused on Hall's pioneering contribution to the entertainment industry, stating, "for a couple of decades, J.C. Hall provided more classical and substantial theater to Americans

"SO NOW THE TALL, HANDSOME MAN WHO LOVED KANSAS CITY IS GONE. HE DID NOT INVENT THE GREETING CARD, OF COURSE, BUT HE MADE IT POPULAR. . . IT WOULD HAVE HAPPENED ANYWAY, BUT NOT WITH THE TENDERNESS AND AFFECTION AND TASTE THAT WERE INHERENT IN THE CHARACTER OF JOYCE C. HALL."

—*Kansas City Times*

OPPOSITE PAGE, NEAR RIGHT: *Don and J. C. Hall in the mid-1960s.*

FAR RIGHT: *Don, Don Jr., and David Hall.*

> *"He was simple but complex. He was plain spoken yet every inch the gentleman. He had one of the most fertile minds I've ever known.*
>
> *— Franklin G. Murphy, longtime Hallmark board member and former chairman of the Times Mirror Company.*

than any man before or since." The "old man" (as he often referred to himself in memos to his staff) would surely have loved that line.

Hall's inspiring business success was only part of the story, of course. Local newspapers, especially, paid tribute to the less sensational aspects of Hall's life. "Morality and integrity were words used universally Friday to describe Mr. Hall," wrote a staff writer for the *Kansas City Times*. Citing his dynamism in developing Crown Center, the *Times'* sister publication, the *Kansas City Star*, summed up a long lead article with the simple sentence, "Joyce C. Hall was a man who made things happen."

But Hall was perhaps best eulogized by *Kansas City Times* columnist Arthur S. Brisbane, who wrote of the indelible link between the man and his adopted hometown:

"Kansas City, which welcomed a humble Joyce Hall in 1910, long has had a special stake in the man. Mr. Hall's success fulfilled Kansas City's image of itself as a city of opportunity, a burgeoning young metropolis with a future."

"(Joyce C. Hall) entered the realm of myth, a realm where mortal man, transformed by his own industry and good sense, becomes something more than just a man. He becomes an institution, the proverbial great man, the chairman of the board."

The passing of J.C. Hall marked the end of an extraordinary life, but it didn't necessarily mark the end of an era at Hallmark. The fact is, Hall's spirit, his energy, and most importantly, his commitment to the company had long ago been instilled in his son, Don, who had been at the helm of the company for 16 years at the time of his father's death. The Halls had long worked toward a smooth transition of power from generation to generation, and this effort was never more obvious—or appreciated—than at the time of Joyce Hall's death.

The following year, Don Hall assumed chairmanship of Hallmark. He also retained the office of CEO. Had he cared to look back over his more than 30 years at the company, he could do so with a great degree of satisfaction. The business had grown exponentially on his watch but had managed to retain many aspects of its family company feel. But Don Hall was always more inclined to look toward the future, and in that future he took even more satisfaction because he knew that his own children, by then young adults, had absorbed the same beliefs and values that had successfully led the company through its first generational transfer of leadership.

Changes at the Top

If a casual observer were to have taken stock of Hallmark in 1955, he would have seen a direct reflection of its founder, Joyce C. Hall. Hall's mark, "OK JC," was literally applied to every product before it was produced.

Similarly, by the early 1980s, the company bore the distinctive stamp of Donald Hall. Far larger, more diversified, more technologically adept, a more empowered and autonomous management team—all of these had been elements of the younger Hall's vision for the company. By any account, Don Hall's nearly two decades of leading the company had been an astonishing success. He was by no means finished, of course. There was much more he intended to accomplish. But by the early 1980s, Don Hall perceived a need to reach beyond his own vision of what Hallmark should be. He would rely upon some trusted compatriots, both experienced and new to the company.

In 1983, Hall promoted David Hughes to president of Hallmark. Hughes was a longtime Hallmark executive and an even longer-time friend of Don Hall. He had served as chief operating officer of the company since 1979. With the promotion, he became the first person outside the Hall family to hold the president's office.

Hallmark had long carried a reputation of promoting from within, and like Hughes, the vast majority of Hallmark's management team had worked its way up through the ranks. But Don Hall wasn't averse to looking outside the company for talent. In the same year that Hall promoted Hughes to president, he recruited two men whose careers he had followed for many years—each of whom possessed a kind of experience that was hard to match.

The first was Robert (Bob) Kipp, who for the previous 10 years had served as city manager of Kansas City. Hall had come to know Kipp when the former had served as chairman of the Kansas City Civic Council in the mid-1970s. The two developed a mutual respect,

David Hughes and Don Hall

Bob Kipp

and long before Kipp announced plans to retire as city manager in the summer of 1983, Hall had made it clear that his skill and service would be of great value in the private sector. In August of 1983, Hall proudly announced that Kipp had joined the Hallmark team and would become CEO of Crown Center Redevelopment Corporation.

"Through the years I have expressed my hope to Bob that he would never leave Kansas City without giving local companies and institutions an opportunity to keep him and his family in the community. When it became known that Bob was leaving his position at city hall, he and I discussed his options and his preference to enter the business community. I am delighted that he has accepted the Crown Center presidency. We feel very lucky to have him."

—Don Hall, 1983

With his keen understanding of urban development, well-established management credentials, close ties to local government, and intimate knowledge of the Crown Center development, Hall had found a man uniquely qualified to run the Crown Center subsidiary.

Kipp was thrilled at the opportunity to lead Crown Center's further development. "They had worked with the top-level urban planners of that time," he explains. "Edward Larrabee Barnes was heavily involved in the design, and Victor Gruen literally wrote the book on mixed-use communities." For a student of urban planning and management, Crown Center was, according to Kipp, "a very big deal."

But there was another reason Kipp accepted Don Hall's offer without hesitation—and that was Don Hall himself. In 1977, Kipp had been invited to join the Hall Family Foundation board at a planning retreat in Colorado. The experience made an indelible impression on him. "That's when I really got to see

David Hughes: Right-Hand Man

David Hughes remembers J.C. Hall's frustration at his long deliberation before accepting a job at Hallmark. "I think Mr. Hall was expecting that if offered a job I'd jump immediately," says Hughes. "He wasn't used to having people delay."

Hughes' hesitation wasn't over the job or the company—he knew Hallmark well enough by reputation. The issue was Don Hall. "I didn't want to screw up our friendship," explains Hughes. "I thought if things didn't work out at the company, it could affect our friendship, so I was very apprehensive. If I hadn't known Don I probably would have accepted right away."

After months of contemplation, Hughes did accept a job at Hallmark, with the impressive title of executive assistant to the executive vice president (Hughes laughs over that one), and in 1958 he joined his friend Don Hall at his family's rapidly growing company. His worries about their friendship not surviving have proved warrantless—it's still going strong after more than 65 years.

Hughes met Don Hall in the former's final year of high school in Kansas City. The two headed in different directions for college—Hall to Dartmouth and Hughes to Princeton—but they stayed in touch and saw each other back in Kansas City on breaks. After Princeton, Hughes went on to Harvard Business School (on his second try, he points out for the record—he was turned down the first time), and upon completion of his MBA he served 14 months in the air force, finally returning to Kansas City in 1953 to work for another Hall family friend, Charles Kimball, at the Midwest Research Institute. That same year he proudly served as Don Hall's best man at the Halls' November wedding.

Five years later, Hughes signed on at Hallmark. "When they first hired me I don't think they knew what to do with me," he remembers with a laugh. "They put me under Ed Goodman who was executive vice president, and I think that was just a place to put me while they got to know me and let me get to know the company."

Soon enough, the company found plenty to do with Hughes. Hallmark's product lines were expanding rapidly, and J.C. Hall assigned Hughes to coordinate the "line planners" in charge of them. No one had a name for it at the time, but as Hughes says, "We kind of developed our own form of product management."

"They'd been flying by the seat of their pants," says Hughes. "We developed procedures and criteria and figured out the most efficient way to get products through the production system." During a period when Hallmark was introducing so many new products—stationery, puzzles, candles, frames,

gift books, and more—the old ways, Hughes knew, just wouldn't have worked.

So adept was Hughes at this work that within less than a decade he was named vice president of product management. In the early 1970s, his leadership role evolved and expanded as he was named executive vice president of marketing.

From his earliest years at Hallmark, Hughes represented a new breed of Hallmark manager. Though he was hired by J.C. Hall and apprenticed by one of his key lieutenants, Goodman, Hughes was precisely the kind of person that Don Hall had in mind when he began his quest to bring more professional and modern management principles to Hallmark. He could think on his feet and wasn't afraid to make his own decisions without running to the boss to ask permission.

In 1979, David Hughes was named chief operating officer, and in 1983 he was promoted to president. He was only the third person in the company's history to hold the post and the first outside of the Hall family. For Don Hall, the decision was an easy one. There was no one he trusted more than his old friend. The two men share the kind of easy, honest rapport that only develops over time.

"He wasn't afraid to let me know it when he thought I was wrong," says Hall. "I could always count on Dave to tell me what he really thought." He pauses for a beat and smiles. "...which he did a little too often for my taste."

The timing of Hughes' tenure at Hallmark provided him with an unusual perspective—he joined the company at a time when it had definitively outgrown its status as a successful entrepreneurial shop, and as one of its top executives, he helped steer the company beyond its adolescence into a position of market dominance. He learned about the business from the "old-timers," some who had been around in the company's nascency, but before long he stood as the archetype of what a modern, self-efficient manager could and should be.

For 15 years after that, Hughes continued to serve on the Hall Family Foundation's board of directors, finally stepping down in 2005. Though fully retired now, Hughes knows that he'll always be a part of Hallmark. After all, he's still the chairman of the board's best friend, and that's a role impossible to replace.

Asked about the importance of David Hughes in her husband's life, Adele Hall sums it up succinctly, "He was Don's best man 55 years ago, and he's still his best man today."

the depth of Don's understanding and belief in corporate social responsibility," says Kipp.

"In the United States, corporations aren't preordained. Corporations are enabled to exist by government. So those corporations have a responsibility to the larger community, in addition to their responsibility to their own business. It was refreshing to find in a big corporation a CEO— Don Hall—who held those same beliefs. I wouldn't say he's unique in that, but you'd have to search a long time to find his equal."

—Bob Kipp

Much of Hallmark's tremendous growth during Don Hall's tenure as CEO had come as a direct result of business diversification. It was a strategy Hall believed in and was determined to stick with. In 1978, he had asked Irvine O. Hockaday Jr., the young CEO of Kansas City Southern Industries to join the Hallmark board of directors. Hall was impressed with the moves Hockaday had made to diversify Kansas City Southern, and by the early 1980s, he began speaking to the executive about a job change. What remained to be determined was just what job that would be.

Left to right: David Hughes, Bob Stark, Don Hall, and Irv Hockaday

To answer that question, Hall arranged a meeting that would set the company's management course for the next several years. He recalls the meeting well.

"I arranged for Harvey Thomas, an industrial psychologist that we had worked with for many years, to facilitate a three-day meeting. I asked him and his wife, Dave Hughes and his wife, and Irv Hockaday and his wife to go down to Florida and spend three days with Adele and me. In those three days we decided what we would do about Irv joining the company, what Dave's position would be, and what I would be. It was a marvelous discussion. Everybody came out with what they wanted to do, and we decided our steps for the next few years."

It was in that meeting that it was decided that Hughes would assume presidency of the company, which he did on June 14, 1983. Hockaday joined the company as executive vice president. But it was also determined in advance that if all went according to plan, the new Hallmark vice president would become CEO after a few years of service.

To outsiders, the arrangement may have seemed an unlikely abdication of power for a CEO to engineer, but for Don Hall, establishing the shared leadership structure was merely an extension of what he had been advocating for decades.

Interviewed by the *Kansas City Times* in the mid-1980s, Hall reminded that he never intended to keep a stranglehold on company leadership. "It's just my management style as opposed to Dad's," he explained. "My style is much more participatory management."

On January 1, 1986, just as the three men had discussed in their Florida meeting a few years earlier, David Hughes stepped aside as president of Hallmark to become vice chairman of the company. Hockaday was named president and chief executive officer. Together with Don Hall, the three comprised what Hall termed, "the office of the chairman." Robert Stark, head of Hallmark's Social Expression Group that oversaw all domestic and international greeting cards and related product, was named executive vice president. He joined Hall, Hughes, and Hockaday on a newly formed "policy committee" which would set Hallmark's direction on key issues affecting its future.

What all this rearrangement meant was that for the first time in the company's 73-year history, someone other than a Hall family member would be acting as chief executive officer. Just the same, Don Hall had no hesitation about giving up the CEO position. He had confidence in the team he had put together, and besides, he reminds, "I had been doing that for about 20 years. It was time to get some fresh ideas in there."

Irv Hockaday: Challenging Convention and Extending the Hallmark Brand

"Irv brought a style and approach to Hallmark that was probably different from most of the executives that grew up there, and I truly believe that's why Don hired him. He was not afraid to take risks. He was not afraid to state different opinions. He was not afraid to take action when he thought it was needed. It wasn't without some ripples, but that kind of input and direction was pretty vital for us at that particular time. He was a marvelous addition to the company."

—Jack Winne, retired Hallmark vice president

Irvine (Irv) O. Hockaday Jr. accomplished much in his 16 years at the head of Hallmark Cards, but he will likely best be remembered for his relentless efforts to move the company beyond its core business.

Hockaday's reputation as a skilled diversifier of business was one of the key factors that led Don Hall to recruit him to Hallmark shortly after becoming company chairman in the early 1980s. By then, Hall was well acquainted with the young president of Kansas City Southern Industries—a publicly traded transportation and financial services company. The two had begun crossing paths in Kansas City civic and business corridors in the early 1970s. Impressed with the executive's sharp mind, Hall asked Hockaday to join the Hallmark board of directors in 1978.

By 1983, after nearly 30 years at the helm of Hallmark, Don Hall was ready to transition out of day-to-day management. His older son, Don Jr., who was finishing up his MBA at the time, would rejoin the company full time upon graduation. In Hockaday, Don Hall saw a man who could ably lead the company, while Don Jr. gained operational and leadership experience.

Hockaday's initial reaction to Hall's offer was to pass. "I was having a good time and was energized by what I was doing at the time," he explains. But a combination of factors brought a change of heart. "The Hallmark brand was, and is, an extraordinary brand," he explains, "so, that attracted me. Also, I knew Don and Dave Hughes well and it seemed it would be a wonderful opportunity to work with exceptional people."

Hockaday was hired as executive vice president in 1983 and was named president and CEO three years later. He inherited leadership of a company that dominated its industry and enjoyed consistent annual growth. Still, as he looked at demographic trends, Hockaday worried. "If one posited that mathematical reality meant that Hallmark could not continue to grow its unit sales of greeting cards the way it had, and if you looked at the trends in demographics and declining birth rates, it was not unreasonable to say there will come a time when the growth as we've known it can not be sustained," he says in a measured tone. "It seemed to me we needed to understand what the potential limits of the Hallmark brand were."

Exploring the reach and range of the Hallmark brand became one of Hockaday's prime objectives. Hockaday oversaw significant expansion in Hallmark's international business with acquisitions of greeting card companies in the Netherlands, Mexico, the United Kingdom, and Japan. With each international play, Hallmark gained valuable insights.

"I was very supportive of international expansion because I felt that growth was inevitably going to slow in the domestic market, and therefore we should explore whether the greeting card habit translated to other cultures," explains Hockaday. "We weren't sure whether you could create this sort of mindset, this almost genetic predilection to buying greeting cards in other places. We gave it a fling in China. That culture didn't seem as receptive, but certainly in the English-speaking parts of the world, it seemed to me we should explore the possibility."

Hockaday's most ambitious moves were in the entertainment sector. Cable television was experiencing a tremendous boom at the time, and he hoped that Hallmark could become a player in the industry. He pursued business opportunities both on the systems side—with a 1990 partnership with Jones Intercable—and on the programming end, acquiring television production company RHI Entertainment in 1994. That business was later recast as the Hallmark Entertainment Network and launched the Hallmark Channel in 2001.

Subsequent moves within the entertainment sector followed over the next several years, but ultimately, Hockaday concedes that the television business didn't provide the brand-extending boost he had hoped it would.

"It was disappointing, perhaps, because we didn't seem to find—I didn't seem to find—a winning formula that could demonstrate the possibilities," says Hockaday, "but I would have been more disappointed if we hadn't at least looked and explored."

Hockaday retired as Hallmark's CEO and from the company's board of directors in 2001, but he still retains close ties to the company, serving on the boards of both the Hall Family Foundation and Crown Media Holdings, the public company that owns and operates the Hallmark Channel.

"He broadened our range of businesses, initiated important internal changes, and generated significant growth. Perhaps most importantly, he helped ready us for the future."

—Don Hall, on Irv Hockaday

BOB STARK: THE OPERATOR

In his 35 years with Hallmark, Robert (Bob) Stark held some lofty positions, including executive vice president and president of the Social Expression Group. Though proud of what he accomplished in Hallmark's executive corridors, Stark would not have anyone think of him as merely an august administrator. "I was the operating guy," Stark says in a booming voice. "I was not the theorist, the strategist, the dreamer of big dreams or whatever. I was the operator."

> *"Good execution of a mediocre strategy will always beat poor execution of a good strategy."*
> — *Bob Stark*

Stark always saw himself as the man in the trenches, even when he reached the very top echelons of senior management. His journey toward those top posts began in 1958 when he joined the company as a management trainee.

"I was fortunate enough to have rotated through a lot of the aspects of the business," says Stark. "I spent time in accounting and finance, management information systems, product management and product distribution, and ran the Canadian operation early in my career." That last assignment is one Stark takes particular relish in discussing. He served two tours at Hallmark's Canadian subsidiary in Toronto, the first as chief financial officer and the second, from 1970 to 1973, as president. "It was a break-even operation up until then, but when I went back in 1970 we started making some money. I think there is a direct correlation there," he says with a mischievous grin.

Stark also counts himself fortunate to have worked for Hallmark in the latter years of J.C. Hall's active involvement. He speaks with a sense of awe about the founder's "towering" presence and his instincts about which cards would perform. "He had mental telepathy about it," marvels Stark. "We started a research department and spent tons of money to find out what people wanted, but he just knew."

Traditionally, Hallmark executives have tended to be low-key and circumspect—politely midwestern. Stark never fit that mold. Direct, headstrong, and occasionally loud, he was never afraid to play the provocateur. Voluble and good-natured, he is a font of spirited axioms. One imparted often to his employees was, "If you don't know where you're going, any road will lead you there."

Stark knew where he was going. His broad range of experiences gave him a formidable working knowledge of the place. And his passion for the business has never diminished. "Bob Stark bleeds Hallmark," says one former associate.

Though he retired in 1993, Stark is still a frequent visitor to Hallmark's executive offices—his presence usually announced by boisterous, genial greetings well before he comes into view. Walking past his old office, he notes—not for the first time—that it is unoccupied, as it has been since he retired. "They're still looking for someone who can fill it," he deadpans. Eyes roll and smiles spread. That's Bob Stark for you.

EXPANDING THE HALLMARK VISION

The early years of Irv Hockaday's leadership at Hallmark would be marked by a consistent wave of expansion, acquistions, and exploration into new markets outside the social expressions category. But the strategic acquisition that has proved most enduring was actually finalized before he held the company's top spot.

In 1984, Hallmark acquired Binney & Smith, an 81-year-old company famous to every grade-schooler in America as the maker of Crayola crayons. The acquisition brought together two venerable family-owned companies with more than a few shared values. David Hughes, who as president and chief operating officer of Hallmark at the time helped consummate the deal, remembers that the Binney acquisiton was a perfect fit for Hallmark but required some patience.

"We talked to them and looked at the figures and went to visit and it just was a perfect fit. They ran a manufacturing operation very much like Hallmark—clean and organized. But they said they didn't want to sell, and we didn't want to go in with a hostile takeover. So we left it by saying, 'Well, if you ever decide to sell, call us.'"

About a year later, the Binney executive did call, and in just a few months the deal was done. It was a classic win-win. Binney & Smith gained marketing clout and access to broader markets though Hallmark's huge network of independent retailers and international presence. Hallmark picked up a category-dominant brand and gained access to the youth market, traditionally difficult to reach with greeting cards.

On the heels of the Binney & Smith deal, Hallmark bought a minority share in the SFN company, a leading textbook publisher that also owned several publishing and broadcasting subsidiaries. Two years later, it acquired the Univision Station Group, a group of Spanish-language television stations and Univision, Inc., the largest Spanish-language television network in the U.S.

"There was a strategic dimension to Binney & Smith. The mom that bought crayons for the kid was the same consumer that the Hallmark brand had built up huge equity with. There was not a strategic dimension to SFN or Univision. I wouldn't call those typical diversifications. That was more an investment management approach."
—*Irv Hockaday*

The company sold SFN after only about a year when Hallmark was made what Hockaday calls "an offer we couldn't refuse" from a Canadian publisher. The Univision deal didn't work out as well for the company.

Hallmark sold Univision to an independent investor in 1992 for roughly what it paid for the company in 1988. But Hockaday candidly admits that the "opportunity costs" of trying to make a go of the Spanish-language cable business were high. "The guy who bought it from us ended up making a ton of money," says Hockaday. "He knew exactly what to do. The idea was a really good one," he explains, "but we didn't know how to execute it. He did." The lesson learned by Hockaday and Hallmark was to truly understand a business sector well before jumping in, or failing that, to have a partner that does.

During the same period, Hallmark acquired a small group of cable television systems and in 1991 established a new subsidiary called Crown Media, Inc. to oversee the business. In 1995, it would sell Crown Media in a move that signaled its move out of cable systems operations. Instead, the company decided to put its energies into entertainment production and development. In 1994, it established Hallmark Entertainment, Inc., a subsidiary that would eventually develop multiple cable television channels and be spun off as a publicly traded company named Crown Media Holdings. In 2001, Crown Media launched the Hallmark Channel in U.S. cable markets.

LEFT: *In 1985, Hallmark celebrated its 75th anniversary. Among the many highlights of the diamond-anniversary year was the opening of the Hallmark Visitors Center on January 10. For the center's main entrance, Hallmark commissioned one of its artists, Don Dubowski, to design an enormous, 25' by 8' mural called* The Four Seasons. *One hundred different artisans and technicians worked together to execute Dubowski's design in copper, brass, and magnesium.*

MARJOLEIN BASTIN: FILLING NATURE'S SKETCHBOOK

"Parents can hardly guess what can happen when they put their children in the garden or in the grass," says Dutch artist Marjolein Bastin.

Marjolein's earliest memory is lying in the grass as a toddler outside her family's home near Utrecht, The Netherlands, absorbing the sights, sounds, and smells of the natural world around her. Little did her mother know that when she lifted little Marjolein from her baby carriage and placed her into the embrace of nature, she was placing nature into the embrace of Marjolein.

As a little girl, Marjolein collected and treasured simple items from nature – pinecones, seeds, and flowers. As soon as she was able to hold a pencil and paintbrush, she began trying to capture the beauty of nature in her sketches and paintings. "It was my way of holding forever the impression I loved so much in nature," she says.

Marjolein continued to pursue those impressions as she grew and developed her talent as an artist, ultimately attending the Academy of Arts in Arnhem, The Netherlands. Shortly after completing her studies there, her work came to be publicly recognized when she was asked to illustrate a one-page feature for the popular Dutch women's weekly *Libelle*.

A Hallmark designer discovered Marjolein's artwork while on a trip to Holland in the early 1990s, initiating a relationship that has spanned 20 years. Today, stationery and greeting cards bearing Marjolein's work are among the company's best-selling offerings.

Marjolein's work is enjoyed the world over. In addition to her partnership with Hallmark, she provides ongoing contributions to *Libelle*. She also writes and illustrates children's books featuring the character Vera the Mouse. Through her art and words, Marjolein offers people a simple reminder to pause and enjoy nature and allow it to be a source of serenity, energy, and healing.

Her workday often begins as early as 6:00 a.m. and extends into the evening, as she sits at her worktable, which inevitably is crowded with flowers or other treasures found on long daily walks. Brush in hand, she brings her special relationship with the world full circle: Nature captivates her, and she captures it to share with others.

9

10

"ZOMERSCHOON" 1620   "ABSALON" 1780

"BESSIE" 1847   "GLORIA"

◆ Ronald Reagan begins his second term as the 40th president.

◆ In February, the price of a first-class stamp rises from 20 to 22 cents.

◆ Mikhail Gorbachev becomes general secretary of the Communist party and de facto leader of the USSR. Breaking dramatically from party positions, he champions *glasnost* (openness) and *perestroika* (a market-oriented economy) and promises broad political, social, and economic liberalization.

◆ British meteorologists announce discovery of a hole in the ozone layer, which blocks ultraviolet rays from Earth.

◆ The Kansas City Royals come from three games behind to beat the cross-state St. Louis Cardinals four games to three in the 1985 World Series.

◆ An extra second is added to the calendar year.

◆ Nintendo video games are introduced.

◆ The collision of matter and antimatter is achieved by the Fermi National Labs atom smasher in Illinois. It allowed the Fermilab physicists to observe the first full demonstration of Einstein's famous equation $E=mc^2$.

◆ Pop music star Madonna launches her first road show, the Virgin Tour. Joining Madonna at the top of the pop charts in 1985 are Wham!, Foreigner, Chaka Khan, Tears for Fears, and Dire Straits.

◆ U.S. Route 66 is officially decommissioned.

◆ The *Argo* research submarine run by Dr. Robert Ballard finds the *Titanic*, resting 13,100 feet below the surface. It was split in two but largely intact.

◆ Coca-Cola introduces "New Coke" in an attempt to attract younger drinkers. The launch is an abject failure. In less than three months, the company reintroduces the original formula, calling it Coke Classic.

◆ The Montgomery Ward Company discontinues its product catalog after 113 years of continual publication. Started in 1872, Montgomery Ward is considered the world's first mail-order business.

◆ The Discovery Channel debuts on cable television.

◆ In 1986, Westwood, Kansas-based United Telecommunications and GTE Corporation of Connecticut merge into what becomes Sprint Corp., which will make its headquarters in the Kansas City area.

Taking Care of the Core

Hallmark's moves into media and other ancillary businesses made plenty of headlines throughout the 1980s and '90s, but the greeting card business still produced the vast majority of the company's revenue. In a 1985 interview with the *Kansas City Times*, Irv Hockaday emphasized that the non-greeting card ventures he pursued tended to give an inaccurate perception of Hallmark's primary focus. "It's a little bit like watching a magician perform," he said. "His most active hand is what you watch, and you lose sight of what is going on in the other hand."

The "other hand" at Hallmark was plenty full. When the Social Expressions Group—which managed the greeting card business—was formed in 1984, it accounted for 90 percent of Hallmark's revenue. In the mid-1980s, the company would take several major steps to assure that those revenues kept flowing.

In 1986, Hallmark launched Shoebox Greetings, a line of humorous greeting cards that carried the tagline, "(a tiny little division of Hallmark)." That parenthetical qualifier wasn't far off—the division *was* pretty tiny, with a staff of artists and writers that numbered only around 25. But the small team's output was huge. At the time, the Shoebox launch—including around 800 cards—was the largest product introduction in Hallmark history. It was also remarkably quick. In an era when it usually took 18 months to two years to bring a new card line to market, the team assembled to launch Shoebox pulled it off in just six months.

Shoebox cards (named for the humble containers that held J.C. Hall's inventory of postcards in 1910) were different from Hallmark's established humor cards and represented a direct response to humor trends in the greeting card market. They were timely, topical, unexpected, and edgy.

Homer Evans, a retired Hallmark vice president who led the Shoebox initiative, recalls the impetus for development of the new line and the urgency with which it was undertaken. "Our retailers and our field sales force had a lot to say to us about what competition was doing to us,"

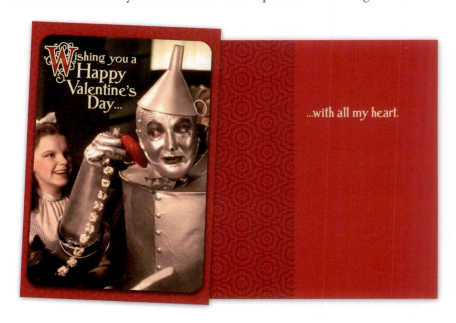

Evans recalls. "People who had exploited this new direction in humor were capturing a lot of space in Hallmark stores, and it was time to do something about it."

Hallmark did something about it and did it quickly. Within just a few months after launching, Shoebox accomplished the almost unthinkable. The "tiny little division of Hallmark" had redefined—or at the very least, greatly broadened—what was understood to be "Hallmark humor."

The tone and direction of the line wasn't dictated by Evans or any other Hallmark executive, but rather, it was set by the creative team charged with launching Shoebox. The hand-picked crew was told only to come up with an "alternative" line. What "alternative" meant was up to them. As editorial manager of the line throughout its development and launch, Steve Finken had a lot to do with figuring that out.

"We had long discussions about what the identity of this line would be. We had focus groups tell us that women weren't finding humor cards for them. They wanted humor cards with messages, not just jokes. They wanted a realistic, conversational voice. They wanted something fresh, with current references to the culture around them. And they wanted the illustrations that represented them to be realistic, attractive, and up-to-date, not so cartoonish."

—*Steve Finken*

The new line was loose, casual, and rooted in real life. According to Finken, although it was created from a youthful mindset, it appealed to people of all ages. There were no licensed "stars" in the Shoebox line when it debuted—no Snoopy or Mickey Mouse—but the line would soon create break-out stars of its own. Recurring characters, like the crabby, brazen, old bat Maxine and the young, acerbic, man-weary Denise gave voice to millions of card buyers. Both characters would take on a life beyond cards, appearing on a broad range of products—and in Maxine's case—even enjoying a multi-year run as a syndicated newspaper cartoon.

Shoebox was no small risk. Some worried that Shoebox's casual art style and impertinent humor might tarnish Hallmark's image. But the first sales figures proved that the strategy, created in chaos and laughter, had been successful. When the numbers came in, they showed Shoebox cards outselling the main Hallmark card line by over 12 percent.

A quarter-century after Shoebox debuted as a spirited experiment in greeting card humor, it has become an institution. Since the line's inception, more than 2 billion Shoebox cards have been sold. Writers and artists have come and gone—and many have come and stayed—but every workday, a team of around two dozen very creative individuals keeps the funny coming in this "tiny little division of Hallmark."

Taking care of the core business meant more than just refreshing and broadening the greeting card and product lines. A strong partnership with retailers had long been a key to Hallmark's success, and in 1986, Hallmark underscored its commitment to its best retailers by launching the Gold Crown store program.

The Gold Crown program was designed to provide independently owned card and gift stores the most complete selection of Hallmark merchandise along with unprecedented levels of service, sales information, and marketing and promotional assistance. For stores to receive the Hallmark Gold Crown designation, they had to meet exacting standards and demonstrate a commitment to professional retailing. The Gold Crown concept was a new idea at the time, but its philosophy can be traced all the way back to J.C. Hall's boyhood realizations about the importance of maintaining well-run retail operations. By the end of its first year, nearly 4,500 stores had enrolled in the Hallmark Gold Crown program.

LEFT: *Warner Bros. has been a solid partner for Hallmark for a quarter of a century. The collaborative relationship, which began in the mid-1980s, brought all-time favorites such as Looney Tunes, Scooby-Doo, DC Comics (including Batman and Superman), Hanna Barbera, Wizard of Oz™, and Gone With The Wind to the Hallmark licensing portfolio.*

An Irreverent, Semitrue History of Shoebox Cards
As told by Bill Gray (a tiny, little division of the tiny, little division)

Writers who brought a quirky sense of humor to the new Shoebox Greetings line included (back row) Dan Taylor, Kevin Kinzer, Bill Bridgeman, Steve Finken, Bill Gray, Mark Oatman, Chris Brethwaite, Rich Warwick, Myra Zirkle, (front row) DeeAnn Stewart, Allyson Cook, Leslie Kemp, and Scott Oppenheimer.

In the beginning was the joke. And it was funny.

A quarter-century ago, a group of hand-picked writers and artists—and if you're going to hand-pick writers, watch out for thorns—pulled up stakes, index cards, colored pencils, pens, and typewriters and left the Hallmark mothership for an outer building and a new adventure.

They took with them all the vital tools a writer needs: yo-yos, balls, dartboards, radios, movie posters, stuffed animals, and anything else that would keep them from having to actually write.

They called the new card line "Shoebox" because humor was afoot.

Shoebox was the answer to a number of questions consumers were asking: Why don't cards sound like us? Why don't they talk the way we talk? Why do hot dogs come in packages of eight, but buns come in packages of 10?

People still loved traditional Hallmark cards—and always will—but they also wanted newer, hipper, more realistic ways to say "Happy Birthday!" or "Get Well!" or "My cat can speak Portuguese!"

And so the writers at Shoebox squirreled themselves away in their cubicles to write jokes all day, every day. At the end of the day they gathered in a little room to read all of their efforts out loud. Laughter rolled like funny thunder, hilarity rained down on them, and that's all the weather references I can think of right now.

The jokes were handed over to the loving hands of artists who had acquired grown-up skills without ever losing the imagination, joy, and sense of freedom of kids with new crayons. (You have to talk like that about artists, or they get all pouty.) Together, they turned out a line of cards that looked and sounded just like real people would look and sound if they were a tad more attractive and really, really funny.

Very soon the Tiny Little Division of Hallmark became very big indeed. A quarter of a century and couple gazillion jokes later we're still here, although a couple of us are about to finish gnawing through the ankle chains. And folks are still standing in front of card racks, saying, "Read this one! It sounds just like your sister's friend Amber!" and trying not to laugh that embarrassing snorty laugh.

And that's what we call happily ever after.

KINDA MAKES YOU WANT TO BROADEN YOUR SOCIAL CIRCLE A LITTLE, DOESN'T IT?

It's your birthday.

Eat all the crap you want.

Wow! No way! It has an inside, too!

This just gets better and better!

WOW! You got a card!

A real, honest-to-goodness card!

Not an e-mail.

Not a text message.

But a true Birthday Card just for you!

Celebrate for 10 minutes and tell your buddies it was more like 3 hours.

PEACE in your heart...

Bless You Mama

FRIENDS ARE THE FROSTING ON THE BIRTHDAY CAKE OF LIFE!

RAMSTAD

Being on your own means that you can do the things you want, make your own decisions, take responsibility for your own happiness. But it can sometimes be kind of lonely...

It means a lot to me that you respect my decisions and accept me for who I am.

Para Ti
En Este Día de las Madres

Que DIOS Los Bendiga Al Celebrar Su Aniversario

Shoebox was Hallmark's largest new product rollout of the 1980s but far from its only one. In 1987, Hallmark introduced Mahogany cards to serve the African American market. That same year, Ambassador (Hallmark's mass-market greeting card division) rolled out its first nontraditional humor line, called "My Thoughts Exactly." The company undertook another major launch in 1989 with the innovative "Just How I Feel" line of cards and related products. This line broke new ground by offering sincere sentiments that addressed real-life situations like divorce, addiction recovery, and terminal illness. Hallmark extended its ethnic product reach with a new Spanish-language card line, called "Primor," introduced in 1991.

The 1990s would see further expansion of Hallmark's core business and ever broader efforts to extend the Hallmark brand into other categories. Hallmark made a strong move into the Asian market in 1994 by entering into a joint venture with Aesop, Ltd., a leading publisher of greeting cards in Japan. It would buy the company outright in 1997 and rename it Nihon Hallmark KK. Several other acquisitions were made throughout the decade to strengthen the company's position in European and U.K. markets. Closer to home, the company purchased InterArt Holding Corporation, an innovative greeting card publisher based in Bloomington, Indiana, in 1998. That subsidiary would be renamed Sunrise Greetings in 2005.

BEYOND BRICKS AND MORTAR

In 1993, the U.S. National Science Foundation, the primary financier of the global computer grid called the Internet, made significant changes to the network's technological backbone that made transferring digital information 30 times faster. That breakthrough, more than any that preceded it, brought the Internet into broad public and business use. Almost instantaneously, a new lexicon was born as words like "Web site," "domain name," and "browser" found their way into common usage.

Hallmark, like millions of other businesses, raced to develop ways to apply this new communication platform to its business model.

"Those were like the days of the Wild West. Land grabs in the digital sense occurred in the form of 'cyber squatters' who tried to lay claim to space before the big brands became aware of the Internet's potential. Even individuals who later became industry giants like Bill Gates thought that desktop computing would always be a much bigger deal than the networking aspects of the Internet."
—*John Sullivan, former Sr. Vice President, Hallmark.com*

The company formed Hallmark Connections to develop and market interactive electronic greeting cards and related products in 1994. Two years later, Hallmark Connections paired with Microsoft to develop Greetings Workshop, computer software that allowed customers to create personalized products on home computers. Around the same time, in 1996, Hallmark launched its official company Web site, Hallmark.com. The first incarnation of Hallmark's Web site didn't offer much more than basic company news and information, but it would shortly be eclipsed by ever more ambitious and engaging content. Within a few years, it became one of the 50 most trafficked Web sites in the world as Hallmark.com began to serve as a multilevel portal to the company, complete with e-cards, animations, and interactive features.

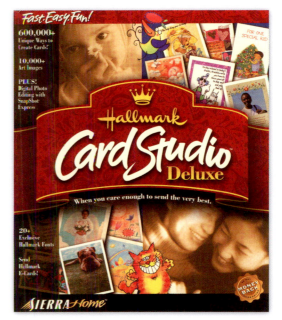

TOP: *In partnership with software company Sierra Home, Hallmark provided the creative content to launch a new line of personalization products called "Hallmark Card Studio" in 2000, replacing the Greetings Workshop line. "Hallmark Card Studio" has partnered with the software company Nova Development since 2004.*

ABOVE: *The characters hoops&yoyo were adapted by illustrator Bob Holt for life on the Internet. Their e-card debut on Hallmark.com was July 4, 2003. The above animation cells are from the hoops&yoyo animation series, Campfire Stories: "The Runaway Marshmallow," Part I. The complete series can be seen on hoopsandyoyo.com.*

ENDING THE MILLENNIUM ON A STRONG NOTE

By the 1990s, the depth and breadth of Hallmark's greeting card offerings dwarfed the competition. But Hallmark was hardly finished. Between 1997 and the end of the decade, Hallmark would experience wave after wave of new product roll-outs. It began with the enormous launch of the Expressions from Hallmark line.

Much like the Ambassador line, introduced 37 years before, Expressions from Hallmark was developed specifically for the mass-market retail channel (drug, discount, and grocery stores). Boosted by a year-long ad campaign including TV spots and back-cover ads in more than 100 national magazines, the new line was initially installed in 5,000 stores.

The launch of Expressions came 10 years after the debut of Shoebox Greetings, and according to Ellen Junger, Hallmark senior vice president of marketing, what Shoebox was to the 1980s, Expressions from Hallmark was to the 1990s.

"Shoebox and Expressions were both major milestones, but they accomplished different things," Junger explains. "Shoebox broadened what Hallmark stood for and got us into the alternative card business. Expressions really drove a big increase in market share for us because it allowed Hallmark to compete more effectively in the mass channel."

The impact of the Expressions line was tremendous. "We went from having two lines—Hallmark and Ambassador—to three and basically grew everything by about 30 percent," says Junger. "Then you add in all the work we were doing around innovation for Gold Crown stores and all the product launches—it was a very busy time from a product launch standpoint."

The company pulled off two other major card line launches just two years later, in 1999.

The Warm Wishes line brought hundreds of 99-cent cards to more than 17,000 retail outlets nationwide. The line, according to Junger, "was part of Hallmark's strategy to broaden its range of price points and grow category share at the lower end of the spectrum." A second major release in 1999 was a Spanish-language line called "Hallmark en Español," which included 1,000 cards.

Hallmark began the new millennium with another debut—an alternative line of square cards called Fresh Ink. Aimed at 18 to 29 year-olds, Fresh Ink's approach was irreverent, urbane, honest, and quirky. A national television and print-ad campaign introduced the 500-card line with the tagline, "Say something real. Fresh Ink."

"Expressions" from Hallmark (top), "Fresh Ink" (center) and "Warm Wishes" were three milestone card lines that Hallmark launched in the 1990s to provide consumers with more options in pricing, retail channel, and—in the case of "Fresh Ink"—the attitude and style of the cards themselves.

TAKING THE REINS

At the end of the 20th century, Hallmark celebrated its 90th year in business. With roughly 4 billion dollars in consolidated net revenue per year, Hallmark was one of the largest privately held businesses in the world. In December of 2001, Hallmark president and chief executive officer Irvine O. Hockaday announced that he would retire at year's end.

"As Hockaday's role in the Hallmark story proves, family businesses can benefit from outsider blood while maintaining the integrity of a family-owned business."
—The Chief Executive, *Jennifer Gilbert, Dec. 2001*

Hockaday had led the company through one of the most dynamic periods of its 90-plus-year existence, tapping new markets, testing new waters, and extending Hallmark's reach into a wide array of business categories. There were hits and misses to be sure, but at the end of his tenure, one important number speaks volumes. By 2001, fully 40 percent of Hallmark's total revenues derived from non-greeting card business—an increase of 30 percent over roughly a decade and a half. Clearly, Hockaday had taken Don Hall's mission to diversify the business and run with it.

The same company announcement that carried news of Hockaday's retirement also delivered official word on the company's new president and CEO.

Sixteen years after his father had stepped out of the chief executive role—and 92 years after his grandfather founded the company with help from his two great uncles—Donald J. Hall, Jr. was named Hallmark's chief executive officer—only the fourth in company history.

In a nearly 30 year career at Hallmark, Donald Hall, Jr. had already held several key positions within the company—most recently vice president of product development. He had served as vice chairman of the board since 1996. As part of the same reshuffling that moved Donald Hall, Jr. to the top spot, his younger brother, David Hall, returned to the parent company following a three-year stint as vice president at Hallmark's Binney & Smith subsidiary in Pennsylvania. David Hall would take on the position of senior vice president of human resources.

It was January 1, 2002. After 16 years, family leadership had returned to Hallmark.

With the goal of expanding its distribution and broadening its product offering, Hallmark made three important acquisitions in the late 1990s. In 1997, the company acquired West Kennebunk, Maine-based William Arthur, long considered one of the finest makers of high end, customized stationery (bottom image at left). The following year, Hallmark purchased InterArt Holding Corporation, an innovative greeting card company based in Bloomington, Indiana (middle image). In 1999, Hallmark acquired DaySpring Cards, a leading manufacturer of Christian personal-expression products based in Siloam Springs, Arkansas (top).

John Wagner: The Man (Yes, Man) Behind Maxine

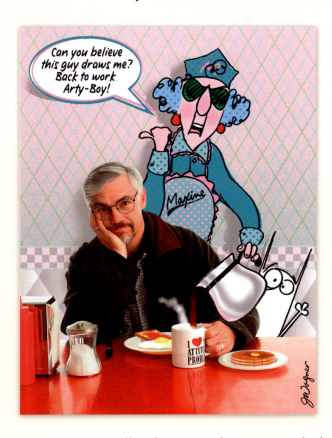

The one question Hallmark artists and writers get asked more than any other is, "Where do you get your ideas?" If John Wagner, creator of the sharp-tongued cartoon character Maxine, has told the story of her origins once, he's told it a hundred times—on *Good Morning America* and *CNN*, to *People* magazine, *USA Today,* and to dozens of newspapers and TV stations across the country.

Yet his face still brightens with fond amusement as he tells it again. "My mom and maiden aunts were the inspiration for Maxine," he says. "When you have that many older women around all the time, you pick up on a few of their quirks."

Wagner was the first art studio manager for Shoebox Greetings in 1986 when he first drew Maxine. The new card line was trying to connect with card senders with a fresh type of female character. They were women with attitude, insightful, funny— like the popular Denise character drawn by Denise Chevalier. Wagner thought the line needed an older character, too. So with a few passes of his pen he created the no-BS grouch who would be known for years only as "John's old lady."

Maxine was born. Her first card sold well, so there was another, and another. At one point there were 40 Maxine cards in the Shoebox line. Wagner is quick to point out that Maxine's take-no-prisoners world view and stinging turn of phrase is the work of Shoebox writers, who seem to relish letting Maxine say those things most of us are too polite, or sheepish, to say. But Wagner creates her distinctive look, from her chemically tortured hair, aviator shades, and

perpetual snarl, right down to her housecoat and bunny slippers. He's even given her a canine best friend, Floyd, who plays her straight man without saying a word.

As Maxine's greeting card popularity grew, she suddenly took on a life of her own. "I knew Maxine was popular one day when security called me down to the lobby," Wagner recalls. "There was a woman waiting there who had dressed up like Maxine and wanted to meet me."

Then Wagner's mom got involved. Toni Wagner, who helped inspire the character, was a willing conspirator in Maxine's publicity boom. Toni began dressing up as Maxine and attending special events at Gold Crown stores and nursing homes throughout New England, where she lived.

"My dad would drive her around. . .she called him her chauffer-gofer," Wagner remembers. "She'd get into her funny hat, housecoat, and bunny slippers. They were quite the cute couple."

Maxine hit it big in 1995 with a *People* magazine article featuring Toni and John. From then until her death 10 years later, Toni took on the Maxine persona in countless interviews with national and local media.

Since her creation, Maxine has appeared on millions of cards, t-shirts, coffee mugs, Keepsake Ornaments, dolls, and other gifts. She's had her own syndicated newspaper strip, her own Christmas television special, and been the subject of calendars and books—with her recent book, *It's Not Menopause...I'm Just Like This,* selling over 400,000 copies. She even had her own fan club with 17,000 registered members. Maxine has become one of Hallmark's hottest properties, which the company licenses out to other manufacturers. She's moved into new digital media too, with her Web site, Maxine.com, boasting 10,000 bookmarked users who check in for her daily *Crabby Road* cartoon.

These days Wagner is devoted to Maxine full time. And if he's grown a little weary of the old sourpuss, he doesn't let on. In fact, he talks with excitement about plans to celebrate the old girl's 25th birthday. He knows he'll have to tell the story of her creation a dozen more times, but he won't mind. To him, it's almost as if Maxine is family—and, of course, she is.

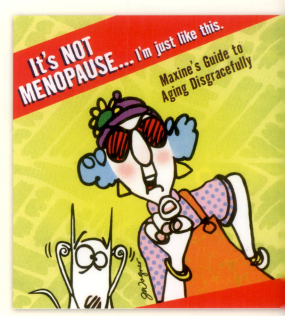

Another Birthday and you've still got it!

But nobody wants to see it.

Happy Birthday

Christmas is just plain weird.

There are easier things than meeting a good man.

Nailing Jell-O to a tree, for instance.

What other time of year do you sit in front of a dead tree in the living room and eat candy out of your socks?

CHAPTER TEN

A Second Century, A Third Generation

(2002 AND BEYOND)

"One faces the future with one's past."

— Pearl S. Buck

O N JANUARY 1, 2002, DON HALL, JR. BECAME CEO OF HALLMARK CARDS. THE JOB WAS NEW, BUT HE WAS WELL ACQUAINTED WITH THE ENVIRONMENT. LIKE HIS OWN FATHER, HE HAD VIRTUALLY grown up in the business.

Some of his earliest memories included playing in his dad's office on Saturday mornings while the elder Hall caught up on the week's work. Now, 36 years after his father had first taken over formal leadership of the company, that office was his.

Much was the same in the eighth-floor executive area of Hallmark Cards—including a few of the faces a young Don Hall, Jr. might have encountered on those childhood visits to the office. But in the dawning years of the 21st century, the world surrounding that office was changing—and changing fast.

The ground was shifting in 2002. An America still shaken from the terrorist attacks of September 11, 2001, was on the cusp of war in the Middle East. And while the domestic economy continued to grow, the rapidly emerging economies of China and India vastly outpaced that of the U.S.

A years-long dot-com bubble effectively burst in 2001, but the high-tech industry still set the pace for innovation and captured the lion's share of interest from investors and from a consumer public that eagerly embraced the latest technological wonder. When Apple's iPod was introduced in the fall of 2001, it—and the mp3 digital audio recording format that it utilized— changed the way much of the world purchased and listened to music. (Within less than six years, sales of the iPod would reach 100 million units). Change has always been a constant. But the sheer speed and global nature of 21st-century change would have been almost unfathomable just a decade before.

Despite the fluidly changing environment, Don Hall, Jr. showed early on that his leadership style would be deliberate and focused. His decisions as the company's new leader were clear-headed and considered, even if they weren't always easy. He had the counsel of his father, his brother, and a circle of trusted advisors, but he also had what he considered a reliable roadmap: the company's Beliefs and Values statement.

"One of the first things we focused on was a reaffirmation of our beliefs and values," says Hall of his transition to the

company's top spot. "We didn't view them as historical, but as critical to our future success."

This reexamination led to some important priority shifts. For one, Hall explains, they decided to focus less on the size of the company and more on the needs of the consumers it served—both greeting card buyers and sellers. Echoing his father and grandfather before him, Don Hall, Jr. explains, "We're only successful if our retailers are successful. We're only successful if we meet certain fundamental needs, and in order to do that we needed to have certain capabilities."

First among these capabilities was the company's creative resources. Almost immediately upon assuming leadership, Hall designated the creative division as a corporate entity, elevating its importance in the company. "Previously, it would have been considered a production area," explains Hall. "But we envisioned creative as central to our brand. We thought it was time to refocus on the brand, on creative, on product and our customers."

In other words, Hall thought it was time to bring emphasis back to the core business.

"We felt that corporately we had been too focused on our entertainment areas," he continues. "We had been putting increasing

---

BELOW: *Even as a child, Don Hall, Jr. was a frequent visitor to the Hallmark offices. In this photo, taken in the late 1950s, the Hall family gathers in J.C. Hall's office. Standing behind Don, Jr. are (left to right) J.C., Elizabeth, Adele, and Don Hall, holding daughter Margi.*

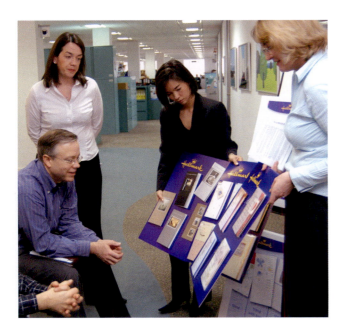

levels of resources toward that business and we wanted to pull that back and apply those resources in other places."

Hallmark sold its television production and distribution business, Hallmark Entertainment, Inc., a few years later. By 2006, the company's sole presence in the television entertainment category consisted of its long-running Hallmark Hall of Fame series and the Hallmark Channel, which by 2004 ranked as a top-10 U.S. cable network.

While he was determined to give the core greeting card and gift business the attention it deserved, Hallmark's new CEO did not turn his back on the idea that Hallmark should pursue other, ancillary business opportunities. They just needed to make sense in the context of Hallmark's core capabilities.

As he considered Hallmark's business opportunities, Hall was determined to learn from the company's diversification hits and misses over the previous decades. Among its acquisitions, the most resounding success had been Binney & Smith, the maker of Crayola crayons. Hall believes that a good portion of that success derived from the fact that the acquisition was a natural complement to Hallmark. The business was built on a strong brand foundation. Creativity and emotion were central to its product development and its relationship with consumers. All were things that Hallmark understood and knew how to use in building a successful business.

In 1999, Mark Schwab, then Hallmark's senior vice president of strategy and marketing, was dispatched to Easton, Pennsylvania, to become president and CEO of Binney & Smith and revitalize that business. Schwab, who earlier had launched the Hallmark Keepsake Ornament business and led Hallmark's product discovery and development division, streamlined the business, emphasized product innovation and strengthened the Crayola brand presence in the marketplace.

In 2007, the company changed its name to Crayola and found itself in the enviable position of serving as the "category captain" in the children's creative experiences aisle of most major retailers. By the time Schwab retired in 2009, the company was enjoying record-breaking revenues, solid customer partnerships and a steady stream of product innovation.

"With regard to future expansion," says Hall, "we're looking for things that will extend the reach and relevance of our brand and build off of the knowledge and capability that we have, and will over the long term be viable businesses."

TOP: *Don Hall, Jr. is a longtime member of the board of trustees of the United Way of Greater Kansas City. He served as chair of the group from 2002 to 2004, during which time he helped lead a complicated effort to reorganize four local United Way organizations into one unified body. In this photo, Hall receives a gavel in recognition of his two years of leadership. Presenting the honor at the organization's annual meeting in March 2004 is incoming United Way chairman, Jimmie Stark.*

MIDDLE: *Mark Schwab retired in January 2009 from a 30-year Hallmark career, during which he oversaw the launch of the Hallmark Keepsake Ornament collectibles business and a major transformation of Crayola.*

LEFT: *On a 2004 trip to Hallmark UK headquarters in Bradford, England, CEO Don Hall, Jr. reviewed new greeting cards developed for Clinton Cards, the United Kingdom's largest greeting card retail chain. From the left are Don Hall, Jr., Geri Davies, Lina Hansard, and Belinda Cockburn.*

DON HALL, JR.: NO SHORTCUTS TO THE TOP

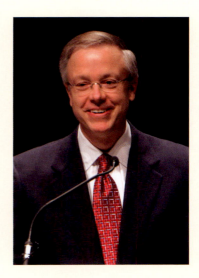

In the mid-1980s, Don Hall, Jr. spent a year working on a large lithography press as a trainee in Hallmark's graphic arts division. Far from the company's executive office suites, this is where the most elemental work of greeting card production happens—where ink meets paper. Ken West was the man in charge of Hallmark's graphics production at the time, and one of Hall's supervisors and key mentors was an experienced lithographer named Wayne Herran. The two veteran printers shared a passion for their craft that Hall will never forget.

"I remember listening to Wayne and Ken talk about color theory and lithography, and the importance of quality lithography relative to our business," says Hall. "And before Ken sent me to work with our press operators, I remember him saying, 'You'll find that when you get a little bit of the ink under your fingernails, it'll never go away. Your love of this business will permeate your whole system.'

"It was really through that experience that I realized that I really loved this business and the product that we make, and that I realized the tremendous commitment that Hallmarkers were making to our business."

"When I worked with the press operators, I was in awe of their craftsmanship, their attentiveness to quality, their desire to always improve. It was really inspiring. Everyone had a great sense of pride in what we were doing and how we were doing it."

That job as an apprentice lithographer wasn't the first that the elder son of Don Hall had held at company headquarters—not by a long shot. He began working at Hallmark part-time in his teenage years, and there would be multitudinous jobs along the way before Hall would be prepared for the company's top spot.

But it was that job, and others like it—where he worked side-by-side with fellow Hallmarkers in production, packaging, the photography lab, and customer service—where Don Hall, Jr. truly earned his status as a Hallmarker.

"I felt good about the company before that," says Hall, "but it was through those work experiences that I really came to appreciate the significance of what everybody was working on."

Hall's résumé shows that he held nearly 20 distinct jobs

in at least a dozen different departments on his long tour through Hallmark. But the path he took was anything but random.

From the time he took his first part-time job at Hallmark as an assistant in the company's photographic department as a teenager, Don Hall, Jr. had been intrigued and excited by the work the company did. By the time he had earned his MBA from the University of Kansas in 1983, he was increasingly certain that he wanted to work in the business. The question was where to start.

Planning an appropriate career path for Hall fell to Jack Winne, a Hallmark human resources director, and Charles Egan, with input from Don Hall and Don, Jr.

The result was a roadmap specifically designed to give Hall varied and meaningful experiences within the company. He started with customer service and field sales and then moved into the product areas, working as a line planner and product manager. Along the way he held mid-level management positions, but never until he had worked at a lower level within the department he led.

"When I went into this it was with an objective to play a meaningful role, a very conscious desire to contribute in a way that could help the company," Hall explains. The plan was designed so that Hall's path through the company would expose him to all facets of the business from concept to retail. In the early 1990s he worked in specialty store development, gaining valuable insight into the retail side of the business.

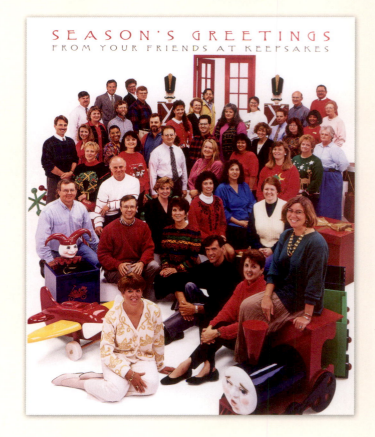

"Don Hall made it clear to HR that he wanted his sons to move up just as far as their own interests and talents took them and not just because of their name."
—Bob Kipp

In 1993, Hall was named general manager of the company's Keepsakes business unit. He counts his time leading Hallmark's ornament division among his most formative experiences.

"One of the things I learned through my experience with Keepsakes is that innovation is the best way to spark growth," says Hall. "That was one of the most innovative areas of our company and one of the areas where creative was the most engaged in terms of identifying the opportunities."

Maintaining Hallmark's long-held status as a creative powerhouse has always been one of Hall's passions, so it was fitting that he first became a corporate officer as vice president of Hallmark's creative division in 1995. As head of creative, Hall worked to bring emphasis back to what he considered to be the engine of Hallmark's core business. In Don Hall, Jr., Hallmark artists and writers found a kindred soul and a real advocate. "He made it very clear that if you had any concern you could walk up and talk to him about it," recalls a 23-year veteran artist. "He was extremely visible and accessible."

Hall was voted onto Hallmark's board of directors in 1990 and became vice-chair in 1996. He served as vice president of product development and then executive vice president of strategy and development before taking over as CEO in 2002.

Myriad challenges awaited Don Hall, Jr. when he stepped into the job once held by his father and grandfather, but his thoughtfully conceived, broad-based, and patient journey to that position had prepared him well. It's easy to assume that a father's eldest son will succeed him in leading a family company, but on Don Hall, Jr.'s journey, the easy road was never taken.

Though decades have passed, Hall has continued to draw on the professionalism, dedication, and passion of the co-workers who inspired him when his career at Hallmark was just beginning. And he never has gotten that ink out from under his fingernails.

RIGHT: *In 2002 Hallmark debuted the Maya Angelou Life Mosaic Collection of cards and gifts in its Hallmark Gold Crown stores.*

LEFT: *Before he was CEO of Hallmark Cards, Don Hall, Jr., was general manager of Hallmark Keepsake Ornaments from 1993-1995. He joined the Keepsakes staff for a photo that ran on the cover of the Keepsake Ornament Club newsletter in December 1994.*

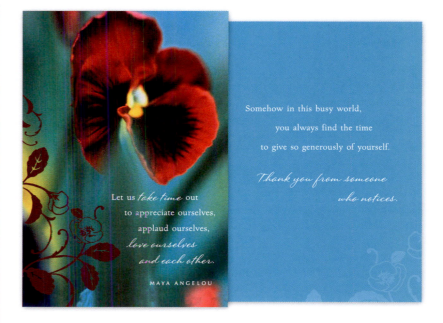

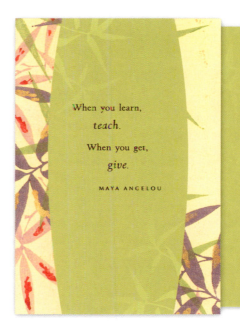

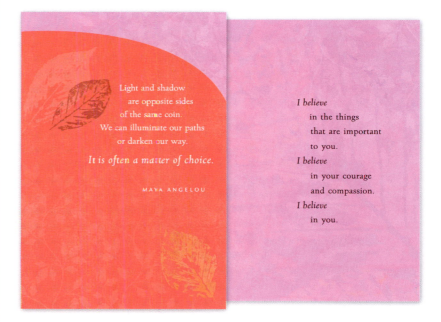

ENHANCING RELATIONSHIPS, ENRICHING LIVES

Don Hall, Jr. is an ardent believer in the power of—and importance of—the Hallmark brand. When he became CEO of Hallmark in 2002, he asked that a statement be created that would capture the "essence" of the Hallmark brand—one that could serve as a daily inspiration to Hallmark employees.

Ed Cunningham, a 40 year veteran of Hallmark's editorial department, was asked to write a piece "from the heart." He wrote the statement in one afternoon. It is reproduced to the right.

That same year, Hallmark undertook several initiatives that reflected the spirit and inspiration of its new brand essence statement. The flurry of activity would touch nearly every part of the core business while reaffirming Hallmark's commitment to both its mass-channel business and its specialty retailers.

One of the largest initiatives of the decade was the creation of an exclusive greeting card line for the nation's largest retailer. Hallmark launched its Connections From Hallmark line in Walmart stores in 2003. The sheer size of the initiative required an unprecedented creative and logistical effort. The line, currently sold in two-thirds of Walmart's 3,600 stores, includes roughly 3,000 greeting cards developed exclusively for Walmart. Hallmark, with plenty of input and help from Walmart, delivered this tremendous output of product in just one year.

While Connections From Hallmark was certainly attention grabbing, it wasn't only Walmart that benefitted from Hallmark's push to reinvigorate its presence in the mass-market channels. Long-term key accounts in the drugstore category, like Walgreens and CVS, also saw an influx of new and innovative product.

Hallmark specialty retailers—its independently operated Hallmark Gold Crown stores—likewise benefitted from the company's renewed commitment to its product lines and retailer services. In 2003, Hallmark hired Jim Boike to lead the development of a long-term vision for Hallmark's retail business. Boike had spent the previous 14 years at Williams-Sonoma, the last two as executive vice president and chief operating officer.

Good changeThe move signaled Hall's commitment to the independent retail network and his belief that Hallmark Gold Crown stores presented the best retail stage for the Hallmark brand.

"Jim's understanding of the consumer, product and visual merchandising helped define the recent evolution of the store environment," says Don. "The people, products, service and operating standards he advanced have elevated the Hallmark brand experience for consumers who shop in Hallmark Gold Crown."

ENRICHING LIVES

Hallmark is here
to help people
define and express
the very best in themselves,
to serve their spirit of kindness,
their need to comfort and to heal,
to love and be loved,
to laugh and to celebrate,
to reach out and to remember.

We are here
to offer gifts of thoughtfulness,
messages of care,
moments of beauty created to heighten
the pleasure of giving, the thrill of receiving
and the joy of sharing.

We are here
to commemorate the smallest events
and the largest milestones,
to affirm our respect for humanity,
our belief in its future
and our unwavering reverence
for the sweetness and fullness of life.

We are here
to make connections
with timely humor and timeless inspiration,
with gentle affection and genuine surprise,
with light and music and color,
with stirring images
and powerful stories
that speak to what is universal
in the human heart.

We are here
to enhance relationships,
to enrich lives,
to play our unique
and cherished role
in the always changing,
never changing seasons
of friendship and family and love.

"I THINK THERE'S STILL A WONDERFUL FEELING ABOUT THE HALLMARK BRAND, AND I THINK WHAT'S MOST INTERESTING IS THAT PEOPLE REALLY FEEL THAT THE BRAND HAS BEEN IMPORTANT IN THEIR LIVES AT IMPORTANT TIMES. PEOPLE TRUST THE BRAND. THEY FEEL IT HAS DEEP EMOTIONAL CONNECTION AND RELEVANCY. EVEN WITH YOUNGER CONSUMERS WHO MAY NOT HAVE HAD ALL THE HISTORY WITH THE BRAND, THERE'S A GREAT FEELING OF RELEVANCY."

—*Don Hall, Jr.*

RIGHT AND ABOVE: Launched in 2003, Connections From Hallmark was created to meet the needs of Walmart consumers. Sold in about two-thirds of Walmart's 3,600 U.S. stores, the Connections brand has won Walmart's top-supplier honors for its flexible, innovative, and fast-to-market strategies, as well as for its focus on birthday sending and cards for kids.

BELOW: In the summer of 2006, Hallmark launched Hallmark Magazine. *Designed to bridge the gap between sophisticated lifestyle titles and traditional women's publications, the bimonthly women's magazine focused on family, friends, home, communities, and celebrations. Despite strong support from a base of consumers that had reached 800,000 by 2008, the company discontinued publishing early in 2009. In a statement to the media, Don Hall, Jr. lamented the magazine's closing. "In just under three years, the staff accomplished a great deal, creating a product that beautifully reflected the brand and reached consumers in new ways. But, with the overall magazine industry clearly struggling for the foreseeable future, we could not justify further investment."*

LEFT: *The early years of Don Hall, Jr.'s leadership saw Hallmark extending its brand in numerous, but calculated ways. In addition to the Maya Angelou Life Mosaic Collection, Hallmark also introduced The American Girls Collection of gifts and personal expression products in 2002. The line was designed to reinforce the bond among girls, mothers, and grandmothers. In the same year, the company launched Hallmark Chocolatier, a line of Hallmark-branded chocolates through a licensing agreement with Alpine Confections. The year before, a subsidiary floral business called Hallmark Flowers was launched. In 2003, Hallmark unveiled a comprehensive revision of its Spanish-language greeting card line with the introduction of Sinceremente Hallmark. The line is distributed in the U.S., Puerto Rico, and Mexico.*

Internally, Hallmark calls the part of the company that deals with its core business—that is, its greeting card, gift wrap, and partyware divisions—the Personal Expression Group. The divisions that comprise the Personal Expression Group are responsible for roughly 75 percent of all Hallmark revenue. Needless to say, the person responsible for this business has an extremely critical job.

From 1997 to 2005, that person was Don Fletcher. Fletcher had started his career at Hallmark in 1967 and worked his way up through the ranks in various product and marketing positions. Along the way, he distinguished himself as one of Hallmark's most accomplished and respected leaders. His skill at building relationships was valuable not only within the company, but also in working with the company's key customers.

With the multi-front surge of activity in Hallmark's product groups in 2003 and 2004, the company benefitted greatly from Fletcher's experience and steady demeanor. In Fletcher, Don Hall, Jr. had no doubts that he had the right man in a remarkably complex job.

"Don Fletcher was an incredible mentor—not only for me and my brother, but for so many Hallmark managers," explains Hall. "He was a transformational leader with an unwavering commitment to product leadership. Even today, probably half the senior managers here would still point to him as a mentor who was generous in sharing his insights and experience."

In 2004, after 37 years with the company, Fletcher told Don Hall, Jr. that he intended to retire. Fletcher's impending departure would leave the company with a considerable leadership void to fill. But it also presented an intriguing opportunity to bring an even greater level of family leadership to the 95-year-old family company.

As the executive directly in charge of the majority of Hallmark's divisions, the president of the Personal Expression Group is generally considered the number two spot in the company. Early in 2005, the company announced that Fletcher's position would be filled by David Hall. Don Hall, Jr.'s younger brother was already a senior vice president and had served on the company's board of directors since 1996. But now, for the first time in its history, two descendants of J.C. Hall would concurrently occupy the top spots at Hallmark.

David Hall had the great benefit of working side-by-side with Don Fletcher for the first six months of 2005. The two worked together on every facet of the job—the practiced executive imparting his 38 years of knowledge and experience to his successor. On July 1, Fletcher ended his illustrious career at Hallmark and David Hall took on full responsibility for the Personal Expression Group.

LEFT: *Don Fletcher, a 38-year Hallmark veteran, served as president of Hallmark's Personal Expression Group from 1997 to 2004 and was an important mentor to countless Hallmark managers.*

BELOW: *(left to right) Don, Jr. and David Hall*

"THEY HAVE AN EXTRAORDINARY RELATIONSHIP—AND IT'S GENUINE. I'M NOT SURE I'VE EVER SEEN ANYTHING LIKE IT."

—*Irv Hockaday, on Don, Jr. and David Hall*

GUIDED BY VALUES

Hallmark has always been a company with a strong sense of purpose. Its guiding precepts—to make personal connections, to enhance relationships, and to enrich lives—are elemental to everything it does. Such tenets serve to keep the company grounded, but at the same time mandate that it constantly evolve to keep pace with societal change and shifting customer needs.

Clear evidence of such evolution at Hallmark is a corporate-wide internal initiative called "business transformation." The effort—kicked off in 2006 and ongoing—is, according to David Hall, "about focusing on the end results that we want to get and changing the way we work to get there." From that broad purpose statement, Hallmark's business transformation project has launched roughly 40 initiatives, covering everything from reducing product-to-market cycle times, to fostering innovation in products and how they are marketed, to bringing more flexibility to the company's supply chain. Several of the initiatives revolve around upgrading and streamlining the company's technology.

"In the past, when we wanted to effect change, we'd say, 'We'll work a little bit harder and we'll change the outcomes,'" explains David Hall. "But what we finally realized was that we have to really change the way the game is played—so we've fundamentally changed the way we think about product. We've focused much more heavily on innovation as opposed to trying to refresh several thousand stock numbers every year."

Though the term, "business transformation," is of the moment, the idea—that a company should re-examine its basic assumptions and look for new ways to improve—is certainly nothing new. "My grandfather did this," points out David Hall. "He never would have used the word 'transformation,' but he was always looking for ways to significantly change the way things were done in order to better meet the needs of our customers."

"Innovation" has been a watchword for both David and Don Hall, Jr. throughout the first decade of the 21st century. Either will tell you that innovations are made in all areas of the company, but the most obvious evidence is in the greeting card aisle of the local drugstore, or, to an even greater extent, at one of Hallmark's Gold Crown stores, where the company's newest products normally debut. The past decade has brought an explosion of products that offer what Hallmark calls "an amplified experience."

Leading the amplified experience were Cards With Sound, introduced in 2006 and Cards With Motion which hit the market the following year. The sound cards—which play an audio clip when opened—were a hit from the beginning.

The story of the creation and introduction of Cards With Sound has already entered into Hallmark lore. The line began

Song: Best of My Love *by The Emotions*

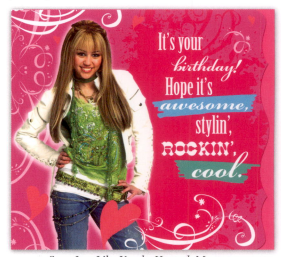

Song: Just Like You *by Hannah Montana*

Song: Bad to the Bone *by George Thorogood and the Destroyers*

ABOVE: *Hallmark's Cards With Sound line took the market by storm when it debuted in Gold Crown stores in 2006. With greatly enhanced digital and audio technology, original song clips from original artists, and complementary artwork and sentiments, the cards were a great leap forward in the sound card category. Subsequent additions to the line expanded its range, including cards with sound clips from movies, TV theme songs, vintage commercial jingles, and even recordable cards that allow senders to record their own message to add before a prerecorded song. At the time of this writing, well over 2,000 Hallmark cards incorporate sound technology.*

"THE SHARED EXPERIENCE
PEOPLE HAVE WITH MUSIC,
WHEN COMBINED WITH
A MESSAGE THAT ONLY
HALLMARK CAN DELIVER,
SATISFIED A CONSUMER
NEED THAT HAD NOT BEEN
ADDRESSED IN THE
MARKETPLACE."

—*David Hall, on the success
of Cards With Sound*

with an audacious directive from Don, Jr. and David Hall and Jim Boike to a small group of creative and retail managers. "We challenged the group to come up with a new product line to be in stores by July," Hall explains. "We didn't tell them what it should be but said, 'It has to be big, it has to be buzz-worthy, and it has to make people say, 'Wow!'" That challenge was leveled at year-end in 2005. With just a few months to deliver a winning new line, the group—assisted by hundreds of other Hallmarkers from across all company divisions—rose to the challenge. The resulting line has been delivering "Wows!" and sales ever since.

David Hall holds up sound cards as one prominent example of Hallmark's renewed innovative spirit—but only one among many. "As we've muscled up on innovations more, consumers have responded," he says. "The spirit of innovation has really transferred into all of our product categories," says Hall, "and even beyond product."

Hall is quick to offer other examples. Another recent favorite is the company's line of fUNZIPS—whimsically styled, self-sealing gift boxes that are "unwrapped" simply by pulling a perforated strip. Thus, an eager child can unzip an alligator's mouth to reveal the gift inside. Hall points out that development of such products came about only by fundamentally changing the way the company thinks about the concept of gift-giving and receiving.

"We had always approached gift wrap as an act of concealment," explains Hall. "Your main job as the gift-giver was to hide the present you were giving. But when we listened to our customers about their gift-giving experiences, we learned some interesting things. Among these was that fact that there are times when you want to do more than just conceal a present—you want to make opening it an event too. You want to prolong and enrich that experience." As evidence of this subtle, but to Hallmark, meaningful change in approach, the division known for decades as "gift wrap" has recently been renamed, "gift presentation."

ABOVE AND LEFT: *Early in 2006 Hallmark began redefining the category of "gift wrap" as "gift presentation" in order to heighten the experience of giving and opening gifts. New formats including fUNZIPS, decorative boxes with a perforated strip used to open the package, debuted in July 2007. Christmas 2008 saw the debut of Peek-Buster gift bags, with motion-activated sound technology, and the first-of-its-kind adhesive gift wrap with low-tack adhesive on one side that sticks firmly to packages like an over-sized sticky note.*

Don Fletcher: Learning, Leading, and Passing It On

Don Fletcher, who retired as president of Hallmark's Personal Expression Group in 2005, graduated from Drake University in 1967 with a lot of options. Among the many corporate recruiters impressed by the young man was Hallmark's on-campus scout at the time, Jack Winne.

> *"In his early years, he wanted to know as much as he possibly could—first about greeting cards and then about other product areas. He attracted some mentors who wanted to help him—people with incredible levels of experience like (Hans) Archenhold, Jeannette Lee, (Jack) Jonathan, (Homer) Evans, and (Clark) Randall. He took it very seriously, and he developed a deep knowledge of the core business."*
> —Jack Winne, discussing Don Fletcher

But it was an earlier visit to Hallmark with his business fraternity that convinced Fletcher that his future would be in Kansas City.

"We toured Hallmark while we were in town and when I got back to school I told a friend, 'If I ever have the chance, I'm going to go to work for this company because walking through the halls of Hallmark felt just like walking down Main Street of the small farming community where I grew up. Everybody knows everybody by first name. It's very informal, very casual, and very comfortable.'"

The amiable Fletcher fit right in. He was assigned to Hallmark's career development program and had the good fortune to learn the greeting card business from two respected veterans, Homer Evans and Clark Randall—"two of the best mentors a person could have had," remembers Fletcher. "They taught me, and they gave me opportunities."

Fletcher made the most of every opportunity he got. After spending several years working in greeting card marketing and development, he was put in charge of the company's licensed properties business. It wasn't a job he sought out, but he quickly saw the value in the assignment. "It gave me the opportunity to work with a lot of people who weren't Hallmarkers which made me realize how strong an organization we had and also the caliber of people who were employed by Hallmark," he says.

But deep down, Fletcher was always "a product guy." He loved working in the core business and from his early years with the company harbored a desire to head up greeting card development. By the mid-1990s, he achieved that and more. In 1992 he was named vice president of product development and elected an officer of the company. In 1997, he was put in charge of all of Hallmark's greeting card, gift wrap, and party business as the president of the Personal Expression Group.

As much as Fletcher achieved in his 38 years at Hallmark, the last six months of his career were among the most important. He spent them mentoring David Hall in the key job he had held for eight years. For Fletcher, it was the perfect way to wrap things up.

"It gave me an opportunity to watch firsthand how he and Don, Jr. worked together, which furthered my confidence that the two of them working in tandem were going to be a great team to guide Hallmark forward through the opportunities and turbulent waters that would face them in the future," Fletcher says.

As for his protégé, David Hall appreciates that he learned from one of Hallmark's very best. "He was a great leader," says Hall, "One of those who really embodied the notion of treating Hallmarkers the way you want to be treated. He was eminently fair, yet still expected results. If there were a Hall of Fame, Don Fletcher and Jack Winne would be in it."

It's time to start the party, time to break out the kazoo—Hope your day will be amazing, fun, and funky just like you!

LEFT: *Spin-a-Majigs™ made greeting cards a moving experience, literally, when they debuted in Hallmark Gold Crown stores for Valentine's Day 2008. Using a small crank on the cover and a hidden gear box, the cards used a single set of parts to create up to 17 different motions. Some of the cards also featured light and sound.*

OLIVER CHRISTIANSON

BEFORE KIDS

AFTER KIDS

Oliver Christianson has signed his cartoons "Revilo" since college. The fact that Revilo is Oliver spelled backward may help explain his humor—peculiar yet surprisingly familiar, like life seen in a fun-house mirror.

Of course the only explanation really needed is that Revilo is funny. He's made people laugh in the pages of magazines as diverse as Better Homes and Gardens, People, National Lampoon, and Esquire. He's won the "Cartoonist of the Year" award for greeting cards from the National Cartoonists Society.

The Revilo cartoon collection now appears on Hallmark cards, calendars, books, and on the Internet at Revilo.com. But when Christianson started at Hallmark in 1986 cartoons were rarely published on greeting cards. He was one of Hallmark's pioneers in an art form that allows his writing and drawing talents to merge as one integrated, slightly skewed, view of life.

"I think of myself as the court reporter of life," he says. "I really don't have to do any writing. I just listen, look, and write down what I see."

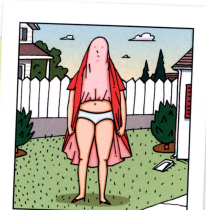

JUDY HAD A SPLIT PERSONALITY. THE TOP HALF WAS INTROVERT, THE BOTTOM WAS NOT.

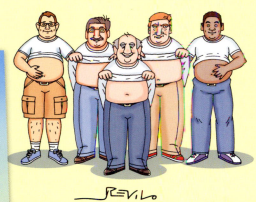

GUYS GONE WILD!
CONTROL YOURSELVES LADIES!

2010 Wall Calendar

Take me! Take me!

No, you're ugly..

COMMON FIGURE FLAWS

BIG HIPS   LONG WAIST, SHORT LEGS   SHORT WAIST, LONG LEGS   POORLY DRAWN HEAD

I THINK THE RUFFLE REALLY MAKES A DIFFERENCE, DON'T YOU?

David Hall: A Passion for the Business

"People have always asked, 'What's your favorite job?' and I've always answered, 'the job I'm in.' I always hated to leave the job I was in…but I always loved the job I went to."
—David Hall

David Hall has held a broad range of jobs within Hallmark Cards. Each assignment has presented its particular challenges, but Hall has met them all in his same signature manner—it might best be described as easy-going determination. Hall brings a gregarious, amiable presence to the office every day. But he also brings a single-minded conviction to making Hallmark the very best.

Hall's zeal for the business is contagious. His enthusiasm is palpable as he discusses his goals around cutting lead times, developing new product offerings, and gaining deeper insights into the wants and needs of the company's customers.

"Dave had a passion for wanting to do it and do it right, and with that kind of mindset I was very confident that he would bring to the assignment what it was going to take to be successful and surely take it beyond where I had taken it."
—Don Fletcher, David Hall's predecessor as president of Hallmark's Personal Expression Group

There's no shortage of issues that require Hall's attention—or benefit from his passionate approach toward the business. As president of the Personal Expression Group, David Hall has operating responsibility for all aspects of Hallmark's North American and International businesses. He also serves on the boards of directors for Hallmark, and the Hallmark Corporate Foundation.

Just as his brother did, David Hall took a lengthy and deliberate path through several departments of Hallmark before landing in his current position in 2005. His odyssey began in the early 1980s when he worked summer internships while earning his undergraduate degree. He worked two years in product development and finance jobs before heading off to law school at the University of Kansas. Three years later, with law degree in hand, he returned to Hallmark to talk about the future—a favorite subject of David Hall's.

"I would sit down and talk with Jack Winne, who was a great guy at developing people," Hall says. "And I'd also talk with Don and with Dad and get their input— early on it was probably more direction than input," he jokes. "We talked about what would be good experiences and building blocks, so that I would develop an understanding of the business—but also do some real work. This was about accountability and responsibility and having things that I had to deliver, and not a lot of safety nets."

"It's a question I've often been asked, 'Did you always know you were going to work here?' I don't think I did always know that, and that in a large part is because Dad never made it an expectation. Dad was wonderful about it. He would talk about work if you wanted to, but he would never force it. He instilled this feeling in me that he would love it if I did, and he would be totally supportive if I didn't. I think that made it more enticing to come to work here."
—David Hall

The goal—to learn a lot about the company and the business through exposure to various departments—was the same for David Hall as it was for his brother, but early on, David pointed out the benefit of mixing things up a bit.

"Over time it felt as though the building blocks were really similar to Don's, and I started to think, 'Gosh if this does work out that we both want to work here over time, does it make sense for us to have the exact same experiences or does it make sense for them to be different?' Also, we're different people and have different interests."

They had different educational backgrounds too. With his law degree, it was natural that David Hall would spend some time in Hallmark's legal department. He served as a staff attorney for four years, but never doubted that he would wind up back on the product side of the business. "I never thought that was going to be my path," he says of corporate law. "But what I learned in my four years of being a lawyer has been extremely helpful in my career."

Hall next took on assignments in the public affairs and human resources offices and then as director of retailer relations and communications. In 1998, he oversaw the integration of a subsidiary greeting card company newly acquired by Hallmark.

But it was his next assignment that Hall considers one of the most formative of his career. In 1999, he packed up his family and moved to Easton, Pennsylvania to take the job of vice president for U.S. marketing and sales at Hallmark subsidiary, Binney & Smith (now called Crayola). He admits to being conflicted, initially at least, about the move. "I always loved the work in Kansas City. I hated leaving here," he says. "But I loved working out there."

"The first time I walked into the manufacturing facility at Crayola Crayons, I said almost exactly the same words that everybody says the first time they walk through the plant: 'This smell reminds me of my childhood.'"
—David Hall

Though he found many similarities in the two companies and their respective corporate cultures, Hall also found the change

As Crayola celebrated its 100th anniversary in 2003, Dave (left) and Don Hall enjoyed the festivities, riding in the Crayola Centennial Parade as it passed through Center Square in downtown Easton, Pennsylvania.

refreshing and eye-opening. "It was very healthy, I think, to get outside the comfort zone of what is Hallmark in Kansas City," Hall explains. "It was a bit more contained—a smaller yet fairly good-sized business—so you could really see how the choices you made on a Monday could make a difference on a Tuesday. It was a great learning experience. While Crayola, like Hallmark, is a great consumer brand, it's a very different business. And there was something about that that I found intellectually fun."

In 2002, Hall moved back to Kansas City to take the job of vice president of human resources. "We moved to Pennsylvania with three kids and came back with four," Hall says with a laugh. But that wasn't all that had changed. At the same time, his brother was also moving into his new job as president and CEO. In this most challenging position, Don Hall, Jr. would no doubt need plenty of support. Having his brother back on the hometown team gave him an ally he could always count on—and that arrangement became even more vital when David Hall was named president of the Personal Expression Group in 2005.

"There's so much going on at any given time that it's helpful for us to divide and conquer," says Hall. "We take advantage of the fact that there are two of us. On rare occasions, after hashing through an issue, we might find ourselves on opposite sides of the answer, but when a decision has been made, there's never anything but bulletproof support afterward."

ABOVE: *The popular characters hoops&yoyo got their start in Hallmark artist Bob Holt's basement in 2001, with Bob fiddling around on the drawing of a little green bunny. Bob liked his funny bunny. For a Hallmark.com e-card, Bob made the bunny pink, gave it a kitty's ears, and the green bunny became Hallmark's pink kitty, which Bob eventually named hoops. When hoops needed an e-cards sidekick, Bob brought back the green bunny and named it yoyo.*

Thus from wacky origins the duo's on-line popularity grew and spawned plush characters, profitable sound cards, and a crazily popular web site that launched in 2004. Much of hoops&yoyo's fame lies in their hilariously unscripted gab-fests. Their voices are recorded (and speeded up) in a Hallmark studio, with Bob as yoyo and artist pal Mike Adair voicing hoops.

There's something subversive in their wisecracking anarchy, but wholesome too. From the heap of fan letters and email, Bob says his favorite points to hoops&yoyo's innocent appeal: "I come to your site because you guys make me smile, even on bad days."

Now More Than Ever

The chapter of Hallmark's history that began on January 1, 2002, is still unfolding today. And in the fascinating timeline of this extraordinary company, this period is in many ways the most dramatic of all. As it celebrates its one-hundredth anniversary, the company dominates its industry as at no time in its history. But that industry is a mature one in which growth comes hard. The challenges faced by Don Hall, Jr., David Hall, and all Hallmarkers are daunting and real.

In late 2007, the United States entered into a lengthy and severe economic recession. Pressured by a collapse in an overextended housing market, banks in the U.S. and Europe failed. Credit for businesses and consumers evaporated as banks quit lending. By the following year a domino effect brought down stock markets all over the world. As the economy shrunk, businesses did too—if they didn't go bankrupt altogether. The unemployment rate soared to levels not seen in decades.

Conventional wisdom holds that greeting cards are a recession-proof business. That wisdom is wrong. Hallmark's chairman, Don Hall, was a child during the Great Depression of the 1930s. He reminds that the company's revenues plummeted during those difficult years. "Many people assume that in tough economic times people would give up gifts and send cards instead, but not so," says Hall. "Economic ups and downs affect this business directly. If people don't have money, they can't spend it. If people aren't in stores, they can't buy."

Keeping perspective can be difficult in times of crisis, but Hallmark has always been a company that has taken the long view—and a company that has persevered through economic and natural disasters.

"No one in this building has faced a time like this," says David Hall of the current economic climate, "but this company has. This company has weathered two world wars. It's weathered a devastating fire and a tragic flood. It's weathered the Great Depression. And what's allowed us to withstand these things is an ability to not lose sight of who we are, to not lose sight of what the consumer needs, and to focus on what we have to get done, not on what we are victimized by."

About our character
CREATIVE

THE VERY BEST

LEFT AND ABOVE: *Five timeless brand traits—the "5 Things"—are intended to guide all Hallmarkers in pursuit of the company's vision of creating a more emotionally connected world by making a genuine difference in every life, every day. As Don Hall, Jr. explains it, "The world around us will evolve, and so will the ways we bring these timeless attributes to life. But the foundation of our approach will stay the same. We will continue to share our values, our understanding of others, our positive outlook, our creativity, and our passion for doing things right."*

CARING ENOUGH

The values so fiercely upheld by Hallmark were not arrived at by happenstance. They are a direct reflection of the values of J.C. Hall and his descendants. The company's well-known slogan, too, is a window into that value set. It is composed of nine words, but can perhaps be distilled down to two: "best," which describes the company's constant goal regarding its products and services, and "care."

That word, "care," more than any other, lies at the heart of this singular company that grew up in the nation's heartland." To Hallmark, this care exists on many levels—it is the care it shows to its customers, the care it feels for its employees, and the care it helps to communicate every time one of its products is given by one person to another. It is this fundamental caring that distinguishes Hallmark even in difficult times.

Addressing employees in the early months of 2009, Don Hall, Jr. acknowledged the severe economic conditions and resulting downturn in the company's financial performance. "It's no exaggeration to say that this recession will test us in ways that most of us have never been tested before," he told the group. "But," he continued, "I firmly believe that this moment in time is full of opportunity."

The work we've done in recent years to build critical capabilities is helping us respond to the economic crisis," said Hall. "Creating Hallmark's future will require us to effectively address our company's most pressing challenges so we can emerge from the recession with the strength, capabilities, and resiliency to thrive."

"NOW IS THE TIME TO CHALLENGE OURSELVES, THE TIME TO HAVE A RELENTLESS CONSUMER FOCUS, AN INSATIABLE CURIOSITY ABOUT THE WORLD, FLEXIBILITY IN EVERYTHING WE DO, GREATER ACCOUNTABILITY, THE COURAGE TO ACT AND THE DETERMINATION TO WIN."

—*Don Hall, Jr., 2009*

BARBARA LOOTS

EACH DAY IS LIKE A WORK OF ART
THAT'S YET TO BE DESIGNED,
AN EMPTY CANVAS WAITING
FOR THE DREAMS THAT FILL YOUR MIND...
YOUR TALENTS AND YOUR STRENGTHS
ARE LIKE THE COLORS YOU CAN USE
TO PAINT THE PICTURES OF YOUR LIFE
IN ANY WAY YOU CHOOSE...

THEY'RE SURE TO
BE ORIGINAL,
AND ALL THE WORLD
WILL KNOW
THE INNER PERSONALITY
YOUR WORDS AND ACTIONS SHOW.

SO LET THE COLORS OF YOUR LIFE
EACH DAY CREATE A NEW
AND BEAUTIFUL EXPRESSION
OF THE ONE AND ONLY YOU.

Barbara Loots began writing for Hallmark in 1967 at age 20. By the time she retired as a writing stylist in 2008, she'd seen big changes in the ways Americans wanted to express themselves to one another. "We'd gone from saying nothing in a pretty way to saying authentic things in a real way," she says. "You could start seeing it in the '70s and '80s as we began to acknowledge the realities of life, which weren't always so happy."

Even Loots' real-life messages were usually written in the pretty style for which she's celebrated. At Hallmark, where writing with regular rhyme and meter is known as verse and everything else is prose, Loots is still the acknowledged "Queen of Verse." It's an art form she clearly loves. "When you put in rhyme and meter," she explains, "you give words the music that people enjoy."

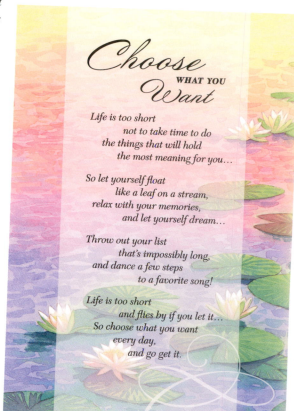

Choose WHAT YOU Want

Life is too short
not to take time to do
the things that will hold
the most meaning for you...

So let yourself float
like a leaf on a stream,
relax with your memories,
and let yourself dream...

Throw out your list
that's impossibly long,
and dance a few steps
to a favorite song!

Life is too short
and flies by if you let it...
So choose what you want
every day,
and go get it.

A Story About You

Who in their life
hasn't planted a peach pit
just hoping that somehow
a seedling would grow?
And then they move on
to some other adventure,
and if it comes up—
well, they don't even know.

That's one way
of picturing your style of living.
You've planted ideas
and dreams unaware.
You've noticed somebody
whose heart needs attention
and planted a positive feeling in there.
It's part of your nature.
You may not remember
the kind and encouraging
things that you've done...

But everywhere,
"peach pits"
are growing like crazy,
and people are blooming.
(I know it—I'm one.)

Happy Birthday

ALWAYS CHANGING, NEVER CHANGING

It seems entirely appropriate that Hallmark's brand essence statement, written by a long-term staff writer in 2003, reads like a hybrid of a mission statement and a poem. The final line sums up the company's reason for being, vividly and concisely.

We are here to enhance relationships, to enrich lives,
to play our unique and cherished role in the
always changing, never changing seasons
of friendship and family and love.

To survive for 100 years, a company must be "always changing," and Hallmark—from its bootstraps beginnings in 1910 to its market-leader status today—has changed constantly. Its early move from postcards to greeting cards took it from a stagnant industry to a burgeoning one. Its subsequent decision to print its own cards gave it flexibility and control of quality. Its ceaseless drive to modernize, innovate, and push technology forward helped it to distinguish its product and outpace competition. Its exploration into other businesses gave it a broader platform for success. And its early embrace of digital technology positioned it for continued growth, both within its core business and beyond. Along the way, Hallmark didn't just change—it consistently changed the industry that it helped create.

But, in spite of all the changes in the company and in the world in which it operates, many things at Hallmark have not changed—and never will.

Hallmark's commitment to producing high-quality product is legendary. It was the stake J.C. Hall put in the ground in the company's earliest years as publishers.

"I think this business can continue to grow during any
of our lifetimes, and beyond our lifetime, if we keep
the quality the best—and you don't follow competition
but lead it. And you guard your integrity because
it's your greatest asset. And work."

—J.C. Hall, 1950s

That commitment runs from the company's top management down through every level of employment. Don Hall recalls more than once being called down to the production floor by an operator who had literally stopped the presses because he didn't think a particular design was up to Hallmark standards. In each instance, he agreed with the pressman and pulled the card from the line. At Hallmark, commitment to quality and respect for the opinions of employees have always gone hand-in-hand.

It's difficult—if not impossible—to get Don Hall to discuss

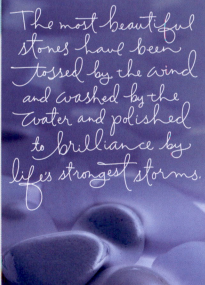

ABOVE: *The Journeys line launched in mid-February 2007 as a collection of 176 encouragement cards that addressed a range of difficult topics not traditionally approached in greeting cards, such as cancer, job loss, and even the empty-nest syndrome. The line also offered cards designed for youngsters aged 12–16 that used kid-friendly language to explore real-life situations. To spread the word about Journeys cards, Hallmark used an integrated marketing approach that included magazine, radio, and Internet advertising.*

his accomplishments during his 60-plus year tenure with the company his father founded. But getting him to talk about his passions is easy. "The three passions I've had in this company through the years are excellence of product, the importance and proper treatment of employees, and the proper place of a corporation in a community."

Don Hall's commitment to community involvement and charitable organizations is the stake *he* put in the ground when he entered the Kansas City civic and business arena in the 1950s. What he has achieved in these areas is as important to him as anything he accomplished in the Hallmark boardroom.

This commitment is alive and well in the company now run by his sons. In 2005, Hallmark announced a pioneering alliance with UNICEF—the world's leading child health, protection, and advocacy organization. Two years later, Hallmark launched (PRODUCT) RED™ greeting cards, partnering with (RED)™—a global organization committed to eliminating AIDS in Africa.

The ways in which Hallmark makes a difference in its community and in the world may change—but its commitment to doing so never will.

One Hundred Years and Counting

Running a successful business is not easy. In fact, the average lifespan for all firms in this country, regardless of size, is generally considered to be about 13 years.

Running a successful family business—and maintaining family ownership of the business through multiple generations—is more difficult still. According to Dr. Joseph Astrachan, editor of *Family Business Review*, only 30 percent of family-owned companies will go on to be run by a second generation. Fewer still make it to a third.

Hallmark has always been a company that has beat the odds. Its continued success—as a third-generation, family-run company—has depended upon multiple factors. Its growth into one of a handful of truly iconic American brands throughout the 20th century and into the 21st is testament to the entrepreneurial spirit and spunk of its founder, the bold leadership and long-term vision of his son, and the focus, agility, and innovative zeal of the current generation of Hall family leadership. A remarkable capacity for hard work has been a genetic trait common to them all.

> *"Hallmark is now in the hands of the third generation and that third generation is firmly established, clearly entrenched, has a vast and superior knowledge of the business, and is carrying on in a tradition that the first and second generations would be extremely supportive of—and there aren't too many privately owned companies where the third generation would be described in that way. The foundation is there for success in the future."*
>
> *—Don Fletcher, former president of Hallmark's Personal Expression Group*

But Don Hall, Jr. and David Hall are both smart enough to know that no matter how hard they work, that work would be in vain if not for the dedication of the thousands of employees who proudly call themselves Hallmarkers. The future is never certain for any company, but as David Hall confidently says, "At the end of the day, we've not found any challenges that dedicated Hallmarkers can't overcome."

When J.C. Hall was building the company that would become Hallmark in the early 20th century, he was constantly faced with decisions that would set and alter the course of the business. Asked in retirement how he was so often able to make the right decisions, he answered simply, "the vapors of past experience."

Hallmark embarks on its second century with a tremendous store of past experience. From its soft-spoken but big-thinking chairman of the board, to its experienced executive leadership group, and right down to every one of its more than 14,000

"A FULL ONE-THIRD OF THE COMPANIES LISTED IN THE 1970 FORTUNE 500 . . . HAD VANISHED BY 1983 — ACQUIRED, MERGED, OR BROKEN TO PIECES."

—Arie de Geus, author of The Living Company

LEFT: *Hallmark launched its full (PRODUCT) RED™ line in Gold Crown stores in January 2008 with gifts, gift wrap, greeting cards—including a large proportion of song cards—and high hopes that its socially-aware connection would appeal to young consumers. In fact, Hallmark estimated that consumers ages 18–34 represented 19 percent of all (PRODUCT) RED™ sales, from which a portion of Hallmark's profits were shared with the Global Fund to help fight AIDS in Africa.*

"I'VE SAID MANY TIMES, I'VE NEVER SEEN A GREETING CARD SENT IN ANGER. IT'S MARVELOUS TO BE IN A BUSINESS WHERE YOUR SOLE EFFORTS ARE DIRECTED AT IMPROVING SOMEBODY'S FEELINGS."

—Don Hall

employees, there lies a vast, deep, well of collective expertise, of acuity, and insight. It is exceedingly clear that these people know what they are doing.

But into this tremendous reservoir of experience flows a constant stream of new ideas and fresh perspectives. The company remains the envy of its industry—and of every industry—because it combines the strength and stability of a seasoned market leader with the energy and passion of a start-up.

Any time a company reaches a one-hundredth anniversary in business, it is worth noting. For this company, the occasion provides a unique opportunity to look back with gratitude, nostalgia, wonder, and pride, and to look forward with excitement, ambition, and the determination to build upon a remarkable past.

dimpled feet...

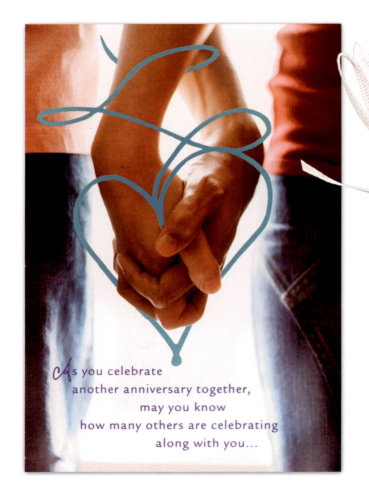

As you celebrate
another anniversary together,
may you know
how many others are celebrating
along with you...

You taught me to tie my shoes,
love my friends, help my neighbors—

Hallmark often features its newest and freshest cards in small collections that are displayed separately from the large core line. These cards from recent anniversary, baby congratulations, and Mother's Day collections use photography, which research shows is especially popular with card buyers when used with simple, emotional messages.

Hallmark has never been a company to think small. But to say that the company thinks big only in terms of the number of products it sells on an annual basis doesn't nearly do it justice. Rather, Hallmark—and Hallmarkers—think big when they define the mission for their company and the role that they expect the company's products to play in people's lives.

The goals the company sets for itself are lofty—its standards legendarily high. In an address to employees early in 2008, Don Hall, Jr. said of Hallmark, "We will be the company that creates a more emotionally connected world by making a genuine difference in every life, every day." That's no small ambition. But Hall is serious about the company's vision and mission. His confidence in the company's ability to deliver on such promises comes, he says, not from anything he or his brother may do, but from the talent and commitment of the people he sees around him every day.

"There is a sense of a shared mission with all Hallmarkers," says Hall. "One of the exciting things about this moment in time is the fact that the original mission and vision of the company is broadly embraced by the employees of today."

Everything else that Hallmark does, Hall contends, depends upon those shared values and that sense of common mission. "The product innovations, the consumer insights, the creative breakthroughs—all of these things are made possible because of the passion and values that are embodied in Hallmarkers—and those are the same values that my grandfather and father worked to create."

This fundamental faith in the commitment and creativity of Hallmarkers assures Hall that the company will always be uniquely qualified to bring relevance, creativity, and caring to emotional connections between people—whether those connections are made through ink-on-paper greetings, digital media, or in ways not yet imagined.

As chairman of the board—and father of the CEO—Don Hall necessarily stays current with company's broad strategies and major initiatives. But he very much enjoys watching the next generation lead the company that means so much to him. In assessing the future, he exhibits the philosophical perspective of one who has seen the company evolve and grow through eight of its 10 decades.

"Our products might change a great deal," Hall says, "and methods of delivery might change—certainly production and all matter of other things will change over this next century. But the need for caring for other people will always be a constant."

Don Hall, and his father before him, built Hallmark's unmatched reputation and helped establish it as a brand that is trusted, respected, and cherished the world over. Each generation stands on the shoulders of the generation that preceded it. Today, Don Hall's sons are charged with upholding the lofty legacy of the company that still insists on giving its customers the very best. It's a responsibility that the third generation of Halls takes very seriously.

No one who has had the pleasure of spending time talking to Don Hall and his two sons could help but notice how very much alike the men are in their approach to business, to life, and to the people around them. Much has been passed from father to sons—work ethic, integrity, humility, seriousness, and an honest-to-goodness affinity for the business of making personal, emotional connections.

David and Don Hall, Jr. have no doubt heard their father ruminate on the relevance of Hallmark's place in the social fabric. The sons echo the father but add their own perspective.

"The ways people express themselves change over time, but the need to express themselves and connect emotionally is enduring. Our job now is to imagine the possibilities for the future."
—Don Hall, Jr.

Though it has traced the course of this extraordinary company throughout 100 years, this book is not a history of Hallmark Cards, because that history is still being written. As it has for a century, Hallmark continues to play "its unique and cherished role in the always changing, never changing seasons of friendship and family and love." One hundred years is but a marker in time. The story continues.

"Our commitment to helping people enrich their lives through their emotional connection with others will always continue," says Don Hall, Jr. "And our brand will always be grounded in that basis of trust and the shared commitment of all Hallmarkers to the quality of those expressions—that desire to be relevant and authentic."

Or to put it more simply, as long as people care enough to send the very best, Hallmark stands ready and committed to help them do it.

Page 5: © 2010 Maya Angelou
Page 8: (bottom left) Library of Congress, Prints & Photographs Division, LC-USZ62-57524
Page 10: Library of Congress, Prints & Photographs Division, LC-USZC4-5117
Page 11: UNION PACIFIC RAILROAD, Licensed by Looking Good Licensing
Page 15: www.wikimedia.org
Page 15: (bottom) Library of Congress Prints and Photographs Division, LC-USZC4-4411
Page 19: www.wikimedia.org
Page 20: Library of Congress, Prints & Photographs Division, John C.H. Grabill Collection, LC-DIG-ppmsc-02600
Page 21: Library of Congress, Prints & Photographs Division, LC-USZC4-12466
Page 24: (top) Milstein Division of United States History, Local History & Genealogy, The New York Public Library, Astor, Lenox and Tilden Foundations
Page 30: Missouri Valley Special Collections, Kansas City Public Library, Kansas City, Missouri
Page 31: (top) Missouri Valley Special Collections, Kansas City Public Library, Kansas City, Missouri
Page 32: (both) Missouri Valley Special Collections, Kansas City Public Library, Kansas City, Missouri
Page 33: Library of Congress, Geography and Map Division, g4164k pm004290
Page 34: (top images) Missouri Valley Special Collections, Kansas City Public Library, Kansas City, Missouri
Page 47: (top) Library of Congress, Prints and Photographs Division, LC-USZC4-1502
Page 47: (middle) Library of Congress, Prints and Photographs Division, LC-USZC4-595
Page 47: (bottom) Australian War Memorial
Page 52: (bottom) Library of Congress, Prints and Photographs Division, LC-USZ62-90030
Page 56: © Disney
Page 61: (top left) NOAA George Marsh Album
Page 61: (top right) Library of Congress Prints and Photographs Division Washington, DC, cph 3g08199
Page 61: (middle) Library of Congress Prints and Photographs Division Washington, DC, LC-USF34- 009058-C
Page 61: (bottom) Library of Congress Prints and Photographs Division Washington, DC, LC-USF34- 009740-C
Page 62: (top) Library of Congress Prints and Photographs Division Washington, DC, LC-USZ62-74620
Page 62: (bottom) Joseph H. "Jack" Wally, Jr. (1913-2006) Collection (KC0329) in Western Historical Manuscript Collection-Kansas City
Page 63: (top left) Library of Congress Prints and Photographs Division Washington, DC, Library of Congress Prints and Photographs Division Washington, DC, , LC-GLB23- 0930
Page 63: (top right) Dr. Kenneth J. LaBudde Department of Special Collections, University of Missouri-Kansas City
Page 63: (bottom left) Dr. Kenneth J. LaBudde Department of Special Collections, University of Missouri-Kansas City
Page 63: (bottom right) Missouri Valley Special Collections, Kansas City Public Library, Kansas City, Missouri
Page 63: Dr. Kenneth J. LaBudde Department of Special Collections, University of Missouri-Kansas City
Page 75: (top left) National Portrait Gallery, Smithsonian Institution (NPG.2004.159)
Page 80-81 (top) National Archives and Records Administration, General Record of the Department of the Navy, 1798-1974 (80-G-16871)
Page 82: (top) National Archives and Records Administration, Howard R. Hollem, April 1942. 208-AA-352V-4
Page 82: (middle) National Archives and Records Administration, (NWDNS-179-WP-1563)
Page 82: (bottom) Ralph Iligan/National Association of Manufacturers/University of North Texas Libraries/http://digital.library.unt.edu/data/govdocs/atoz/02/meta-dc-1806.tkl
Page 84: (top left) National Archives and Records Administration, Record Group 26, Records of the U.S. Coast Guard (26-G-2343)
Page 84: (bottom right) National Archives and Records Administration, 111-sc-197661
Page 84-85: U.S. Coast Guard Collection in the U.S. National Archives (26-g-2517)

Age 85: (top) National Archives and Records Administration, (531217)
Page 85: (middle) National Archives and Records Administration (26-G-3394.)
Page 86: (top left) National Archives and Records Administration (208-AA-322H-1)
Page 86: (top right) Alfred Eisenstaedt/Time & Life Pictures/Getty Images
Page 87: (top) National Archives and Records Administration, Records of the Office of the Chief Signal Officer (111-SC-210241)
Page 87: (bottom) Ed Clark/Time & Life Pictures/Getty Images
Page 98: (left) Missouri Valley Special Collections, Kansas City Public Library, Kansas City, Missouri
Page 99: From an original illustration by Norman Rockwell in the Hallmark Art Collection
Page 115: (top) Courtesy of General Motors
Page 115: (bottom) Courtesy of Zenith Electronics
Pages 134-135: Illustration by Johne Richardson
Pages 144-145: PEANUTS ©United Feature Syndicate, Inc.
Page 152: Armed Forces Radio and Television Service
Page 160: (middle) Photo by Jon Farmer
Page 160: (bottom left) Photo by Erik Heinila
Page 165: PEANUTS ©United Feature Syndicate, Inc.
Page 176: Photo by Rick Stare
Page 177: Photos by Fred L. Kautt
Page 178: Photo by Fred L. Kautt
Page 179: Photos by Fred L. Kautt
Page 180: (top) Photo by Fred L. Kautt
Page 180-181: (bottom) Photo by Michael J. Reagan
Page 181: (top left) Photo by Fred L. Kautt
Page 181: (top right) Photo by Mark McCabe
Pages 182-183: Photos by Chris Duh
Page 187: (bottom right) Photograph by Victor Keppler, Courtesy the Harris Corporation.
Page 191: (top left) Chevrolet, Corvette Emblems and Body Design are General Motors Trademarks used under license to Hallmark Cards, Inc.
Page 194: Photo courtesy of The Kansas City Star
Page 195: (top) Photos by Henry Clark
Page 195: (middle left) Photo by Randy Stanley
Page 195: (bottom left) Photo by Chris Duh
Pages 198-199: Photos by Jeff Nightingale/Courtesy of The Nelson-Atkins Museum of Art
Page 201: (top right) Photo by Mike Sinclair, 2008
Page 203: Photo by Michael J. Reagan
Page 204: Photo by Fred L. Kautt
Page 205: Diagram courtesy of The Kansas City Star
Pages 208-209: Photos by Steve Wilson and Donald Lesko
Pages 220-221: Photo by Steve Wilson
Pages 222-223: © Marjolein Bastin
Page 224: THE WIZARD OF OZ and all related characters and elements are trademarks of and © Turner Entertainment Co. Judy Garland as Dorothy from THE WIZARD OF OZ. (s10)
Page 225: BATMAN, SUPERMAN and all related characters and elements are trademarks of and © DC Comics. (s10)
Page 242: (top left/middle/right) Copyright © 2010 American Girl, LLC. All rights reserved. The trademark The American Girl Collection is used under license from American Girl, LLC. (bottom left) © Disney
Page 245: (bottom) BATMAN, SUPERMAN and all related characters and elements are trademarks of and © DC Comics. (s10)
Page 254: Hallmark is a proud partner of (PRODUCT)RED™

All other images are from Hallmark Cards, Inc., and its subsidiaries, the Hallmark Archives, the personal collection of the Hall Family, or in the public domain.